FALSE
ARREST

FALSE ARREST: THE JOYCE LUKEZIC STORY

Joyce Lukezic and Ted Schwarz

NEW HORIZON PRESS
Far Hills, New Jersey

Library of Congress Catalog Card Number: 89-63990

Joyce Lukezic
Ted Schwarz
    False Arrest

ISBN 0-88282-050-8
New Horizon Press

AUTHOR'S NOTE

This is the actual experience of a real person, Joyce Lukezic. The personalities, events, actions and conversations portrayed within the story have been reconstructed from extensive interviews and research, utilizing court documents, letters, personal papers, press accounts and the memories of participants. In an effort to safeguard the privacy of certain individuals, the author has changed their names and, in some cases, altered otherwise identifying characteristics. Events involving the characters happened as described: only minor details have been altered.

CONTENTS

PROLOGUE

If Joyce Lukezic noticed the men as she drove into the driveway of her Phoenix, Arizona, home, they did not register in her mind. She was with her daughter, Eden, having purchased doughnuts for breakfast, a special treat to share before starting the day's chores.

"Joyce Lukezic?" asked one of the men as she stepped from her car. He was well dressed, broad shouldered, the suit barely containing his muscular arms.

"Yes?" she said, smiling. An insurance salesman, perhaps, though he had no briefcase.

"Phoenix police. I have a warrant for your arrest."

And then they moved. Eight or ten, she was too shocked to count. All of them dwarfing her 5'4" frame.

She saw badges. Guns. Felt hands grab her arms.

Against the car, forced to lean off balance, an officer positioned to sweep her feet from under her if she tried to flee.

There were words, all blurred together. "Kidnapping . . . Accomplice to murder . . . Right to remain silent . . . Right to an attorney . . ."

For a moment she felt the frisk. Like television, only different. More thorough. Her clothing checked inch-by-inch, a crushing motion used so that anything concealed would be detected. The hands were quick, professional. Any weapon she might have hidden, from a razor blade to a .45-caliber automatic, would be uncovered.

But there were no guns, no knives, no weapons of any kind.

"Give me your wrist." Her right arm pulled behind her back, the steel cuff tightening against the skin.

Then the left hand. Her balance gone. Someone keeping her from falling while the cuffs held her fast.

Eden, shocked, stood by the door, staring in horror. Her eyes searched the faces of the detectives, then settled on her mother, seeking answers. All she saw was shock, fear, confusion. She withdrew into the house to call her stepfather at work. Maybe he could make sense of what was happening. Maybe he could stop the nightmare. Maybe he . . .

A hand took Joyce's arm. Into the back of the car. Watch your head, Joyce. Low ceiling.

Falling onto the seat. Awkward. Trying to sit with her wrists cuffed behind her back.

Looking out the windows. Thoughts jumbled. Never hugged the children. Never said goodbye.

Neighbors staring. Suburban housewives don't get arrested. Not in that neighborhood.

Scandals. There were scandals. Too loud parties on prom night. Teenagers sharing an illegal beer. Philandering husbands. Cheating wives.

Not murder. Not Joyce.

"Have you ever been arrested before, Joyce?"

The voice was in front. One of the cops. Got to focus. Got to think. "What?"

"Have you ever been arrested before?"

"No. Never. Not for anything." She shifted to see him better. Face a blur. Shock.

"When you go, you really go First Class, don't you?"

The car passed Park Central Shopping Center. The kids like going there. Lots of stores. Good prices.

"School starts tomorrow, doesn't it, Joyce?" asked the driver. "Your kids happy about going back?"

Try to focus. Think. Shoulders aching. It's the end of August. Of course school starts tomorrow. Have to pack lunches.

But I can't pack their lunches. Not with my wrists handcuffed. Not with these men saying I'm under arrest.

My God! I'm under arrest.

The police station. Madison Street jail. Drive around the back. Reporters everywhere. Cameras. Voices. Detectives. Jeff Smith. Familiar face. Ron sent him. Ron's not here but Jeff is. Shouting over the crowd. "Don't worry, Joyce. Everything's going to be okay!"

And a lawyer. Larry Debus. Ron's lawyer. Ron must have called him. But where's Ron? Why didn't he come?

"Hey, Joyce, over here!" A stranger's voice. Turn. Light flashing. News photographer.

"You have anything to say, Joyce?" "How does it feel to get arrested?" "Smile for the camera, Joyce." "Over here." So many voices. So many faces. Cameras growing from their eyes.

Hide my face. Desperately want to hide my face. Can't do it. They keep moving me. Why does everyone crowd around me? Why don't they stay away? Why don't they tell me what's going on?

Into a room. Chairs, a table, big glass window. Not in the hall anymore. Not with the reporters. Just an investigator. Dan Ryan. And the cops.

Then Ryan stepped from the room for a moment. Smile on his face. Hands above his head. Like a boxer after a victory. The winner. He's making the sign of a champion. He's playing to the crowd. My God, he's playing to the crowd like a fighter prancing around the ring after a knock-out punch.

Then back into the room for questions. But Joyce had one for him. "Why did you do that?" Her voice was calm, curious. "Why did you make that victory sign?"

And then it all changed. The carnival atmosphere was

over. The room was silent, cold. His eyes were intense, like laser beams that could burn their way through her head. Then he spoke, calmly, deliberately, an edge to his voice that was harder than anything she had ever heard. "Because I want to see you die in the gas chamber."

PART ONE

TO LIVE AND
DIE IN PHOENIX

Chapter 1

THE MURDERS

The dark sedan moved steadily through the streets of Phoenix, Arizona, the three men inside looking as though they were going to a party. It was December 31, 1980, New Year's Eve, and the entire city was decorated for celebration. Restaurants, bars, and nightclubs had banners, streamers, and live bands playing everything from big band jazz to country swing to punk rock. Revelers wore tuxedos to one club, jeans to another, and Fredericks of Hollywood outlandish to a third. Hookers had more business than they could handle, and bartenders delighted in dwindling stocks.

Along the residential areas, the partying was only slightly more subdued. Cars were parked everywhere as people gathered with friends to toast the new year. The music coming from the houses came from stereos, but the dancing, drinking, and flirting were just as intense as in the hotel ballrooms and bars.

Uniformed police were heavily on patrol, watching for individuals driving erratically. This would be a night for countless auto stops, checks for people driving under the influence. Only the detectives expected a certain amount of peace. Homicide had had three cases that day, an unusually high number, but they finished with their work early enough for partying. Detective Larry Martinsen, for example, arrived home at 7:30 p.m., plenty of time to change clothes and enjoy the night with his wife. Uniformed patrolmen would handle the city, bar fights and family feuds dominating whatever calls did not relate to traffic.

Cab companies were working to further reduce the chance of tragedy. Many had arrangements with area bars to shuttle the intoxicated to their homes, often without charge. College students were using a designated driver program in which one person, the designated driver, would refrain from drinking anything alcoholic.

For Joyce and Ron Lukezic, New Year's Eve was a night for celebration. Ron Lukezic and his partner, Patrick Redmond, had had another good year, their income in the six-figure range. They jointly owned a successful printing company, one which appeared to be about to expand. The only tension between the men related to a printing contract in Las Vegas that they had recently decided against taking. The contract would have increased their gross by as much as six million dollars per year, but there were strings attached. They would have to share some of their company's ownership with the people involved, allegedly people believed to be connected with organized crime.

Ron Lukezic, the more ambitious of the two, had wanted the deal. His partner, satisfied with the success they already enjoyed, wanted nothing to do with the arrangement. The arguments had continued for weeks. New Year's Eve, though, was not a time when the feud was in anyone's mind. It was a night for partying, a night when Ron, always a heavy drinker, had to make no apologies for excessive indulgence.

Joyce sat in the bedroom, applying her make-up. She was an attractive woman in her late 30s, living in a nice home in a good neighborhood. She owned her own small business, a medical personnel placement company her brother had helped her start, and delighted in the ways her three children were maturing. After seeing a marriage go sour and relocating 2,000 miles from her home town of Boston, life was falling into place. She had achieved what many people considered the American dream, the only stress coming from what she perceived to be a possible estrangement from her husband. Ron had a reputation as a philanderer. They both had hot tempers. There had been some arguments and angry words. Still, she knew that all marriages had their trouble spots, and, though several times lately she had caught Ron looking strangely at her teenaged daughter, she dismissed the disturbing thought and relegated such problems to the back of her mind. Perhaps it was her imagination, misplaced jealousy. He was still her best friend, a man who could make her laugh, a man whose company she enjoyed. Besides, with the coming of the new year, everything seemed brighter. Every problem seemed capable of correction.

The car containing the three men braked smoothly to a stop near 320 West El Camino, a street of upper income homes in one of the area's most desirable neighborhoods. The men knew there were only two entrances to the house that was their target, and they had been briefed as to their locations. They also knew that Patrick and Marilyn Redmond, along with Marilyn's mother, Helen Phelps, would be alone in the house. There was still time before the Redmonds' guests for the evening would be arriving.

They had come prepared. Seven hours earlier, at noon that day, they had stopped at Long's Drug on West Baseline Road in Mesa. They were dressed in business suits, inconspicuous except for the fact that two of them were black. There were a limited number of blacks living in the area.

The white man bought three pairs of inexpensive surgical gloves for fifty-seven cents, paying in cash, then accidentally dropping a penny on the floor. Mrs. Laura Avery was nearby, spotted the cent, and pointed it out to him. For some reason, she also noticed his appearance—brown suit jacket, brown boots, and a silver and turquoise ring on his right ring finger, the turquoise stone slightly larger than normal. The man thanked her, went over to the two blacks who had just purchased a large roll of adhesive tape, and, together, they left.

The men had the gloves and the adhesive tape that night as they approached the house. The white man approached the front door. The black men stayed behind for a moment so they would not be spotted until after the door had been opened to the white man. Phoenix, like Mesa, had few blacks. Even a casually-dressed white stranger would be perceived as more trustworthy than well-dressed black men. However, once the door was open, the two blacks moved quickly forward, one going to the carport entrance, the other moving around towards the back of the house.

The white man did his work smoothly. He removed his wallet from his pocket, preparing to show a badge and other credentials when someone answered his knock. It was a scene he had played out hundreds of times in the past when he was on the Phoenix police force.

Police work was long in the past, but the lessons of his earlier career had stayed with him. Identify yourself as a police officer and you have the edge. It didn't matter whether the person was suspected of a crime or an innocent citizen who might have some knowledge that would be of help. The reaction was always the same.

First there was the feeling of guilt. "Then they really did see me roll through that stop sign as I pulled onto McDowell?" Or, "They found out that my birthday was a week ago and I still haven't renewed my license." Or, for the most neurotic, "I never realized I could still be charged for stealing that cap gun from Woolworth's thirty years ago when I was nine."

Then there was the relief. "It's just routine. We're doing some checking on a person who has been seen in this neighborhood and we're wondering if you might have noticed something that will help."

That's when they invited you inside. That's when they would tell you anything because they were so delighted that your presence had nothing to do with the events they feared.

This time it was different. This time when the man held up his credentials, his other hand holding a revolver just out of view, he no longer worked for the police force. This time when he revealed the gun and his partners entered through the other entrance, effectively trapping everyone in the house in their line of fire if they resisted, he was on the other side of the law.

If any thoughts went through Patrick Redmond's mind at the time he answered the door and found himself facing a revolver, they were probably reflections of the warnings he had received from friends in the past. "You keep talking about all that gold and silver you keep around the house. Somebody's going to rob you."

But neither Patrick nor Marilyn Redmond ever listened. They had worked hard for what they owned. They took pride not only in possessing it but also keeping it where others could see it. Their jewelry was flashy and frequently worn. Their lifestyle was flamboyant, constantly broadcasting the fact that they were successful. Being able to lead such a life was always more important to them than the risk of loss. They were fatalistic about the idea of robbers entering their home and did not worry about it.

Marilyn Redmond was in the master bedroom when there was a knock at the door. She had forgotten her cigarettes and the coin purse filled with quarters she would use for betting when they played cards that night.

When Marilyn returned to the entrance area, she

heard her husband calling to her. She opened the door leading to the laundry room and saw Pat, with a black man holding a gun on him. The man was tall, nicely dressed, wearing a brown leather jacket, a dark shirt, and dark pants. She had no idea who he was or what he wanted. All she could do was stare at him until he walked towards her, took her arm, and asked, "Who else is here?"

"My mother," she responded.

"Where?"

"In the kitchen." It was around the corner at an angle where Marilyn could see the woman, but the man holding the gun could not.

"Go get her or tell her to come here."

Marilyn left Pat and the man with the gun. Although she could see others in the house, she could not really tell who they were or what they were doing. She went into the kitchen and said, "Mother, we are being robbed."

The women returned; Marilyn was ordered to close the draperies in the dining room and living room. She knew there was nothing to be done except to go along with what was happening and see what would take place.

When she returned to the family room, Pat was being guarded by one of the men, but her mother was no longer there. She called the dog and restrained him. He was not vicious, but she feared the men might kill the animal to be certain everything would be okay. She held onto its collar, taking the dog into the bathroom, then shutting the door. The animal would be safe from harm there.

Marilyn and one of the black men went to the back of the house, her husband remained in the living room with the white man. When they reached the bedroom, she saw that the other black man was standing guard over her mother who was lying quietly on the bed.

The men asked for jewelry, opening a drawer under the vanity and studying the items in the jewelry case she kept there. "That's all junk," he said. "We don't want that.

Where is all your good stuff? We were told you were rich. Where is all your gold? Where is the safe? Do you have any guns?"

"Yes," Marilyn replied, explaining that there was a gun in the night stand and some shotguns in the closet. She led him to the weapons, removing them from the closet and placing them on the floor. During all this time, the white man remained in the other room with Pat whom he referred to as "Mr. Bigshot."

Marilyn realized that this was not a random robbery. The men had been told that they had gold, money. The family had been specifically targeted.

Pat was also brought into the bedroom. All three were now isolated from any avenue of escape except by rushing past the three well-armed intruders. They were ordered to take off their personal jewelry and also emptied their purses and wallets, yielding several hundred dollars in cash.

Then all three were ordered to lie on the bed, their hands behind them. The robbers took out adhesive tape, using it to bind their victims' hands behind their backs.

"We know you've got more money. Where is your safe?"

Marilyn Redmond replied, "We were robbed a few years ago and there is nothing here. We don't have a safe. We have a safety deposit box."

Then the men went through the dresser drawers, searching for something to use as gags.

There may have been some comfort in the victims' helplessness as socks were stuffed in each of their mouths to silence them. This was a residential neighborhood where gun shots might be heard by others. If the men meant to kill them, why render them helpless and silent? Probably they would be left like that, freeing themselves after the robbers had gone.

"We don't need these two any more," said one of the

men. And then Marilyn heard two shots being fired. After that, she heard nothing.

The first bullet shattered Patrick Redmond's skull, sending blood, bits of hair, tissue, bone, and brain splattering against the wall. He was dead instantly, a gaping, gory hole destroying the life that had once existed.

The other two bullets were fired so quickly, neither of the women had time to grieve. Marilyn's mother was dead instantly. Marilyn would prove luckier, the freak chance of an odd angle of entry sending the bullet ricocheting around the skull without damaging enough of the brain to cause death. She lost consciousness, her wound severe enough that her body seemed lifeless.

One of the men had a razor sharp chef's knife which he used to slash Patrick Redmond's throat. Then he turned to Helen Phelps, repeating his action. Yet for some reason he did not follow through with Marilyn, apparently not realizing that her seemingly dead body was still strong enough that survival was possible.

And then they were gone.

It seemed like hours before Marilyn Redmond regained consciousness. She lifted her head slightly, thinking that if she didn't get up and get out to the back door, nobody would be able to come inside and find them. She glanced at the clock radio next to her, saw it was around seven-twenty, and was surprised how swiftly everything had taken place.

Marilyn rested a few seconds, listening to the quiet, making certain that the killers were gone. Then she rolled over onto the floor, sat up, and scooted across the carpet. She pushed with her hands and pulled with her feet until she got back out to the center of the family room, coming to rest by an end table.

Verna and Floyd Kelley expected the night to be a relatively quiet one. Floyd was a concrete contractor who had known the Redmonds for eight to ten years. The Redmonds, a man named Bob Gladden, and his date, Delpha Brooks, would all be enjoying food, drink, and a friendly card game played for quarters. The games, whether with the Kelleys or others, were frequent enough that Marilyn Redmond always kept a container of quarters in the bedroom.

Bob Gladden, a self-employed plumber, was planning to arrive a little later than the seven p.m. time the Redmonds had suggested. They would be together for several hours and the exact time of arrival was not critical.

There was no answer when the Kelleys knocked at the Redmonds' door, but the carport held the van and the Cadillac they owned, and the door was unlocked.

Everything inside seemed as it should be. The organ, the Christmas tree, the television set, the fireplace, all the things expected in the family room. Then he saw Marilyn, lying on her stomach, head turned sideways. She had worked the sock gag from her mouth, but her hands were taped behind her back. A knot on her jaw indicated that she had been hit or had bumped her chin.

"My God, Marilyn, what happened."

"We've been robbed."

"What can we do?" they asked.

"Ice," she whispered.

Verna went into the kitchen, returning with some ice wrapped in a towel. She also brought a knife to cut the tape.

"Negroes," she said, then added that it was three men. Kelley immediately had his wife call for the Paramedics and the police, warning her to not go in the bedroom. He had already gone back to check on Pat and Helen Phelps, realized they were dead, and wanted to prevent his wife from seeing the carnage.

Kelley also went out to his car at some point, touching the hood. He never knew why he did it, could not remember when. But he left a few drops of Marilyn's blood on the metal. It was just enough to warrant impounding his car, to briefly cause the detectives to wonder if he was involved.

He wasn't. It was just to have been a quiet evening with friends.

It was 8:30 p.m. when Detective Larry Martinsen knew that his New Year's Eve plans would have to be canceled. He ordinarily worked the day shift, a homicide specialist, being called at night only when a case did not seem routine.

The patrolmen who arrived to help Marilyn secured the crime scene, contacting the night detectives who routinely rolled on such cases. They were the generalists, as likely to be at the scene of a robbery as they were to appear at a domestic shooting. Frequently they encountered the classic "smoking gun," a man or woman holding a revolver, an automatic, or perhaps a rifle, the weapon's barrel still warm. The killer would be in shock, in tears, or gloating in triumph, never quite certain what happened, just knowing that life would never again be the same. It was only with the unusual, the cases that were in no way routine, that the night detectives were ordered to call in the specialists.

There was no smoking gun in the Redmond murder case, no obvious suspect. The immediate family was either dead or near death. There was no sign of forced entry, yet a robbery had obviously taken place. And black men were suspects, something foreign for the neighborhood. The night detectives had to call in the specialists, and one of the first to be reached was Martinsen. For his promptness in responding on one of the hardest nights of the year to reach anyone, he was named the case agent in charge.

Ron and Joyce Lukezic also had their evening's plans abruptly altered by the murders. The night detectives called them to the scene, seeking whatever assistance Patrick's business partner might be able to provide. The Redmonds also had children. Someone had to shield them from the nightmare sight in their parents' bedroom. Somebody had to . . .

Suddenly the plans for partying changed. The Lukezics quickly drove to the Redmonds' home. Shocked, they answered questions about the business, the Redmonds' personal life, the possibility of unknown enemies. And always the answers were the same. No one would want to hurt them. No one would have a grudge against them. No one could do such a thing. It had to be a robbery. It had to be killers who learned of Patrick Redmond's talk of the gold and silver he kept in his home.

The crime scene was relatively crowded when Detective Martinsen arrived. Uniformed officers and paramedics had been inside the home, working to save Marilyn Redmond before securing the crime scene. There were police and neighbors milling about, television, radio, and newspaper reporters taking pictures, interviewing anyone who seemed to have some piece of information, and waiting to see what was going to happen.

Martinsen was briefed outside. Then he walked inside, observing the crime scene. He was looking for the unusual, the unexpected, something out of place or indicative of what might have happened. Were there shell casings ejected from an automatic? Blood stains? Drawers opened? Broken windows? Signs of a struggle?

In the family room were torn pieces of Marilyn Redmond's clothing, pieces of adhesive tape still stuck to the sleeves. The clothing and tape had been cut away by the paramedics in order to treat her wounds. The items had been left behind, the men knowing that the type of tape, the way she had been bound, or some other aspect of what was there could help pinpoint the murderers.

The night would be a long one because the technical experts always preceded the police, checking for fingerprints, fibers, blood stains, and anything else that might be lost if someone walked in ahead of them. The preservation of clues meant far more than satisfying anyone's curiosity. Everything would be done slowly, methodically, and, if something unexpected was encountered by Martinsen or the other men, it would be photographed, measured, triangulated, and noted on crime scene sketches. They would be there until almost six in the morning, making certain that every clue to the identity of the killers could be found.

At the same time that they were looking, other officers had taken a statement from Marilyn Redmond just before she lapsed back into unconsciousness. Three men, she told them. Two blacks, one white. There were few other details, but they had a start and they released the information to the news media.

The reaction was swift. Three black males had been talking about the murder in the east side of Phoenix near the 1600 block of Washington. Someone overheard both their conversation and the news on the television. The person made an anonymous telephone call and patrol cars were dispatched. The men were stopped, taken to the station for questioning, fingerprinted, their backgrounds checked. But they had no connection with the case. It was not going to be solved so easily.

Joyce Lukezic knew about law and order the way most honest citizens understand it, through television. During the fifty minute hour that comprises each program, everything is simple, black-and-white, a situation that, no matter how seemingly perplexing, actually travels from A to Z in a straight line. The police are the good guys, willing to do anything, including risk their careers, to solve a crime. The bad guys are well defined and obvious to the viewer who may have even been a first-hand witness to the crime at the beginning of the show. If somehow there is a mistake, a lawyer enters the courtroom like Perry Mason, brilliantly defends the accused and gains a tearful confession from the guilty party before the final credits roll. Everything is clearly defined, good and bad, with no shades of gray.

Reality is quite different. In real life there is a symbiotic relationship among cops and robbers, lawyers and prosecutors, politicians and the media. In real life there is an unspoken, unwritten hierarchy of crime that determines which cases will be thoroughly investigated, which cases are most likely to be solved.

First there are the criminals, the majority of whom are so inept that ninety-five percent of all crimes that are solved are solved within the first five minutes of police arriving on the crime scene. Sometimes this means that the criminal is still there, as often happens when an argument between friends leads to a shooting death.

At other times the case may not be solved for months, but when it is solved, the key factor will be an item of evidence—a fingerprint, an accidentally discarded piece of jewelry, an overlooked calendar entry—discovered during the initial investigation of the crime scene. The truly intelligent criminal, or the total psychopath whose actions defy rational logic, may never be caught.

Then there are the crimes themselves. Certain crimes are more important to the general public than others. A series of unsolved muggings in the parking area of a luxury shopping mall will likely receive more police and press attention than the serial murders of black, AIDS-infected prostitutes in trash-riddled alleys within high-crime, low-income ghetto areas. The latter are more serious, but the people who buy newspapers generally do not live in that section of the city, do not use such prostitutes, and may inwardly view the death of AIDS carriers as a public service. On the other hand, many of the readers do shop in the luxury malls where muggers are perceived as very personal dangers. They want the person who has intruded in their world, endangering their safety and making them fearful, to be arrested, locked away, never to be seen among decent people again.

The press understands the relative merits of crime and puts pressure where their readers will applaud such actions. This forces the politicians to demand action from law enforcement officers in order for the voters to feel their elected officials are effective. The law enforcement officers assign their "top men", or create a task force to show they are aggressively handling the problem. There will be confidential hot lines, rewards offered through the aid of civic groups, and other efforts. But all that really happens is that everyone has passed the buck, protecting themselves against criticism. The press can say they did their part by exposing a danger to society. The mayor states that the police were empowered to handle the matter. And the police explain that the unwillingness of citizens to come forward with the information needed to take the criminal off the streets has hampered their efforts to resolve the matter.

The criminals understand their role in the system as well. Often they are pawns, supporting players upon a stage where police, lawyers, and judges have all the leading roles. No one cares about prostitutes plying their trade, since their activities involve the voluntary participation of consenting adults. But civic leaders have learned that periodic sweeps of the prostitutes makes for good television coverage. Cameras record police protecting the community morals, judges handing down sentences, and the "system" working. The fact that the girls are back on the streets within a day or two is not a concern. They are all part of a show that sometimes seems to have been running almost as long as the profession itself.

Junkies shooting up with dope are unsightly more than menacing, but the public applauds narcotics cops who hustle them off to jail. The streets look nicer and the detectives gain excellent arrest statistics for their efforts. The fact that the real problem areas—the large-scale suppliers, the lack of social service intervention in dysfunctional families where kids may escape family violence through drug use—are often ignored is usually overlooked. Arrest statistics are up, the junkies are no longer in the parks and doorways, and the public can again walk safe streets.

In Arizona, the legislature had gone a step further in protecting its citizens from the criminals. A law had been passed in which a person could be convicted of a crime strictly on the word of another individual who had confessed to that crime. The courts did not have to produce witnesses or physical evidence to corroborate the testimony of the admitted perpetrator. Not only did the law make people guilty until proven innocent, it also offered an incentive for lying. A criminal could confess to a crime, then plea bargain a lesser sentence by naming an innocent person without an alibi as the "partner."

The mindset that established a law enabling a man to be jailed, solely on the uncorroborated testimony of a criminal, seemed to have no bearing on a woman such as Joyce Lukezic. She was a housewife, a mother, a woman who would feel a twinge of guilt if she pocketed a quarter found in the coin return slot of a pay telephone. She had no idea that she was slowly being drawn into a web of intrigue and legal perversion that could ultimately result in the loss of her life.

The killing of Patrick Redmond was a media case, if only by default. Nothing exciting happens on New Year's Eve for the reporters and photographers who blanket the streets, trying to make each year's events somehow more colorful than the previous one's. There will be car crash photographs showing the tragedy of the new year coupled with "the first baby born in Phoenix this year" photos. There will be stories about cab companies whose employees take drunks safely home, often without charge. And there will be pictures taken at midnight in swank country clubs and colorful, though slightly disreputable, bars. But murders are not the usual fare of New Year's Eve and, when reports of one go out over the radio, reporters and photographers delightedly converge on the scene. For the first time in years, something new and different would be a part of the night's activities.

There were other factors making the Redmond story newsworthy, of course. The couple had a six-figure income, a nice house, and valuable possessions. Their neighbors were in positions of power and influence within the community. The idea that the Redmonds, a family that enjoyed the good life in a city like Phoenix, could be found in their home bound, gagged, and shot through the head was big news. The fact that it happened on an unusually slow news day just increased public interest.

Despite the immediate news value, the detectives and the politicians knew that the long-term news value would be minimal. There would be a certain amount of rhetoric for a few days. After all, the neighbors were not only voters, they had the kind of money that enabled them to contribute to political campaign drives. If they felt that their streets were no longer safe, they might feel that their elected officials had failed them. The politicians had to be ready to make a call to action if the hue and cry became too strong. However, they also realized that the Redmonds were not community leaders. Another crime in a different part of the city would immediately end the press interest, focusing it on some other location.

Her name was Bindi and she was the first important break in the case. She was a woman allegedly involved with drug deals and prostitution, unstable, as likely to work with law enforcement as against them. She was the type who would tell a detective the truth about a crime she had witnessed, giving such exact details that there was no question of her accuracy, then get mad at him the next day, refusing to repeat anything she had said in a court-room.

Bindi knew she was living in a dangerous world. She made her living from the two most intense passions any-one could have—drugs and sex. She was aware that the two black males who were spending a few days with her over the holidays had been involved with drug dealing and gang activity in Chicago. She also knew that they had served time in jail. But drugs were rough trade and a little violence was normal for the business. What scared her was the realization that they seemed to be talking about something else when they returned to her place after New Year's Eve. They seemed to be talking about murders for hire and that was business with which she had no inten-tion of involving herself.

The call was logged by Silent Witness on January 1st. Silent Witness was a special hotline, untraceable, com-pletely anonymous, that the police used to solicit informa-tion related to crimes in the community. Sometimes there was reward money involved as the impetus for making the telephone call. Sometimes citizens felt the need to do their duty as citizens. And sometimes, as in Bindi's case, the callers were scared. They were involved with something over their heads and the only escape they could see for themselves was through involvement with the police.

Bindi explained to the people who answered about the men who were with her, their conversations, and the possible connection with the Patrick Redmond murders. She provided enough details that seemed to match with what had been learned from Marilyn Redmond that the police considered it worth exploring.

"We were thicker than brothers," Ron Lukezic said to Jack Lavelle of the Phoenix Gazette. It was Friday, January 2, 1981, and he was being interviewed concerning the death of his business partner.

"There was not a greater guy in the world. This man would have given away his car. He would have even carried out his couch, if they just wouldn't have shot him. If anybody was going to blow anybody away, it would have been me."

The same report quoted Police spokesman Sergeant Mike Jahn as saying that there was fairly substantial evidence as to the identify of the killers. But Jahn refused to talk further. He did not want to jeopardize the case.

Joyce Lukezic was in shock because of the murders. She kept trying to figure out what had happened that could have resulted in Patrick's death.

Friends of the Redmonds and the Lukezics gathered in Joyce's home on January 2nd to talk about the murder and share in the grief. They were surprised when the detectives arrived to question Ron, but the questioning was routine. How long had they been business partners?

How long had they known each other? Had anything happened the day of the murder that was unusual, perhaps, with hindsight, hinting at a motive for the murder.

Sally Behm, a secretary for the print shop, told of a rude driver for a paper company who needed cash or a certified check for the $327.58 order they were receiving. Pat Redmond paid cash, peeling the money from a thick wad of bills in a money clip in his pocket.

The detective noted the incident, knowing that love and money were the most common causes of murder. Perhaps the driver had been impressed with the cash Redmond had carried.

Ron mentioned that he and Joyce had planned to fly to Las Vegas for a couple of days and he had given Pat a $2,500 check to cash for him. Redmond had gone to the bank, obtaining twenty-five one-hundred dollar bills. Could a teller have been intrigued? A customer waiting in line?

Then Ron Lukezic further stated that Pat Redmond always carried large sums of money with him. There was usually $1,000 in a money clip and another $2,000 in his wallet.

What about blacks? The killers had been two blacks and a white. Perhaps the color of the men would narrow their search.

Ron Lukezic and Pat Redmond had known few blacks, though. Ron could only think of Claude, Claude's son, and Reiff, none of the men known well enough for him to supply a last name. Claude and his son were private trash collectors, a type of business that was usually thriving in the Phoenix areas. Reiff was an insurance salesman, well dressed, plenty of money.

The list of possible suspects kept growing.

Finally Ron mentioned Chester's, a cocktail lounge at 23rd Ave. and Indian School Road. Pat and Marilyn Redmond were regulars at the lounge, one or both of them drinking there almost every night. All the regulars knew that Pat Redmond flashed his money. All the regulars probably had heard stories about the Redmonds' expensive possessions.

More suspects. Everywhere Pat Redmond walked he seemed to have been carrying a sign screaming, "Mug me, I'm rich." It was a wonder that he had not been the victim of violence before.

Bindi's information was extremely specific. Edward L. McCall was one of the names she provided. He was a white male, approximately forty-five years old, six feet tall.

The black males were Hooper, known as "Hoop,", approximately thirty years old, also six feet tall, and Billy Brice or Bryce. Brice used a number of aliases, including Billy Bounty and William Brice. He was in his early thirties and the tallest of the three, six feet, three inches in height. The black men were believed to live in Chicago. The white male had been booked for assault on December 10, 1979, according to police in suburban Tempe, Arizona. The police did not know for certain who the men were, but they would quickly learn that the Redmond killers had been caught.

The funeral of Pat Redmond was an emotional time for everyone. Ron Lukezic was always a heavy drinker and alcohol affected his reactions. Witnesses felt that he was intoxicated the night of the murder. Later he wept in the lap of a friend, saying, "The Negroes are killing us all." However, the friend remembered that Ron had once been shot in the abdomen by black men during a holdup, a fact that probably resulted in his statement. The death of his business partner seemingly had triggered the memory of that earlier incident.

Don Hume, a printing sales representative who had been with Graphic Dimensions from the time it started, went to the funeral and saw Ron. Actually, it was a memorial service, the formal burial taking place in Ohio. However, Pat Redmond was so respected in Phoenix that the service was jammed with friends and business associates.

"It was very crowded," Hume later stated. "It was held at a mortuary chapel, and it was very packed. In fact, I . . . I stood in the back of the church. I was a little late and had to sit in the back."

Hume mentioned that after the service he went over to talk with Ron Lukezic. "He seemed to be in a state of . . . an extreme state of shock," Hume recalled. "He was crying. He was having considerable trouble controlling himself emotionally and making any statements."

Lukezic went to Hume, embracing his long time employee. "He came and put his hands on my shoulder and said, 'My God, Don, what have I done?' " Hume never forgot the odd incident. He had no idea what Ron Lukezic may have meant by those words.

It was summer before life returned to normal for Joyce and Ron Lukezic. Marilyn Redmond began her slow recovery. She was annoyed and angry that Ron Lukezic was frequently at the hospital, trying to visit her even while she was in the Intensive Care Unit where he was not allowed entry.

There had never been any love lost between Marilyn and Ron. Ron had been Pat's friend and business partner, but he was a heavy drinker and carouser, a man who was on his fourth wife and still had numerous girl friends. Even worse, since Pat was dead, Ron was anxious to make a deal to formally take over the business.

Ron and Pat had been protected by "key man" life

insurance policies, each naming the other as beneficiary. The money was to be used to buy the partner's share of the business in the event of death.

The insurance was viewed as being much too low for the value of the facilities. There was talk of a million dollar offer for the property a year earlier. Yet Ron, when he was finally able to talk with Marilyn, had offered only $250,000.

Marilyn hired a lawyer to arrange for an appraisal and fight Ron Lukezic's offer. The lawyer arranged for an independent appraisal, eventually agreeing with Marilyn concerning the value of the property. In the end, though, she agreed to Ron's terms. She was having trouble eating and swallowing. Part of her jaw was numb. She had lost her husband and was emotionally in bad shape. She took the money, a boat, and a few other items of value. She was too weak and too tired to argue.

But the difficulty over the money was not the primary reason Marilyn Redmond was angry. Marilyn had decided that Ron Lukezic was somehow involved in her husband's murder. She remembered how Ron frequently stated that Pat Redmond was always flashing money and owned large quantities of gold. The fact that the killers were specifically seeking items Ron had talked about concerned her. As she told the police, who took her deposition as soon as she could speak, "He came to the funeral with a shoulder holster and a gun because he was afraid and cried on half a dozen people's shoulders, 'Oh, my God, what did I do?' "

Angrily she had added, "He knew the minute it happened what happened and why."

Words spoken in pain do not represent criminal evidence. All that was certain was that the three men in custody were guilty of the robbery, a fact confirmed through photo identification by Marilyn Redmond. None had named Ron Lukezic. None had named anyone as their tip-off person. And the only other person involved, the woman called "Bindi"—who proved actually to be named Valerie Harper—had told everything she knew when she turned in Hooper, Brice, and McCall.

There seemed no reason to investigate Ron Lukezic, though he obviously gained from the deaths. The police felt it was enough to pursue the guilty parties, looking beyond them only as evidence warranted.

Oddly, Ron Lukezic did suggest to his wife that she find a lawyer who could represent her. Ron had a lawyer for his business, but there was no one Joyce knew to represent her personally. She asked her brother, Arthur Ross, about such representation and he agreed with Ron. It can't hurt, she was told. You never know when you might need one.

Joyce was given several names to call including Thomas Thinnes. Thinnes explained that he might be representing a man named Arnie Merrill who was involved in some way with the Redmond murders. It would not do for him to consider being the lawyer for the wife of Redmond's business partner.

The other attorneys were too busy to bother with Joyce. She had no immediate business for them and they saw no reason to worry about her.

Joyce came to feel the same way. She was in no trouble. The killings did not relate to her. And the idea of paying a lawyer money to represent her at some vague time in the distant future, if ever, seemed a waste of cash. She had made three or four calls to satisfy Ron. She would not bother any further.

Even the newspaper reporters were satisfied with what was taking place. There had been a robbery that had gone awry, leaving two people dead and a third partially disabled. The tragedy offered some excitement for New Year's Eve. It was quickly replaced by other dramas that are constantly a part of daily life. At least that was the case until the day Joyce went for doughnuts with her daughter and life irreversibly changed in ways that simply did not happen to women like her.

Chapter 2

THE MADISON STREET JAIL

It was hot in Phoenix when Joyce was led to the holding tank, an area of the Madison Street jail where women were kept until their hearings came up, they were moved to another jail, or otherwise relocated. The temperature outside was over 110 degrees. Inside the holding area, the air seemed even hotter. There was no air conditioning, seemingly no ventilation. Four large fans were placed in the hallway to stir the air, but even these proved ineffectual.

The heat increased the odor in the area. The aroma of vomit, blood, urine, fecal material, cheap perfume, and disinfectant hung in the air, assaulting the noses of everyone who passed, stinging the eyes of those who had to linger.

There were forty women in the holding tank, a facility built to house no more than a dozen at a time. On one wall were two tiers of three bunks each. The holding tank was not supposed to be used for more than a few hours at a time, the bunks meant for those who were sick or tired.

Along the second wall was a long bench. And by the third side there was a small cubicle holding a single toilet and sink. There was no toilet paper, no sanitary napkins. Personal hygiene was not a consideration because of the short duration the women were intended to stay in the cell. The reality was that some women spent two or three days there, bureaucracy moving slower than expected.

The overcrowded holding area was one of several in the jail. Some held men. Others held bisexuals and male homosexuals. The doors had large barred areas through which the inmates could occasionally see each other. Whenever possible, some of the girls would jump up and down, lifting their skirts to "flash" their pubic area to the cheering men.

Joyce entered the holding area after being finger-printed, photographed, and having her personal posses-sions taken from her. She was aware of the other women yet never truly saw or heard them. There were the prosti-tutes, some yelling and screaming, others sitting sedately on the benches, waiting. A few were obviously past their prime, their bodies scarred from drug injections, slashes of razors, and the ravages of untreated venereal disease. Their clothing was designed to show as much skin as pos-sible. Micro-skirts revealed a hint of their panties as they walked. Blouses were cut to the navel, their breasts barely supported by the fabric. Hair was teased, dyed, bleached, and otherwise altered.

Other prostitutes had been arrested in the better ho-tels. They were well-dressed, sophisticated, with expensive clothing, fashionable perfume, and faces that would seem vaguely familiar around the country club swimming pool. It was obvious, from the way they waited, that this was not their first time in the holding cell; they had experienced the facility before. Many of them were on a first name basis with the guards.

Some of the women were convicted murderers being held in the cell while awaiting a time to testify in other court cases. Others had been in barroom brawls. A few had been arrested for armed robbery, burglary, arson, and extortion. The majority were violent, sullen, and as comfortable with their surroundings as the average person would be in their homes.

Joyce sat huddled on the floor in the corner, saying nothing, doing nothing. There were screams, tears, a cacophony of voices. "Can I have an aspirin?" "Can you tell me the time?" "Can I have some Kotex?" "Do you have a cigarette?" "Can I have a match?" "My lover here yet? He's going to bring me bail."

And there were the jailers calling the women who were to appear in court: "Lopez. Jensen. O'Meara. Bender. Suarez. Botts. Court time."

In the distance was the sound of a typewriter being used in the booking area. And always there was the clanging of the large key used to lock and unlock each cell, the sound of the barred door being moved, the raucous comments of the men and women sexually taunting each other as they moved along the corridor.

Two or three times that day each holding tank was cleaned. A trusty would fill a large container with water and disinfectant, then take a mop and start cleaning the corridor floor. As she would arrive at a holding cell, the door would be opened and all the occupants herded to the next cell to wait while the inside floor was cleaned. Then the inmates would be herded back and the same procedure repeated with the next cell. The water would not be changed until after all the holding cells were swabbed.

Joyce had no idea when dinner was presented to the women in her cell. She had no appetite; she could only stare as the bags of food were passed among the inmates.

Each bag was the same. A date on the outside of the bag indicated when it had been prepared, the food having gone unserved for days.

Inside the bag were two dry bologna sandwiches, an apple or an orange, and a hard-boiled egg. The bread was old, some of the slices having sections of green mold the women either tore off or ate. In addition there was a thin

Kool-Aid mix, one cup per person. The only other liquid came once or twice during the eight-hour shift when each prisoner was allowed out to drink from a water fountain.

Hour after hour Joyce sat, staring, unmoving, unfeeling. Sights and sounds were all around, none of them fully registering. Then, after dinner, her name was called.

Fifty men and women were ushered downstairs to a holding area for initial hearings related to their cases. Her attorney, Larry Debus, was present, the first friendly face she had seen. Debus was tall, well over six feet, powerful, his appearance much like the police officer he had been while working to pay for law school. Those who had known him over the years delighted in his unpretentiousness. While other attorneys displayed diplomas from expensive schools, Debus kept a framed copy of his GED certificate on the wall. The GED was given to high school drop-outs who, as adults, return to classes in order to earn an equivalency diploma. The fact that he had one attested to his personal drive for betterment. The fact that he displayed it showed a lack of pomp in a profession where image was often as respected as substance.

Debus was also a quiet man, seemingly withdrawn at times. During one period of his life, he and his wife spent nine months sailing the world, just the two of them alone on their boat. It was not a typical escape for a defense attorney, a profession that often attracts flamboyant showmen who thrive on an audience every bit as much as actors and entertainers. His lack of aggressiveness was reassuring under the circumstances of the arrest, somehow comforting for Joyce.

He told her not to worry, had her plead innocent, then explained that she would be released as soon as arrangements could be made for a bond. "Don't worry, Joyce," he told her. "You'll be home in no time."

Joyce expected to return to the holding area, but that was not to be. Instead she was transferred to a regular cell in one of the oldest facilities in Phoenix. There would only be four women kept together, approximately double the number originally intended for each unit. Bunk beds lined two of the walls, allowing prisoners to sit and sleep. But the space was such that it was difficult for more than one person at a time to maneuver around the cell. It was as though she was a guinea pig crowded together with three other rodents in a container barely large enough for one.

"Don't worry, Joyce. You'll be home in no time," her attorney had said, and she clung desperately to this belief. Yet even as her mind played back his words, she discovered that one of the women, being held on a charge of second degree murder, had lived in that cramped space for more than six months. She had not met her bail and had to stay there awaiting her trial. She had also been told not to worry, though her lawyer was a public defender. She had also been told that she would be released soon.

Joyce took one of the top bunks because she sensed she would have the most privacy there. She sat down and, taking the sheet she had been given in her hands, wrapped it around her body. She did not crave the warmth. Rather, it was as though the thin material would somehow insulate her from the sounds and the people all around her. It was a barrier; with her body protected by the sheet, no one could hurt her. She was safe, secure, the sounds in the background no more threatening than the noise from a too-loud radio played in the home of a neighbor. And so she slept.

The reality of jail did not occur until morning. She was harshly awakened sometime between five and six A.M. and taken to a day room. There was a long table, food, and a television set kept in such a position that the channel could only be changed by a guard. The set would be kept running from the time everyone awakened until they were all locked up for the night. Meals would be three times a day, each meal lasting only long enough for the women to quickly finish their food. No more than sixteen women would be fed at a time, the cells being opened in shifts. No one could linger because of the risk that someone might become violent.

For the first time Joyce became aware of what was taking place. Most of the women had been in jail before. They had learned the system, learned how to survive in a world where madness was the rule.

Linda, a woman whose latest arrest was for armed robbery, went to the toilet, flushed it, then took a cup and began emptying the bowl. She poured the "clean" water into the sink, emptying cup after cup until the toilet was dry. Then, placing her head deep into the bowl, she shouted, "David, can you hear me?" She listened for a minute, then shouted again, "Hey, one of you mothers, get David to the telephone."

Again there was silence, then Joyce heard a deep male voice say, "What you want, you cunt? You think a little pussy can drag me away from a card game?"

"Don't give me that bullshit, David. A little pussy would make you forget hitting the numbers. So how the hell you doing down there?"

"Shit, girl, ain't nothing to do but talk to the likes of you."

"So come on up, baby. Just tell them guards you want to see your honey. There are four of us up here. We can handle anything you got."

The call became increasingly obscene. Then Annie, a woman charged with prostitution, burglary, and other crimes, demanded her right to use the "telephone." She wanted to talk with someone named Mike.

Hour after hour, unless one of the women had to use the toilet, someone was likely to want to stick her head in the commode so she could talk on the "telephone." The pipes ran through the building in such a way that they served as a link among the cells. With the bowl empty of water, it was possible to carry on conversations. Others might listen in, but no one cared. It was a way for the prisoners to have control over their society. It was a way for them to communicate that none of the guards could stop.

The "telephone system" was also Joyce's first lesson in prison survival. Everything was violence, compromise, and/or adaptation. There was no freedom to move, so freedom came from beating the system, even in so crude a manner as sticking one's head in a filthy toilet bowl in order to communicate with people you could not see.

There were other tricks for survival. Once a week, if they were good and if there was no lockdown of the cells, the women had commissary privileges. They could buy writing paper, stamped envelopes, books, and other things such as instant coffee and tea bags. A hot pot could be created in the cells by filling a cup with water and either instant coffee or tea. Then matches would be burned under the cup, the water inside both heating and acting as protection to keep the cup from bursting into flames.

In some of the cells, bootleg alcohol was made from fruit or fruit cocktail, sugar, and yeast. In others, cigarettes were traded for sex or to arrange a beating. Theirs was a closed society and the prisoners would do anything to feel as though they had some sense of control.

The only service available to Joyce was a small library. The books appeared to have come from hospital book carts, the bindings and pages were always tattered. Many of the books had been damaged, pages or even entire sections removed. Yet even if they had been new books of a type Joyce wanted to read, she could not concentrate. She was overwhelmed by emotions, sights, and sounds that were beyond her comprehension.

First there was the "telephone" system. The sight of women dipping their heads into the toilet bowls, listening to the obscenities of faceless individuals in other cells on other tiers sickened her.

Then there were the "918's," a number designating the emotionally disturbed. These were women who screamed and carried on day and night. Many of them would be released to long-term care, locked mental hospitals. Others would spend their time in prison, though frequently separated from the general population. Still others would serve several months where they were. But no matter what their future, for the moment they were screaming and chattering endlessly, their voices carrying to every cell in the block, no matter how far from the women.

One woman screamed for her mother, begging and pleading to be allowed back in the house. Another chanted obscenities without end until the chant became a meaningless litany of "fuckmefuckmefuckmefuckmefuckme . . ." hour after hour, day after day. Still others carried on conversations about men they had known, dates they were having, and other activities. However, there was no one with whom they were talking. They laughed, cried, and argued vehemently with imaginary beings.

There would come a time when Joyce Lukezic would envy the "918's" ability to live in a world of madness. There would be moments in the time ahead when insanity would be preferable to what she would endure at the hands of others. But for now there was just enough hope that she would soon leave that she chose to escape in other ways.

"I sat on the bed, closed my eyes, and put myself on a boat. I was sailing, alone, a thin, white, sensual dress blowing in the gentle breeze. I had my head back and could feel the light mist striking my face. The sun was out, warming my body, and everything was clean, bright. I was all alone, only the gulls flying around for company. And always I was happy."

There would be other fantasies as well. "I spent a lot

of time with my mother. She had died just a few weeks before my arrest so she was on my mind a lot.

"Sometimes I would be sitting on her lap, being rocked, and she would be telling me everything would be all right. Other times I was in Manhattan with her and we were shopping at Macy's and Gimbel's, and all the other stores. Sometimes I was as young as eight, remembering the dolls, the doll houses, and the other special toys. Sometimes I was fourteen, looking at brightly colored clothing. They were always happy times when we'd come to the city from our home in upstate New York. And if I really concentrated, I could smell the city, feel the clothing, be happy again."

There were thoughts of her children as well. At first she believed that her attorney would gain her release in a day or two. She worried about how the children were getting along, who would take care of them.

Then a day or two stretched into a week, then two. She was helpless, alone with her memories and the fantasies that filled her mind. She began remembering happy times together with her family, sometimes something as simple as reliving making their sandwiches for lunch. She worked to block out the sounds of the toilet telephone, the screaming 918's, the endless game shows on television in the dayroom where they ate, the constant taunting of the guards and the inmates.

Joyce could not remember when it began. There had been the taunts, of course. Her three cellmates, one white, two black, were aware of her case and of her Central Avenue address. The location was common knowledge in Phoenix. It was where the money was. It was where one found families who could afford the luxuries of life. It was a location where the lifestyle was coveted, but the people who enjoyed it were scorned and hated by those who knew they could never afford such surroundings. For a while it seemed that "Central Avenue bitch" was used more often than her name when the cellmates wanted anything from her.

Then there was the touching. The bunks were crowded and reaching the top bunk was not easy for someone as short as Joyce. Frequently she had to use the edge of the lower bunk to boost herself to the top. There was no other furniture, no chair or stool she could use.

"Don't step on my bed, you bitch," said the white inmate, Allison. She was smiling, watching her from below.

"I said, don't step on my bed." She grabbed Joyce's ankle, holding it for a moment, then rubbing her hand up Joyce's lower leg.

Time passed, the touching, the taunting, gradually changing in tone. "You step on my bed, you can just as easily lay down on it." Now the act of holding of her ankle was firmer, the action lasting slightly longer. She studied Joyce's face, making it clear that she was sexually interested.

"Allison wore her hair short, like a stylish man might," said Joyce. "Today it wouldn't seem so harsh, but it was very butch back then. She was definitely a lesbian and I had to face the fact that she was interested in me."

"Come on, Central Avenue bitch. You can stay down here with me."

The other cellmates, Tasha and Jasmine, both blacks, watched, expressionless. They knew what was taking place between Joyce and Allison, knew that the system let a woman like Allison become so aggressive. Whatever was going to happen did not concern them. They lived their lives just inches apart, but that small space might just as well have been a chasm thousands of miles deep. There were unspoken, unwritten rules concerning what one could and could not do, where one would help, where one would suddenly be struck deaf, blind, and mute. Tasha and Jasmine had seen it all before and knew they would see it again. They would only watch, wait, and let the two women handle things themselves.

Joyce never took the time to think about the power structure in the jail cell. There was always racial tension; blacks, whites, Hispanics, and Indians each trying to stay with their own kind, each group hating the other, attempting to gain a feeling of self-respect through a shared bias.

Allison was the leader of Joyce's cell. She was powerful, angry, lusty, and headed back to the penitentiary. She had been in jail, released, committed more crimes, and was being returned. It was the system and she was comfortably a part of it. She knew how to take control of wherever she went. Her leadership was understood by Tasha and Jasmine. No matter what they personally thought of Allison or her actions, they supported her because that was how they stayed alive.

It was afternoon, still early, lunch having been served in the dayroom, the four women returning to their cells. If there was a change in the mood of the women, Joyce was unaware of it. She sensed no tension, no furtive whispering or tell-tale glances on the part of the others. Everything seemed normal as she reached for the top bunk and started to pull herself up.

The hand gripped her ankle. Damn it. More bullshit. All she wanted to do was wrap herself in her sheet, let her mind relax and drift back to the lake, putting herself in the peaceful surroundings that had become her escape.

Suddenly she felt herself being pulled down to the bottom bunk. She lost her grip, her body falling backwards. She felt her knees scrape against the metal frame, her arms striking the side, her head snapping back, then forward, striking the wall as she tried to gain her balance, retain some control.

Joyce tried to twist her body, to lash out. A hand grabbed her hair, twisted it, and tightened the grip. Then her head was pulled back, her neck exposed, any twisting of her face bringing intense pain as though her hair was going to be pulled out by the roots.

Her arms were grabbed and pulled above her, then firmly gripped. Two of them were handling her, holding her. Jasmine and Tasha. Restraining her. Saying nothing. Just keeping her in place.

Joyce tensed her legs, then found Allison straddling her. Allison positioned herself so she was kneeling on Joyce's legs in a manner that made kicking impossible. The woman reached up and pulled the elastic on her clothing, pushing up her blouse, pulling down her slacks, exposing her breasts, her stomach, her pubic area.

"Central Avenue bitch. You've been wanting this. You've been wanting this . . ."

She felt Allison's hands on her thighs, her fingers pushing against the skin, yet she was in too much of a state of shock to realize what was happening. Later she would realize the pressure that had been used. Later she would see the bruising, feel the tenderness, know that there must have been incredible pain her shocked mind had been too numb to feel. But not at that instant. Adrenaline was pumping too rapidly through her helpless body for her to react to anything during those first few seconds.

Suddenly Joyce felt her legs being ripped apart. She bucked, straining against the women who held her before her head was jerked back down against the bed. Her legs spasmed as the muscles tensed in a desperate effort to free herself from the weight of Allison, the pressure of her assailant's hands.

Joyce forced herself to focus on what was being done to her. Foreplay. Allison was engaging in foreplay. Her tongue probed Joyce's most intimate parts, touching, licking, going deeper and deeper as her mouth sucked between Joyce's legs.

Joyce started to scream, felt her hair pulled taut as she arched her back, then had her arms twisted painfully.

She forced herself to silence, knowing the guards were making their rounds, knowing only her assailants could hear her.

A hand moved roughly against her pubic hair, fingers probing deeply, rubbing, abrasive. Joyce tensed her body, breathing rapidly, trying not to think of the pain, not to feel what was happening, not to . . .

She screamed in spite of herself. Allison's fingernails cut deeply against her clitoris, sending paroxysms of pain throughout Joyce's body. Tears came to her eyes as she tried to focus on her assailant, desperate to achieve some human contact that would make Allison ease her actions, free her from the nightmare.

But Allison was flushed, happy, delighting in the assault. Her body moved rhythmically with her hands and tongue, the probings becoming more intense, the friction so rough and rapid that Joyce felt as though someone had taken sandpaper to her genitals. Yet Allison did not seem to notice the pain she was inflicting. It was as though she was achieving orgasm through violence and there was nothing Joyce could do but endure.

Finally Allison shuddered and seemed to relax, her lust at least temporarily sated. Joyce did not know if the other two women would take their turns or if they would use a make-shift weapon to silence her for good. She no longer cared. All she wanted was an end to the pain, the humiliation, the horror. It did not matter whether it came from Allison's lust being sated or from the three women crushing the life from her body. Just so there was an end.

But Jasmine and Natasha had no interest in sexually abusing Joyce. They held her, their muscles flexing with tension each time Joyce struggled, but they made no effort to look at her, to watch Allison's actions. They looked away, to some other time, some other place. Helping with a rape was what one did to survive. But mentally they might have been remembering a favorite meal, a day at the beach, a walk with a boyfriend.

Joyce stared at Allison as she was released from the bed. There was no sign of hate, no sign of anger. There was only peace, a look on Allison's face that seemed to indicate that, at any moment, she would light a cigarette, take a puff, exhale slowly, savoring the smoke, then turn to Joyce and ask, "Was it good for you, too?"

Jasmine and Tasha returned to their bunks, their eyes no different than before the assault. They said nothing to Joyce. They said nothing to Allison. It was as though nothing had happened and, if it had, they were not a part of it.

At first, Joyce was too much in shock to feel the pain. She struggled to her top bunk and began weeping uncontrollably. She cried for the injustice. Then she cried for the pain. She wept from indignity and fear, terror and helplessness. And then she fell asleep, not moving for dinner, to use the toilet, for lights out.

Sometime around 4 A.M. Joyce stirred. The other women were asleep. Bruised and sore she inched down from her bunk to use the open toilet. Her urine burned as she relieved herself, washed in the sink, putting water on her face, cupping her hand for a drink, trying not to think and thinking too much. Then, careful not to awaken Allison, she wearily pulled herself up to the top of the bunk where, weeping once more, she drifted off to sleep.

Ron Lukezic noticed the bruises on Joyce's arm when he came to visit her. She had not tried to reach him to tell him what happened. She had not tried to report the incident to her lawyer or the jail officials. She had learned enough of the system to know that speaking of the rape, pointing the finger at Allison, would only get her in more trouble. Perhaps Allison would retaliate, perhaps someone else. There would be no warning, no outward sign of what was going to take place. One minute she would be standing or walking through a common area. The next moment she would be on the ground, bleeding, her life pulsating from her body with every beat of her ever-weakening heart. And no matter how many people might be present, no one would have heard anything, seen anything, or even admitted to being nearby, regardless of what evidence might exist to the contrary.

But Ron was different. Ron was her husband, the man who claimed he loved her. She could tell Ron. She could share the experience, gain his comfort, his love and understanding. But he did not comfort her. Instead he pressed for details.

How did she do it, Joyce, he wanted to know. Where did she put her tongue? Where did she place her hands? And she was astride you, forcing your legs apart with her legs as she worked on you?

His face seemed to flush, just like Allison's. He had once told her that he fantasized having sex with two women at the same time, though he never mentioned whether or not he achieved that goal. Now he seemed to be living vicariously through Joyce's words, his imagination stirred up by sexual images. He seemed to have forgotten the bruises, to have been unaware of his weeping wife.

Or maybe Joyce was imagining the reaction. Perhaps he really was empathetic. Perhaps she was misinterpreting his expressions, attaching meanings that did not exist in reality. She was uncertain just what was happening. All she knew was that his reaction, or her response to that reaction, was such that they would never again share the emotional intimacy she once thought they had experienced.

Life in the cell continued. Allison never spoke of the incident. She stopped grasping at Joyce's ankle, ceased trying to stroke her leg. There were no more taunts of "Central Avenue bitch," no more sexual innuendoes. It was as though the rape had never happened from the moment it was over until Allison was transferred to the state penitentiary for women.

Jasmine and Tasha also never mentioned the incident. There was not even an unspoken "No hard feelings, Joyce. We're all in this together. We do what we have to do to stay alive. You understand." Joyce was bruised, battered, alternately trying to escape into memories of the past and fighting the desire to weep uncontrollably until all the tears were drained from her body and she was too exhausted to live. And life went on.

It was twenty-one days before all arrangements were made for Joyce's release from jail. Ron had not come to see her very often and this further depressed her but he had made arrangements that bond be met and she was free to go, her trial set far enough in the future that she could at last learn what charges were pending against her.

Joyce arrived home without telling her children she was coming. They were in school so she went to the bathroom, stripped off her clothing, threw it in the washer, then stepped into the shower.

At first everything was normal. She soaped her body, washed her hair, rinsed herself off. Then she took the soap and lathered again, this time harder than the first. She began scrubbing herself, her breasts, her legs, her pubic hair. Every inch of her body was covered, yet she did not feel clean. She rinsed and soaped herself again and again, as though the filth of the jail had been ground so deeply into her pores that anything less than an inch-by-inch scouring of her body might allow the filth to regenerate and infect her home and family. Only when the soap was almost gone, the water cold, and her body wrinkled from the liquid did she stop and dry herself. Then she went to the kitchen, sat down, and waited for the moment when her children would return to her open arms.

Later she would learn of the trials to come. Later she would learn of the contract murders for which she would face the death sentence. Later she would discover that her lawyer would fail her, her husband would disappear, and she would have to prove her innocence of an unsolved crime while living behind bars. For the moment she was content with burying her face against the heads of her children, crying tears of happiness for being reunited, even briefly, with those she loved.

Chapter 3

THE SCHEMERS AND THE DREAMERS

Sometimes it seems as though Arizona is a state of schemers, dreamers, and retirees. It is a new state, the land being a United States territory until 1928, and the frontier mentality is obvious even in the most sophisticated regions. Handguns may be carried openly, violating state law only when concealed. Pick-up trucks are the preferred means of transportation, even among those who can well afford Mercedes, Cadillacs, and other luxury cars. Although temperatures in the state routinely reach 115 degrees and higher during the summer months, gun racks, usually holding either a rifle or shotgun, are more desired pick-up truck accessories than are air conditioners.

There is a myth of friendliness among the people of Arizona, a myth belied by the news. There have been book bannings in the community of St. David, a state ballot declaration, considered anti-semitic by many, that stated that Arizonans were declaring the United States to be a "Christian nation," and wars between polygamous and monogamous Mormons in the northern part of the state. The elderly who retire often isolate themselves in special communities such as Sun City and Green Valley. They fight school bond issues because they have no children and frequently discriminate against the young who wish to buy or rent housing in their areas. In turn, they are attacked by those who say the elderly use a disproportionate number of community services relative to the often small amount of taxes they pay.

Yet fortunes are to be made in Arizona and many families showed their hunger for power and success even before they arrived. Among the early pioneers, one family had sons who earned their grubstake through marriage by being paid large sums of money by a wealthy businessman who desired his ugly daughters wedded. Prominent leaders advanced through connections with organized crime. Land fraud schemes seemed to attract as many career oriented professionals as legitimate real estate. And Arizona was a pioneer in thrift financial institution scandals. Still, despite the need for reform, there was an underlying attitude that if someone couldn't take care of himself, he deserved whatever fate might befall him.

The retirees followed the schemers, sometimes being victimized by land and banking frauds, more often neither knowing nor caring about the problems within the state. They saw a foretaste of heaven in the desert and mountain regions. Sunlight shines more than 3,700 hours throughout the year, an average of more than ten hours a day, seven days a week. There are some periods of mild cold and rain, even in low desert, but snow is rare, lasting no more than a few hours each year. And while traffic has increased dramatically—freeway rush hours being no better than those in New York, Chicago, and Los Angeles—the retirees are mostly located in self-sufficient neighborhoods where there is a sense of peaceful well-being. What does not get done today will be completed *mañana*. And if tomorrow never comes, they have spent their last days in peace.

With the schemers and the retirees came the dreamers. Everything seemed new in the desert: fresh, clean, and filled with promise for people whose futures seemed limited before they arrived. Construction workers earned good wages meeting the housing demands of what once was the fastest growing region of the United States. The military bases employed large numbers of civilians. Tucson was home to major movie studio operations and a regular influx of television, motion picture, and commercial production companies. Phoenix had high tech industries that looked as though they might rival California's famed Silicon Valley. Even Flagstaff, 7,000 feet up in the mountains and seemingly isolated from the world, had the international W.L. Gore Company, manufacturers of materials used in medicine, sporting goods, and other products. Northern Arizona University drew students from as far away as China who sought training in forestry, music, and engineering, among other offerings. The state had a medical school, pharmacy school, law school, professional theater companies, symphony orchestras . . . The list went on and on, giving the impression that no matter what skill someone might have, no matter what they wished to achieve in life, Arizona had something to offer them.

Joyce Dow was that rare exception when she moved to Phoenix. She was neither a dreamer, a schemer, nor a retiree, though her mother had settled in the Sun City community for the elderly. In fact, Joyce had never planned to settle in Arizona. When she divorced Dr. Ed Dow, a physician specializing in pathology, she had two children and a third on the way. His love had degenerated into adultery and violence, and she felt she could no longer live with him. Their marriage ended in 1971. Joyce traveled west with the children to a new home in Colorado, settling in a suburb of Denver. She was trained in biochemistry and medical technology, skills which enabled her to obtain employment wherever she chose to live. However, six months after the move, in the fall of 1975, her mother developed hepatitis as a result of an unusual reaction to aspirin. The illness was very severe and Joyce moved her family immediately. Her brother, Arthur Ross, a successful businessman, was already living in Scottsdale, a Phoenix suburb, the family choosing to draw together in the crisis.

Joyce's father had died many years earlier from a congenital heart condition that would also plague his two children. He was a man in his forties when he was stricken, dying in the then sixteen-year-old Joyce's arms. She had given him mouth-to-mouth resuscitation, desperately trying to revive him.

That death had shattered the family. Emotionally, Joyce's mother had been unable to do more than survive from day to day; even caring for her children became impossible for her. Fortunately Arthur was an adult by then, Joyce turned to him as a father figure. She managed to finish high school and go on to college, rushed into adulthood faster than normal.

Despite the untimely death, the Ross family was left financially comfortable. Although they lived in Boston, Joyce's father had invested in New York City real estate. His wife and children were left shares in apartment buildings and other holdings sufficient to assure enough money to more than cover their needs. They had gone their separate ways until it appeared that their mother now gravely ill might also experience an untimely death, a fact that convinced her to relocate once again.

Joyce's mother survived the hepatitis crisis and Joyce found employment at Diagnostic Laboratories, working as a technologist. Her past experience and training were sufficient for the company to hire her to run their satellite labs.

Phoenix, like so many other sun belt cities of the 1970's, was a lonely town for newly arrived singles. Joyce, though raised as a reformed Jew, was not very religious and seldom attended Temple except on Jewish holidays.

She had neither time nor inclination to join one of the health clubs, and most other events—the Phoenix Symphony, what little live theater existed in the community, and even the museums—offered few opportunities for encountering eligible men. The only option, other than dating someone she might meet at work, was to go to one of the better bars to unwind. It was at the Sahara on Camelback Road that she first met Ron Lukezic.

Ron Lukezic would not be anyone's idea of the perfect leading man for a romantic movie. The first thing anyone noticed was his size. He was tall and fat, more like Orson Welles than Robert Redford. Yet he was outgoing, jovial, a heavy drinker who became even more mellow under the influence. After what Joyce perceived as the physical and emotional ordeal of her previous marriage, Ron appeared to be non-threatening, safe, an alternative worth exploring. Yet she was cautious, refusing to accept his offer to buy her a drink as she sat nursing a glass of wine at the Sahara. All she would do was tell him her name and give him her office telephone number.

Friends and acquaintances laughed about Ron's capacity for liquor. Yet he was a man who never showed any ill effects from what he drank. Whether he started early or late in the day, his mind was quick, his actions friendly, and he always seemed in control. Still, his dates with Joyce were primarily confined to high class bars and restaurants proud of their liquor supplies.

Their relationship grew more serious. Ron became friendly with Joyce's children, taking them all to Disneyland. He and Joyce also traveled to Las Vegas to do some gambling, though even that was always under control. He liked a good time, made a high income, and had the sense to live within his ample means.

Joyce discovered that Ron Lukezic ran a printing company, a business that held no interest for her. She also had little interest in his business partner, Pat Redmond, or

Redmond's wife, Marilyn. The Redmonds also enjoyed drinking and seemed to limit their socializing mostly to activities where they could enjoy alcohol.

Some of the tension among the four of them may have had to do with the fact that Ron had once dated Marilyn, then dumped her as he became involved with other women. Patrick then began dating her, eventually taking her for his wife.

There was also the fact that Joyce was from a radically different background. Patrick was essentially a blue collar worker who had become more successful than he ever thought possible. He was a pressman and took great pride in his skill in the back of the shop.

Eventually Pat's skills led him to become the foreman of the pressmen. It was hard physical labor and required great skill, including the checking of colors under a microscope to be certain the final images would match the originals.

Ron started out as a stripper, the individual who prepared the artwork before it was placed on the printing press. Then Ron, like Pat, also moved up, becoming the manager of the preparation area. He worked in the front office at times, then took over the presidency of the company where both he and Pat were employed. The men worked together and the couples socialized together, Marilyn meeting Ron's various wives—Mary Lou, Jeanetta, and Patty, all the women who preceded Joyce to the altar.

Ron Lukezic was gaining another skill during this period. He was learning how to get large printing orders, bringing in the kind of money that could make a company extremely successful. The Redmonds, Ron, and his wife of the moment also spent considerable time at Chester's, a lounge that held a couple of hundred patrons at a time, many of whom were involved with the printing business. It was a way for Ron to drink, have a good time, and gain more customers.

It was 1975 when Ron Lukezic and Pat Redmond decided to pool their skills to form their own company. Pat handled the dirty work, operating the presses in the back room. Ron handled preparation and sales, the "front end" business. They had only $15,000 to start, spending $10,000 for a color press and borrowing physical space for their business from a mutual friend. The space was a small bay in an industrial park, a location that was more than adequate until they were able to expand. When their business was large enough, they moved into a new building which the owner redesigned to their specifications.

Ron married Joyce after he and Pat became partners, but the socializing among the two wives and husbands was reduced. Not only did Joyce have no interest in Ron's business, she didn't enjoy sitting in Chester's, drinking and talking about printing, about which she had so little concern that she willingly worked out an arrangement at the time of their marriage that she would never benefit from the company. If Ron died, his son by a previous marriage and his mother would benefit. And Joyce, though she enjoyed the lifestyle Ron's income allowed, was financially independent enough so that she could take care of both her needs and those of her children without worrying about Ron's contribution.

Marilyn, by contrast, was frequently in the shop, talking with the employees, keeping herself apprised of what was taking place in the business. She was interested in her husband's work and was known to both the employees and their suppliers. She considered herself a part of the print shop, something to which Joyce could not relate.

At the time of the murders, Ron and Pat had a stock buy-out agreement. Each held 12,500 shares in the company, the key man insurance policies meant to purchase the other person's shares.

Despite their partnership, the two men were very different. Patrick Redmond seemed lacking in ambition for anything greater than his existing accomplishments, delighting in what they were earning, letting alcohol and cards be his way of relaxing when he was not on the job.

There was a gentleness to Patrick that eventually proved lacking in Ron. Joyce recalled one time when they went fishing on a boat. Ron became sick and had to adjourn to the bar. Pat remained topside, eventually catching a large fish. Yet Pat did not have the heart to gaffe it in order to bring it into the boat.

The partners spent time together, yet it was obvious that they were growing estranged. Ron regularly talked against Pat, seeming to feel that Pat was not carrying his share of the workload. Their building had a burglar alarm to which one of the owners had to respond after the security firm made certain no prowlers were on the property, for example. Eventually Joyce was so convinced and angry that Pat was not helping enough that she saw nothing wrong with lying when Ron was called, claiming that he was not with her even though they were in bed together at that moment. This would force them to call Pat, making him go to check to see if anything was wrong. It was against her character to lie, but she had become so fond of the big, fun-loving man, that she would take his side in any argument and often made hot-tempered remarks on Pat's shortcomings.

Ron and Joyce were married in 1977 in Winterhaven, California, then bought a house for themselves and Joyce's three children. Each had a strong sense of independence and a desire to protect what they had developed over the years. That was why Joyce would not share in Ron's $2-million per year printing business and Ron would not share in Joyce's income from her inheritance, her job, and the business she planned to start with the financial backing of her brother, Arthur. The house would be joint property, as would anything the two of them did together, but both were successful enough that they wanted to protect their individual assets.

For the first time in many years, life seemed to be going well for Joyce Lukezic. She had a husband she loved, children who were the focal point of her life, her brother was nearby, and her mother seemed to be recovering from her illness. She delighted in being just another working suburban housewife, watching her family grow into adulthood. Her life was family centered; she was little concerned with the rest of the Phoenix community especially its lawmakers and breakers.

Dan Ryan was a man who was also somewhat of an oddity in Phoenix. He was partially a dreamer, though it was for the betterment of his family's lifestyle. He was also a schemer, though his schemes were in the name of law and order.

Ryan had been a Marine officer who saw action in Vietnam. From there he joined the FBI, establishing a record for competence that combined both commendations and criticism. The strongest complaint against him came from a woman who objected to his smoking a cigar in her presence during an interview in her office.

Ryan left the Bureau after a few years, joining the Treasury Department's Alcohol, Tobacco, and Firearms division in Phoenix, a city he had grown to love. His previous work had been in Chicago where he retained unusually good relations with the Chicago Police Department. Then, after a few years with ATF, he switched to the Maricopa County (Phoenix) office of the County Prosecutor, working as an investigator. His job was working with the Phoenix police, county sheriff's office, and/or on his own as the county attorney designated. The decisions of whether or not to prosecute cases, and how to prosecute them, were all made by the county attorney. Ryan was one of several investigators supplying the background information that might be requested.

Ryan was unusually aggressive as an investigator, delighting in the chase, the capture, and the jailing of felons, according to those who knew him at the time. He seemed to have few ambitions about reaching the top of the career ladder, always staying in the area of investigations. Part of this came from the fact that he seemed to most enjoy field work, and part of this came from an inheritance that made him independently wealthy. As one detective who worked with him would later comment, "If Dan gave someone $500 to help him out, it would be the same as you or me giving the guy a quarter from our pockets. He had that much money and it just didn't mean anything to him."

Joyce Lukezic did not know Dan Ryan before the day of her arrest, had never met him and, so far as she knew, had never seen him. Yet she would soon discover that he had what seemed to her to be a personal vendetta against her. While she was trying to help Marilyn Redmond and the Redmond children through the recovery period following the murder, Ryan was working behind the scenes to send Joyce to death row. Although they had never met, they were mortal enemies locked in a struggle that would change them both for the rest of their lives.

Arnie Kleinfeld was a wise guy. From the time he graduated from high school, he wanted it all—fast cars, good looking women, a party every night. He married, but commitment was for women and suckers. There was too much action for a good looking guy who felt that it was his mission to provide every female with a taste of the best.

For boys, Arnie was someone with whom you could have fun. He was close to his brother, Raymond, a serious student, honest, hard working, seeking a future in business—Arnie's opposite. He was also a friend of Artie Ross,

Joyce's older brother, and a youth who was always close to Raymond. The three of them went hunting and fishing together, sharing laughs, talking about girls, planning for a future that both scared and excited them.

For adolescent high school girls, Arnie was something quite different. He was the type of boy their parents warned them against. He seemed exciting when they were teenagers, although the adults recognized the shallow, lecherous attitude that would eventually cause those same adolescent girls to be glad they did not become more serious about him. However, enough women eventually came under his charm that he never let the good times stop. It was a lifestyle that was flashy, expensive, and beyond the reach of most young men. Even Arnie would later admit that he had to underwrite some of the good times with hustles, scams, and burglaries.

By the time Arnie Kleinfeld Merrill's (he legally changed his name several years before the Redmond murder) name was linked with that of Joyce Lukezic, he had mastered the legal system. He knew how to play to ambitious cops, prosecutors anxious for victory, and the sensitivities of the media. He understood that for the clever career criminal, law enforcement was just another hustle, just another scam.

Arthur Ross, Joyce Lukezic's brother, was the first person in her family to experience the effects of too close an encounter with Arnie Merrill. Ross and Merrill's brother had opened a Phoenix gun shop, a thriving business that was making them a lot of money.

In most states, the owners of gun shops have varying degrees of success. Areas where hunting is popular do better than areas where guns are infrequently used. But Arizona, and especially Phoenix, are havens for gun dealers. There are buyers who wish protection for their home as Ron Lukezic did. Lukezic owned guns because he had been robbed, shot, and was fearful of being threatened again. Other people bought guns because their jobs caused them to come and go at odd hours, because they were in high crime areas, or because they liked the feeling of security they felt guns provided.

Then there were the hunters who sought deer, javelina, wild turkey, and other game that abounded throughout the mountains and deserts of Arizona. It was rare to see pick-up trucks without gun racks and many people routinely carried either a rifle, a shotgun, or both, in their trucks.

Handguns were also popular because Arizona law allowed anyone who owned a handgun to carry it openly. Motorcycle riders routincly wore high powered pistols and revolvers. No one was surprised to see someone walk into a bank with a gun at his hip or in a shoulder holster. Rumor had it that organized crime was working to make Arizona a gambling state, much like Nevada, in part because weapons were so readily accepted, an important factor for the bodyguards of top mobsters.

As a result, gun shops could be more profitable than car dealerships. And the shop that Ross, Kleinfeld, and Merrill were operating was typical of the success possible in the business.

There might not have been any problems for the gun shop had it not been for the fact that Arnie Merrill was not satisfied with being a respectable business man. Despite the openness of weapons in Arizona, there was, as in every area, a black market for unregistered guns. Criminals needed to sell guns they had stolen or to buy guns which they did not want connected to them. And the men who had the connections to supply such weapons were respected by the underworld.

Merrill had begun living a fairly wild life. He was cheating on his wife, hanging out at bars where criminals frequently did their drinking. Merrill made certain that the other patrons were aware that he owned a gun shop.

He also broadly hinted that the shop was where one could go to buy an unregistered gun or to get rid of stolen weapons. He never purchased or sold such weapons, at least not from the existing stock and not with his partners' awareness, but image was always more important than substance for Merrill and he liked the reputation he was getting. What Merrill did not realize was that this reputation was being conveyed to law enforcement officers.

Dan Ryan was working for the Alcohol, Tobacco, and Firearms division of the Treasury Department when rumors concerning illegal gun sales and purchases were making the rounds of the bars. Members of the ATF and the Phoenix Police Department were alerted by "snitches," men and women who revealed the criminal activities of others for money or special favors when they were caught commiting crimes. The snitches told what they had heard about the gun shop and the people who ran it. As a result, law enforcement officials began making periodic checks on the records and inventory, including a surprise weekend raid when the shop was closed. That raid ended in embarrassment because the law enforcement officers had improperly executed their warrant, including entering the wrong address.

No charges were ever brought against the gun store or its owners because there was nothing improper taking place. If the men ever did purchase a stolen weapon for the store, it was because there was no way to know such a situation had arisen. It was an honest mistake, not part of a plot to become a fence for criminals. Yet Merrill talked so much that the word on the street was that Ross and his partners were "too clever" for the cops. They were making fools of law enforcement, so the rumors went, and some of the police believed the street talk. Ryan was allegedly determined to bring charges against Arthur Ross, according to other law enforcement officers. Ryan would not directly comment on his feelings at the time, however, but Ross always felt Ryan had a vendetta against him.

Merrill also began selling legal drugs. He made a deal with a doctor in Tempe, Arizona, a Phoenix suburb, to give him prescriptions for popular prescription drugs such as Quaaludes. Merrill would sell the drugs, many of the buyers thinking that the drugs had been stolen. In fact, the doctor was just doing Merrill a favor and probably never knew what was taking place. The doctor did not financially benefit from the sales, though there may have been some other favors exchanged since the doctor was also a gun collector.

In the meantime Merrill's brother and Artie Ross were expanding and trying to make everything work. The two friends were buying guns, selling guns, and also involved with the custom jewelry business. Merrill was running the shop, receiving money more as a result of his family connections than because of his importance to the businesses.

The final incident that estranged Ross and Kleinfeld from Merrill occurred when Merrill and another man got into a violent argument in a delicatessen. Exactly what happened is uncertain. Some say that the fight was over a woman, though the cause did not matter. Merrill arranged to meet the man with whom he had been verbally sparring in an alley behind the deli later that night.

Neither Arthur Ross nor Ray Kleinfeld were fighters. They were being harassed, in their minds, by investigators looking for stolen weapons. They were wrongfully accused of involvement with criminal activity. And some of the more respectable citizens of Phoenix worried about being involved with them on a personal or business basis for fear the rumors were true.

At the same time, Ross felt that some reputation, good or bad, was important in a community to prevent people from taking advantage of you. As much as he hated Mer-

rill's groundless boasting, he also liked the one side benefit. Sales people handling jewelry on commission, carriers
of the quantities of silver and gold needed for custom
work, and others connected with his jewelry business were
not robbed. Other stores and their personnel might have
an occasional problem, but not Ross, Merrill, and
Kleinfeld. Their reputation with the "bad guys" was such
that they were declared off limits, or so Ross believed.
Thus it was important to him to retain some sort of image,
even one that implied that he was a "tough guy."

Merrill entered the gun and jewelry office near tears.
He was terrified of the fight to come that evening. He knew
he would be beaten at the very least, yet he also felt he
could not avoid the showdown without risking getting
hurt some other way.

Suddenly the three men, all approaching middle age,
were like little kids acting out a bad western. Ross and
Kleinfeld disliked Merrill, their partnership with him near
to being dissolved, but they were not going to let him go to
the alley alone. That night they got in a car and drove
together to meet whatever fate was planned for Merrill.

Merrill got out and walked down the alley as Ross and
Kleinfeld sat in the car. "The other people were coming
down the other end of the alley, you know, like a Clint
Eastwood movie," said Ross, laughing. "Nobody had guns
drawn or anything like that, but God knows what would
have happened. And they happened to see me and his
brother, sitting in the car down the alley, and I had the
motor running. You know, I watch a lot of movies, also.

"Then everything was smoothed over. They came,
they talked, they shook hands, and after that everything
was fine.

"But let me tell you, the stories that went out from
that incident, in Scottsdale, in Phoenix, and around that
area, were horrendous. I mean, this was the gunfight at the
O.K. Corral. We were king shit there. We could do no

wrong. You didn't mess with us." Merrill and his "gang" had become the men who put down the mob.

"Unfortunately that was what started him on his career, whatever his career was," said Ross.

After that time Merrill began his hustles. He could do anything and the bad guys went along. Even worse, the snitches convinced law enforcement that the three men were somehow involved with whatever Merrill did on his own, with no one else's awareness.

"When you think of how foolish you are," said Ross. "The man has no backbone, none at all. He never really worked a full day's work in his life. He tries to skate by and skate on anybody else's back."

And skate by he did. Both Ross and Kleinfeld wanted nothing more to do with Merrill. The two friends were as close as brothers, each willing to do anything for the other. But Merrill had become the ne'er do well brother who wanted to capitalize on image and he wanted to do it in the streets.

Robert Cruz looked like the answer to a businessman's prayers when he entered Arthur Ross's life. Ross, Joyce's brother, was a man who delighted in money, in making deals, in taking profits. "Maybe I wasn't always strictly kosher," he admitted. "But nobody got hurt and any money that had to be paid would have been paid anyway."

Ross was a man who diversified his assets. Over the years he had been involved with the gun shop, a jewelry business, real estate and land development. Just as his father had had the sense to purchase apartment buildings and businesses in Manhattan before values skyrocketed, so Ross could sense an area in transition. He was one of the first developers to spot the potential for profit in Austin, Texas, for example, an area with a 350,000 population, the University of Texas, and the state office buildings. It had a stable, diverse economy, a good-sized population, and the potential for growth. He also saw the profits to be made in Phoenix at a time when the city was about to become one of the fastest growing areas in the United States.

Although Ross was wealthy by most standards, in the high stakes world of land development he was constantly seeking better capitalized partners to help underwrite his projects. One such company was a two-billion-dollar firm out of Canada with whom he arranged to develop some Phoenix property. However, there was a difference of opinion over the financial arrangements between Ross and the Canadian company that resulted in their going to court. Ross felt that his arrangements with the Canadian firm were on a per project basis. The Canadian firm maintained that any Phoenix land development in which Ross engaged was to have profits shared with the Canadians. Although a review of the arrangements indicates that Ross was in the right, this did not prevent the Canadians from suing him in several states where Ross was working.

Ray Kleinfeld's wife was doing some work for Robert Cruz when Arthur Ross got into his financial troubles. It was obvious that even with Ross in the right, the Canadian firm had the assets and the legal clout to bankrupt Ross and his partners. Ross needed additional funds in order to fight the Canadians in court and Robert Cruz seemed to be the answer.

Cruz was a man who said that he made investments, a profession that was fairly common in a city like Phoenix. Men and organizations with large sums of money frequently entered growth communities in the 1970s, investing in real estate partnerships, expanding businesses, and entering other areas where they thought they could make some money. They put a few hundred thousand dollars into one deal, a million dollars into another, until they were assured that their overall profit potential would be quite large. Sometimes these would be wealthy individuals trying to make their family inheritance grow. Sometimes these would be groups of wealthy individuals, such as a number of Orange county physicians who pooled their income and bought houses in Tucson when housing prices were on the rise. The homes were rented to pay for their mortgages, then sold when property prices rose to two or three times the original investment. And sometimes the money came from organized crime.

Robert Cruz's money source was of no concern to Arthur Ross. Ross knew that he was in the right when it came to his fight with the Canadian firm. He knew that the deals with which he was involved were legitimate, potentially profitable, and he did not care who shared the wealth so long as the arrangements were honest.

Eventually there would appear to be two sides to Robert Cruz. One was the legitimate businessman who convinced Ross that he could help with the money. Cruz understood the real estate problems as well as the success that Ross had had in the past. He felt confident that he could easily obtain the money Ross needed to fight the Canadian company, complete the land deal, and end Ross's troubles. He also hinted at "connections" in Chicago, his home town. These "connections" were men who not only could help with the financing, but also it was rumored that they could get the Canadians to stop the legal action against Ross's company. The implication was that the "connections" were part of the Mafia. Later it would be learned that Cruz was related to several individuals who were alleged to be members of organized crime in Illinois. However, he was not personally involved in any way of importance, if at all, according to law enforcement officials.

Ross's company was asked to front some money to the Chicago banks that were going to be involved with the deals. The dollar amount was in the low six figures, an amount that seemed legitimate based on past deals of the same magnitude. Many millions of dollars would be forthcoming from the bank and the relatively small sum Ross had to send seemed in line with normal loan requirements. What was not known was that Cruz had contacts inside the banks such that when the money went to what seemed legitimate purposes, it was then withdrawn and transferred to Cruz personally. The deal was an elaborate scam.

During this period, Ross and his partners acquired an office building. They remodeled sections for themselves, putting in Indian art work and African artifacts from their travels and other businesses. They planned to make a suite available to Joyce Lukezic so she could start her own company. And they discussed Robert Cruz moving to the location.

"I thought this was great," said Ross, delighted to have someone who would be providing him with so much financial assistance located next to him. "I could keep real good tabs on him."

Time passed. Ross went to Chicago, meeting with seemingly legitimate bankers and business people, all of whom assured him that everything would be going as Ross hoped. Then people from Chicago came to Phoenix, meeting with both Ross and Cruz who now maintained his office in the complex. No money was coming. The debt service on the land holdings still had to be paid, and the lawsuits continued to have to be fought. But the future seemed secure. Cruz was a legitimate businessman with all the right connections. Cruz would come through.

It was during this time that Ron Lukezic became more frustrated with Patrick Redmond. The estrangement between the two men had become a case of irreconcilable differences. They argued continuously. Ron wanted to take control of the business, to buy out his partner, to expand in any way he wanted.

Ron Lukezic was successful, though like many successful individuals, he did not have large cash reserves. He had not saved much money and could not afford to handle the buyout himself. He wanted his brother-in-law, Arthur Ross, to do it for him.

"I don't know anything about the printing business," explained Ross, whose past and future business ventures were always in areas he understood and in which he could participate. Besides, "I was, pardon my French, asshole deep in property situation with lawsuits. For me, it's not a viable proposition."

Ron wanted some alternative. Although the men were not close, he knew a little of Ross's activities, mostly through Joyce who was quite close to her brother. "Well what about this Cruz guy?" asked Ron.

"I says, 'I don't know. I'm in the middle of trying to do a transaction with him so far as loaning money. If you want, I'll introduce you to him.' I take him next door and introduce him to him."

Ron talked with Cruz on his own. Ross was too concerned about his own financial troubles to be concerned with his brother-in-law. Ross had never particularly liked Ron, was uncomfortable with a man whose social life revolved around bars. He did not care about Ron's problems in any way.

Time passed, Ross becoming uneasy about the failure of promised funds to appear. Then Ron came to him and said that Cruz told him it would be possible for Ron to get large funds from Las Vegas for handling printing for nightclubs.

" 'That's great,' I told him," said Ross. Then Ron said, "I want to go up there to meet the people. Will you come?"

Ross agreed.

Again everything looked right with Cruz. When the three men reached Las Vegas, their rooms and meals were comped by the casino. Then Cruz started walking around the floor, greeting the pit bosses by name and making it clear that he truly was known as somebody seemingly important. He seemed to know what he was talking about.

The meeting was held in a hotel office. Ron, Cruz, and the hotel executive in charge of printing had their meeting, Ross sitting in but remaining silent.

The meeting was seemingly genuine but the offer seemed less to Ross than Ron eventually believed. As Ross recalled the encounter, "Basically the guy said, 'If you can come in under these prices, give us a quote and we can look at it.' Now the guy in Las Vegas never made any commitment as far as 'no problem, we'll give you the printing' or 'you give us a kickback' or nothing. He never, ever intimated that at all. He said, 'If your quotes are comparable, then I'm sure that we can look at your printing company.' And that's where he left it.

"When we left the room, Cruz said, 'No problem. You come in with the bids and we go the printing.' It wasn't just that hotel. It was another hotel and some other interests, I don't know if it was the Caribbean or what, but he would have all that printing.

"Ron was elated. Bob was very happy. We spent another half day there and then we went back to Phoenix."

There was frustration when Ron returned to Phoenix. Pat was not interested in expansion. He wanted nothing to do with the Las Vegas business, nothing to do with the type of people who might be able to provide such income. Pat understood that a successful bid would bring as much as six million dollars in new income each year, yet he was comfortable with his present success. He did not want the potential for problems that the perceived source of that business might bring.

While Ross was not impressed, Cruz seemed to be.

When he talked with Ross after the trip, Cruz was happy about the way things were going. He explained that he was going to become a partner in Ron's business after the Las Vegas printing contract was issued to Graphic Dimensions.

Robert Cruz came to know Arnie Merrill through Arthur Ross and Ray Kleinfeld. Although Merrill no longer worked with his brother and former friend, he used that relationship to obtain work from Cruz. He also hung around the offices where Arthur Ross was located because of his Cruz connection.

Regardless of what he may have been doing for Cruz, Merrill used his reputation as a bad guy to begin setting up burglaries and robberies. He would work with the men who would commit the crimes, then act as a fence for what they stole. He did not have the courage to commit the crimes himself, but he was quite open about selling what he received from the criminals. He even had the nerve to approach both his brother and Ross with various items after they had dissolved their relationship; the men wanting nothing to do with such goods.

Joyce Lukezic met Robert Cruz in May, 1980 when she was in the process of starting her own business, Diagnostic Stat. The business was going to provide medical technology services to businesses, a field Joyce well understood. Ross was helping her out with office space and venture capital, essentially being a silent partner in the business. Ron also was helpful, arranging for a trade-off in which a commercial artist named Wally Roberts would design the brochure and Ron would handle the printing. The value of the different services was uneven so arrangements were also made for Pat Redmond's yard to be landscaped as well.

Arnie Merrill saw Joyce at the office complex. He was aware that she spent time with her brother. He saw her speaking with Cruz. And he knew that one day such information might help him. The only question was how and when, a question that would not be answered until two lives were destroyed and two others were shattered.

Chapter 4

THE INVESTIGATION

From the FBI files. Transmittal dated January 1981 from the Phoenix office to the Director. The message was marked "Priority." It reads, in part:

"On New Years Eve, three armed gunmen forced their way into Redmond home, Phoenix, bound occupants with tape, ransacked house, and shot all three occupants in head. Mr. Redmond and mother-in-law, Mrs. Phelps, were killed. Mrs. Redmond survived and has furnished descriptive data.

"One suspect, Edward Lonzo McCall, a former Phoenix policeman, has been arrested and charged with the crimes. Two other unsubs are being sought, described as Negro males, from the Chicago area.

"From subjects' conversations during robbery, unsubs used names 'Hooper', 'Bonney', and 'Billy Brice'. Inquiries with Chicago PD to identify unsubs negative to date. Phoenix authorities now have additional name 'Daniel' and believe unsubs may be Daniel William Brice, or Daniel Hooper or possible Daniel Bonney."

After providing additional background, including a Chicago telephone number and descriptions of Brice (aka Bryce and Bonney), the clean cut, well dressed suspect, and Hooper (aka Hoop), the gruff, scarred, stocky suspect, the report continued:

"Investigation by Phoenix office has linked victim

Redmond and subject McCall with subjects of another FBI investigation, of which Chicago office is already aware, case entitled: 'Arthur Paul Ross, aka; et al; RICO (A); co: Px.' Robert Rizzo (Cruz) is also subject of another case entitled: 'Louis Frank Rossanova; et al.

"Victim Redmond's business partner, Ron Lukezik is brother-in-law of Arthur Paul Ross, an associate of Arnold Merrill (TN Arnold M. Kleinfeldt) and Robert Cruz, aka Robert Rizzo, nephew of Chicago mobster Joe Ferriola. Ross and Merrill formerly operated Sun View Development Inc. and other real estate firms. Further, subject McCall operated a Phoenix area repossession firm financed by Merrill.

"Unconfirmed information from police informants suggests printing firm owned by Redmond and Lukezik may have printed large quantity of counterfeit U.S. currency for east coast distribution and Redmond allegedly passed some bills in Phoenix area, an indiscretion that precipitated 'hit contract'.

"This case has received intense media attention in Arizona where three gangland hits have occurred in the past three weeks. Also, there have been two other murders related to the Rossanova case, one in Canada and one in Chicago. Accordingly, it is requested all leads be given expedite coverage."

The transmittal requested information from the Chicago office, including a request to transmit possibly related photographs to the Phoenix office. It ended with the words:

"Armed and dangerous inasmuch as subjects have utilized weapons in commission of murders."

From a handwritten memo dated March 10, 1981 prepared by an FBI special agent for the Special Agent in Charge of the Phoenix office:

"On 2/26/81, Daniel Ryan, Investigator Maricopa County Attorney's Office, Phoenix, advised that William Bracey and Murray Hooper, who were arrested 2/20/81 by the Chicago Police Dept. for the murders of William Patrick Redmond and Alice Phelps in Phoenix, were both members of the Royal Family gang in Chicago. Hooper confessed and implicated both *Arnie Merrill* and *Robert Charles Cruz* stating that Cruz hired himself and Bracey for the Redmond job. Ryan advised that there is a local warrant out for Cruz in Chicago. Ryan further advised that Mrs. Redmond was flown to Chicago and that she identified Bracey and Hooper in a line-up. Ryan advised that Sgt. John Volland, CIU, Chicago Police Dept. is handling the case."

Arnie Merrill was becoming desperate. The Phoenix Police Department was looking for him. The FBI was looking for him. He had finally gained the notoriety he had always desired, only this time the consequences could lead to the gas chamber.

As usual, Merrill was traveling in style. He and his wife, Cathy, were traveling in a late model bronze Cadillac. They were believed to be on their way to Miami or Hollywood, Florida, though the exact destination was uncertain. One of Merrill's children had been contacted, expressed a willingness to cooperate, and suggested that his father might be on his way to Washington, D.C. However, that was discounted as being a probable effort to mislead them.

It was not until April 22, 1981, during a combined law enforcement conference related to the Redmond murders, that Dan Ryan revealed to the FBI agents and others that Merrill had been in contact with him. Ryan explained that Merrill had agreed to talk, explaining that he would be able to involve Robert Cruz with the killings of the Redmonds. Merrill would not say where he was, nor was there any way to locate his position during the call. However, Ryan was certain that Merrill would cooperate and had discussed putting Merrill under the Federal Protective Program when Merrill turned himself in to the authorities.

Merrill finally admitted to himself that this time he had gone too far. He was involved with something from which he could not readily escape. He needed a patsy, a fall guy, and he hoped he had found such a person in the form of Robert Cruz. What he did not realize was that Cruz's involvement with the murders was being determined independently. Witnesses and other evidence was solidly linking Cruz with the murderers. He was being named as the man who arranged for the killings and his fate was being sealed.

The system was no longer working the way Arnie Merrill hoped to play it. He had wanted to confess his role, name Cruz, and get let off with little or no jail time in exchange for helping solve the murders with which he was involved. But his information was reduced in value by the time he told Dan Ryan that he had returned to New York as his hide-out.

Ryan agreed to meet with Merrill near a Nathan's Hot Dog stand in New York. It was a neutral place, an area that was open, a location where Merrill felt safe. What happened next is uncertain because Dan Ryan failed to keep adequate records concerning what took place.

It is only possible to speculate about Dan Ryan at this time. When contacted for an interview, he refused to talk. Thus all information has been pieced together from both those who worked with him and those who felt themselves victimized by him.

The murder case was an important one for Dan Ryan.

It was a media case and certainly more dramatic than many on which he had worked when he was with the Federal agencies. He also seemed to be pleased that, as an investigator for the county attorney's office, he had located one of the primary suspects when the Phoenix police, the FBI, and others involved with the case had failed to find Merrill. In addition, he had earned the respect of Detective Martinsen when the two men went to Chicago to get background on the triggermen. Thus, solving the crime, gaining convictions, had to be important to him.

The exact facts about Arnie Merrill's lies to Ryan when they finally began an interview with a tape recorder going are unknown. However, going against all proper procedure, Ryan repeatedly started and stopped the recorder, leaving others to wonder why. In addition, it was known that Ryan disliked Arthur Ross because of the reputation Ross unjustly gained during his days operating the gun shop. Whatever Ryan's reasons were, an innocent person would be charged with a capital offense. And some people asked was it in order to force the hand of Arthur Ross and make him come forward to confess his "crimes?"

But it may be that Ryan was simply misled, not checking his facts closely enough for the truth to come out.

All that is certain was that from the moment of that recorded interview on April 24, 1981, Joyce Lukezic was about to become the unknowing victim of the criminal justice system. On that date, Arnie Merrill, desperate to save himself from either the gas chamber or life in prison, recognizing that his information about Cruz was no longer valuable, decided to play a wild card. He stated that Joyce Lukezic was the person behind the Redmond murders. It was a bluff he knew was false, yet if it worked, if everyone bought his lies, he would go free. He might have to serve a little time, a few months, perhaps, but he would gladly trade anyone else's life for his own, even an innocent woman.

And so it was that on April 24, 1981, Arnie Merrill told Dan Ryan his story and Dan Ryan centered his case around the difficult-to-believe and easily refuted tale.

Chapter 5

IF WORDS COULD KILL . . .

"Okay. 1978. Joyce Ross or Joyce Lukezic came to me and wanted to know . . . if I knew anybody that would kill her husband, Ron," said Arnie Merrill. He was speaking in New York with investigator Dan Ryan, the interview being tape recorded.

"Why did she want him killed?" asked Ryan.

"She wanted to take over the business."

It was April 24, 1981, and Arnie Merrill, street hustler, was in the process of commiting attempted murder. His weapon was words. His victim was Joyce Lukezic. And Dan Ryan's interview provided the opportunity.

"How much did she want to pay? Did you discuss price . . . or did you know somebody . . . ?"

"I didn't know anybody," said Merrill. "I didn't know anybody that did that kind of stuff."

Merrill told how Joyce wanted him to use his car to run over her husband when he went to lunch each day. But he said that he was not someone who would do anything like that. He didn't know killers and he was a man who would never stoop to murder.

"She tried to kill him?" asked Ryan.

"No, she did try her damnedest to get somebody to do it."

Merrill explained that in September of 1980, the target of Joyce Lukezic's murderous desires had apparently become Patrick Redmond and her vehicle was Robert Cruz. Merrill was asked to go to Cruz's home where he was shown a picture of Redmond. "I asked him where, you know, how he got the picture, and he said from Joyce."

"Joyce, who you know to be Joyce Lukezic," said Ryan.

"Joyce. Joyce Lukezic and Joyce Ross."

"Artie Ross's sister?"

"Artie Ross's sister. He offered us ten thousand dollars to kill Mr. Redmond."

Again Merrill refused to let either himself or his friend get involved. He also told Cruz that he would not let Gill drive the car for the killers, even though the offer was $5,000 just to be the driver.

Merrill claimed to have thought little about the matter until he met with Cruz again around Thanksgiving. Cruz had just returned from Chicago, "And he said Artie tried to screw him when he was in Chicago out of three hundred and fifty thousand dollars, and he had some guys go over Artie's house and told him if he ever wanted his kids to live, to finish school, that he would go along with what he had in mind. And he said he was going to take over a printing company."

"Cruz said that?"

"Yes, at the time."

"Okay."

"And the exact wording I don't remember at that time. Then he said something about Redmond again, and he said within six months we'd get rid of Lukezic, Ron, I didn't even know his last name."

"Yeah. Cruz said that?"

"Yes. Yes."

"And it was your understanding when you talked to

him that he was, that Redmond was, going to get hit, and then six months later Lukezic would get hit . . ."

"Yes."

"And Cruz would take over the business."

"Take over the whole business as payment of . . ."

"Okay."

"Whatever Artie owed him for I think . . ."

Merrill also discussed where he was on New Year's Eve at the time of the murders. He and his wife, Cathy, were home, preparing to attend a New Year's party at the home of his brother, Raymond. There would be many people there—Raymond's wife, Susan, Artie Ross, his parents, Susan Kleinfeld's parents, a man named Joe Scocozzo, and, of course, Ron and Joyce Lukezic.

The party was supposed to start at 7:30, though Arnie and his wife arrived approximately an hour late, Hooper and Bracy having stopped by the Merrill's home after the Redmond murder. Ed McCall did not come by, having dropped off the other two instead. The men admitted killing three people, not realizing that Marilyn Redmond had survived. "And so we get over to the party and the TV was on and I saw the thing."

"It was on the news," said Cathy Merrill. "And we just stood there. We couldn't believe it."

"Peed my pants," said Merrill.

Merrill then described how Joyce watched the television set, never reacting to what she was seeing. She was cold and her actions, coupled with his awareness of the murder, made Merrill physically ill.

Later there would be additional testimony concerning the specifics of Joyce's reaction. It was a reaction that was haunting, one of someone who seemed comfortable with a crime because she had been aware of that crime in advance. He filled in details of where Joyce and Ron were standing when the news came on and how it affected the party. What he did not realize, and what there is no record that Dan Ryan checked, was the fact that at the very moment the Merrills were claiming that Joyce was at the party, the Lukezics were actually being questioned by police detectives at the scene of the crime. Joyce could not have been at the party, because her alibi was established by almost every law enforcement officer involved with the Redmond murders. It was a fact easily uncovered. For Merrill, the statement was a gamble he would win against all odds. For Ryan, a trained federal and county investigator, the statement should have been questioned from the start. Instead, there is no indication he even checked the police reports concerning Joyce Lukezic's location on the night of the murder.

There were other investigations taking place during those months when Joyce thought her life was returning to normal, other pieces of the puzzle seemingly falling into place. Phoenix police, Scottsdale police, Maricopa County Sheriff's investigators, FBI agents and others were all following various leads, comparing unsolved crimes, searching for patterns.

While Arnie Merrill was being sought, new information was being developed concerning Merrill's criminal career. A Scottsdale man named Marvin G. Spiegel had been both burglarized and robbed back in October of 1980. Spiegel was wealthy and had had some valuable jewelry appraised before the crimes occured. During the robbery, adhesive tape was used to bind the victims, an action similar to what occurred with the Redmonds before their murders.

Because of the similarities, detectives explored the possibility that people involved with the Spiegel crimes might also be involved with the Redmond murders. There was little to go on except for the similarities in the items taken and the way in which the victims were rendered helpless. Yet such minor similarities are often the clues that solve a crime. Professional criminals develop patterns that are comfortable for them, each new job so similar to the previous that their actions are almost like fingerprints. Eventually such patterns help the police anticipate the next crime and, in many instances, ensure an arrest when, otherwise, a crime would go unsolved.

Such was the case with the Spiegel crimes and, on January 13, Edward McCall, aka "Deacon," was reported to have been involved. McCall was already in custody for the Redmond murders, the reason an informant had had the courage to come forward. Also named as part of the crime were Michael Dale Gill and George Vincent Campagnoni.

More pieces of the puzzle kept falling into place. Arnie Merrill was named as the probable set-up man for the Spiegel crimes, and Merrill was named as a known association of McCall.

On January 22, 1981, George Campagnoni was arrested in California. He identified Arnie Merrill as the set-up man and also implicated a jewelry appraiser as a probable suspect. The appraiser was also the man who allegedly received the stolen jewelry.

Campagnoni confessed to other crimes. He told of burglarizing the residence of Leonard Romero of Scottsdale, then turning over the proceeds to Arnie Merrill. Campagnoni was on a work-for-hire arrangement, receiving $250 for his efforts instead of getting a piece of the profits.

Because he knew at least one of the killers, Campagnoni was asked about what he knew of the Redmond murder. He said that he had heard that Edward McCall, William Bracey, and someone he knew only as Hooper, were responsible for the killings. He further stated that he had heard that the crimes were set up by Artie Ross.

Artie Ross's name came up again during the investigation. John Morton of Heritage Graphics, another printing firm, explained that he had learned of the Las Vegas printing business. He said that it was his information that Artie Ross was the Las Vegas connection. He said that Ron Lukezic had told him that the printing would be for from three to five casinos and would total approximately $6,000,000 per year. Then he claimed that Ron told him that the Las Vegas people wanted too much money to do business, including money up front and kick-backs.

Ron Lukezic was again interviewed in June, this time in an effort to see his reaction to the information Merrill had provided. The reaction was recorded in the report that stated, in part:

"Investigators indicated to LUKEZIC that information had been received from a subject who is a potential witness in this case, which named LUKEZIC'S wife, JOYCE, as being involved in the REDMOND homicide. LUKEZIC was advised that it had been reported to investigators that JOYCE LUKEZIC provided photographs and information as to REDMOND'S habits, vehicles, and hangouts to persons involved in the homicide. It was also related to LUKEZIC that there was a plan reported which involved REDMOND being killed and six months later, RON LUKEZIC would be killed in a takeover of the Graphic Dimensions printing business. LUKEZIC was also advised that information was received that JOYCE LUKEZIC had approached someone approximately three years ago and inquired as to whether this person would kill her husband, RON LUKEZIC.

"LUKEZIC was visibly and emotionally upset. He denied any knowledge that REDMOND was going to be killed. He also denied any knowledge that his wife, JOYCE, was involved in the homicide."

There were more questions and an additional interview, the next one, on June 18, 1981, in the presence of his attorney. Ron Lukezic was not considered a suspect in the case at that time. He was asked if he knew Billy Bracey and Murray Hooper, or if he had seen them at the home of his brother-in-law. He claimed no knowledge of the men.

Lukezic talked about Robert Cruz as well, saying that Cruz had talked about buying half of the printing business Ron had owned with Pat Redmond. There was little new information gained from the conversation.

Month after month went by, the investigators trying to make sense of the murder. Patterns emerged for most of the men involved. Bracey, Hooper, and McCall were the triggermen. Everyone was certain of that. Robert Cruz had arranged for the specific killers, using contacts he had probably made when he was doing time in jail. If such contacts were not made then, he undoubtedly used the connections he had through relatives in organized crime.

Arnie Merrill was also involved, probably having alerted everyone involved to the gold and jewelry likely to be kept in the Redmond home. He was going to gain financially.

But one question remained. Who was the individual who set-up the murder?

There were only three people who had something to gain from the Las Vegas deal who had not been indicted for the crimes. These were Ron Lukezic, Artie Ross, and Joyce Lukezic.

Ron Lukezic had the most to gain. Ron Lukezic was tired of his partner. He felt that Pat Redmond was a worthless part of their growing business. He called Pat Redmond "as useful as a kickstand on a horse." And he said that Pat was as "useless as a female organ on a boar hog." He complained that Pat could no longer handle his share and, for a while, had John Morton (later of Heritage Graphics) on the payroll to carry Pat's load. He was irate that Pat could not see the possibilities for expansion that the Las Vegas money would have meant. Pat's death would bring him the freedom to do what he wanted with a business that would be one hundred percent his own.

Artie Ross might gain from the Las Vegas deal as well. There could be a substantial finder's fee, perhaps from each of the partners involved. There might be a continuing cut from the Las Vegas money. And, of course, putting this together would make Robert Cruz happy during a time when Cruz was still viewed as having more "muscle" than reality showed was true.

Joyce Lukezic was the wild card suspect in all this. The additional money would enable Joyce and her husband to live better. Yet there were some indications that the marriage was in trouble, that Ron Lukezic was cheating on his wife, that a divorce might be the outcome. The financial arrangements that had been made, the wills, and the other factors that might involve Joyce indicated that the gains she might make would be minimal. Perhaps she could share in some portion of the value of the printing business after the divorce, but the degree of that involvement was unknown. Arizona was a community property state, community property existing only after the marriage. Since Ron had owned the business before he met Joyce, the truth was she had little or nothing to gain.

The alleged future murder of Ron Lukezic also made little sense. The business would definitely be lost then because Ron's family, not Joyce, would benefit. Only Arnie Merrill's statement seemed to indict her, and that made little sense.

Dan Ryan seemed obsessed with Joyce Lukezic's guilt from the time he interviewed Arnie Merrill. The fact that Merrill lied, that his statements were easily determined to be false, seemed to make no difference. The Maricopa County Attorney's office where Dan Ryan worked and was chief investigator on the Redmond case pursued Joyce like hounds chasing a fox into a barn from which there is no escape.

Meanwhile Arnie Merrill was receiving special treatment. He was flown back to Phoenix without handcuffs or normal arrest procedures. Merrill went to a jail that was less crowded than the county facility to which he routinely should have been taken. Merrill received prescription drugs he had been taking and to which, in some cases, such as Valium, he was addicted, in ways that went against routine procedures for other prisoners. Cathy Merrill was helped by Dan Ryan to make payments to the General Motors Acceptance Corporation for her car, including one payment made for her. The criminal backgrounds of both Arnold Merrill and George Campagnoni went completely or partially unrevealed so the court did not have a complete record of all their crimes. Merrill would eventually face a few months in jail when, because of the nature of the case, he otherwise would have been sentenced to life in prison.

Some privileges extended to Merrill as the prosecution's chief witness could be justified by other law enforcement officers, given the nature of this case. Others were viewed as inexcusable. For example, Merrill was allowed to be released from the Maricopa County Jail for periodic conjugal visits with his wife. He was permitted to make approximately twenty-two long distance telephone calls from the Maricopa County Attorney's office, at least some of which were with Dan Ryan's awareness. And no report was filed when Merrill fled custody in order to go to a delicatessen to have lunch with his wife.

More importantly, the defense was not told about Merrill's background. Under the rules of the court system, all information available to the prosecutor must be made available to the defense counsel. Yet Joyce would go through her first trial without her lawyers knowing that there was a pre-sentencing report on Merrill that showed he had been, by his own admission, a Valium addict for the previous ten years of his life. Merrill also took the highly addictive sleeping medication Seconal. Both drugs are meant for extremely short term use.

Both Merrill and Campagnoni were granted a chance to gain immunity from prosecution for all past burglaries and robberies in exchange for their testimonies. They were allowed to plead guilty to one count of Second Degree burglary and one count of theft. This meant that Campagnoni, who had nothing to do with the murders, faced ten years of probation. Merrill, who as an accessory could face the same death penalty as the killers, faced a maximum of eight years in jail. The latter sentence, when actually served by most individuals with similar convictions, would mean just a few months behind bars before parole.

Equally important for the defense and for the reputation of Artie Ross was the hidden background of Campagnoni. He had a previous arrest for assault, a history of drug and alcohol abuse, and was voluntarily in a mental institution for extreme behavior diagnosed as manic-depressive illness. Yet when the defense was given his background, the report indicated that Campagnoni was a first offender without prior arrests or convictions. Even worse, the probation officers were not told that both Merrill and Campagnoni were admittedly involved in the Redmond murder conspiracy.

Joyce Lukezic knew none of what was taking place in the county attorney's office before her arrest and imprisonment. And Joyce knew nothing of the maneuverings taking place after her release, while she was awaiting trial. She viewed the time in jail as a nightmare that could be put behind her. She did not think about the trial. She thought only of her children and her day-to-day concerns. She was an innocent person caught in a situation so ridiculous that there was no way she would ever return to jail. She knew she was innocent. She also felt sure that others would discover the truth. All she had to do was mark time, love her children and try to continue the strained relationship with her husband.

Neither Joyce nor her lawyers knew that powerful members of law enforcement not only agreed with her but had found a person they considered the better suspect—her husband, Ron. For example, on August 5, 1981, a man named Morris Nellum was interviewed by Phoenix Police detectives. Nellum, who was interviewed in Chicago, was a friend of Murray Hooper and frequently served as Hooper's driver since Hooper was unable to operate a car. Nellum had been with Hooper the day before Hooper and Bracey went to Phoenix to kill the Redmonds. They later talked about what took place.

According to the police report filed by Detective Martinsen:

"NELLUM advised that HOOPER told him that HOOPER and BRACEY had gone to Phoenix to do a contract killing. HOOPER indicated that someone in Cicero had paid for the plane fare for them to go to Phoenix. HOOPER told NELLUM that a man was the target of the contract, however when the man was killed, two other people were present and they were also killed. NELLUM advised that HOOPER was very angry at BRACEY because BRACEY had been running off his mouth to people in Arizona and was playing the part of a Casanova with some women in Arizona."

The information Nellum provided concerning the clothing and jewelry worn by Hooper, as well as the weapon he carried, was accurate. He also described the fact that there was an ex-police officer with them, the ex-police officer's trick to enter the house matching Marilyn Redmond's statements.

Nellum described other details of the murder, including the fact that Hooper and Bracey had made a previous trip to Phoenix, meeting with someone named Arnie. He mentioned an earlier murder attempt as well, a chance event tied in with the same contract. According to Nellum, Hooper and Bracey were driving in a van when they spotted Redmond in his car. They wanted to pull alongside and shoot him on the street. However, a third person was with them and that person balked because the murder would have taken place during daylight, a risk factor he felt was unacceptable. This third person was not identified except to say that he was afraid of witnesses to what would have been a murder in broad daylight.

"Nellum advised that he was told that the overall contract involved BRACEY and HOOPER receiving $5,000 each for doing the homicides and monthly payments from a business in Phoenix. He advised that BRACEY and HOOPER were to kill a partner in the business and enable the other partner to take over the business. HOOPER and BRACEY were then to receive a percentage from the business in monthly payments. NELLUM advised that he didn't know the names of any of the people involved in the business." The only names that were mentioned were for one subject who was referred to as either "The Fat Man," "Bob," or "Cruz."

The FBI had access to all the information related to this case, both through its own investigation and through the gathering of law enforcement officers working together to resolve the murders. With all the evidence being revealed, John J. Hinchcliffe, Special Agent In Charge of the Phoenix office of the FBI, officially closed out the Bureau's investigation into the Redmond murders. In a letter dated September 28, 1981, he explained his understanding of the killers and the reason he felt there was no reason for further involvement by the federal government even though the killers had crossed state lines in order to commit the murders. While there were Federal charges that could be brought, it was cheaper to back off and let Arizona prosecute.

Hinchcliffe sent his two-page letter to Paul R. Corradini of the Organized Crime & Racketeering Division of the U.S. Attorney's office in Phoenix, explaining his decision. The Bureau had reviewed the evidence, uncovered the probable killers, and assumed that these were the same men the county would be prosecuting. The letter is chilling in its implications since Joyce Lukezic had already been arrested in front of her daughter, jailed, publicly humiliated, and emotionally battered.

The letter read:

"On New Year's Eve, 1980, three men forced their way into the Phoenix residence of William Patrick Redmond. They bound and gagged Redmond, his wife Marilyn, and her mother, Helen Phelps, then shot them all in the head. Only Mrs. Redmond survived. Investigation by the Phoenix Police Department identified the assailants as Edward Lonzo McCall of Phoenix, and William Bracey and Daniel Hooper both of Chicago. All three were arrested and charged with the murders. Subsequent investigation has established the three were hired for the killings by Robert Cruz, in concert with two of Redmond's former business associations, *Ronald Lukezic* (Author's emphasis) and Arnold Merrill (Kleinfeldt). Local authorities have indicted and arrested Cruz and Kleinfeldt, and the latter has testified against the others before the State Grand Jury.

"Strike Force Attorney Paul R. Corradini had attended the weekly joint conferences in this case with representatives of the FBI, state and local authorities, and is familiar with the entire investigation.

"On August 4, 1981, Special Agent James B. Bolenback discussed the facts of this matter with Mr. Corradini who advised that since all the subjects involved have been arrested and charged, and since the County Attorney's Office is vigorously pursuing prosecution, he would defer any federal prosecution for the killings to the local authorities.

"In view of the above, no further investigation into this matter is being conducted by this office."

Joyce Lukezic's name did not appear. She was never a serious suspect. And Ron Lukezic whose name did, was effectively ignored when the prosecutor went to court.

Chapter 6

THE TRIAL

"I never thought of myself as being on trial for my life. It wasn't that real to me. I felt like I was sitting in the courtroom, looking at the big seal of Arizona on the wall near the judge, and all I could think of was a television courtroom show. I was sitting at the front of the audience, watching Perry Mason. I just couldn't relate what was being said on the witness stand to myself. There was no way to comprehend that the jury could sentence me to death."
Joyce Lukezic

"The police dog's nose, although long and straight, points in only one direction at a time."
Atty. Larry Debus quoting
Sherlock Holmes

There are experiences in life for which no one can prepare—a fire raging out of control in one's home, a child struck down in a crosswalk by a speeding car, or, in Joyce Lukezic's case, an arrest for murder. She had been a suburban housewife devoted to her three children, a businesswoman who believed so strongly in the responsibility of able-bodied people to earn their own ways that she often worked long hours despite an inheritance from her father, and a loyal wife experiencing the anguish of a cheating husband. She could have been anyone's mother, anyone's daughter, anyone's next door neighbor. The idea that she was suddenly approaching middle age with the threat of death in the gas chamber was beyond her ability to comprehend. Real life was not like that.

"I looked upon the court case as something I had to go through to get on with my life. It was going to be like traffic court or something," said Joyce. "You go in, they ask you questions, and then they realize they have the wrong person. They were going to send me home with an apology and everything would be normal. I hadn't done anything wrong and the trial was just a formality. They would know my innocence immediately and I could go home."

Larry Debus, Joyce's lawyer, had not known about the Patrick Redmond murders at the time they occurred. When he remarried, he and his wife decided to fulfill a dream of his by taking a sabbatical and sailing together around the world. He had taken a year from his life, not worrying about crime, law, or defendants. The Redmond death was of no concern until he was asked to represent Joyce after his return. Even then it seemed just another case to be handled to the best of his ability, the drama of the murders, the pre-trial publicity, all essentially history which he learned about only when researching the facts in the case.

Debus was originally going to handle the defense on his own, separate from his friend, attorney Michael Kimerer who had brought him in on the case. Ron Lukezic had originally talked with Kimerer. He knew that the police were asking questions and that he was someone who theoretically had something to gain from his partner's death. As Larry Debus explained, "Ron went to see Kimerer a few times just to have someone hold his hand. But when the police began snooping around Joyce, he decided that she was the one who should be represented."

Kimerer was neither a friend nor an associate of Ron's. Since Ron had not been charged with a crime and

Joyce had, there seemed to be no conflict of interest when, after Debus was brought into the case, Ron specifically wanted both men involved with Joyce's defense. However, Debus would act as the primary attorney.

Preparations for a murder trial are far less dramatic than the potential penalty might indicate. Most of the effort goes into reading police reports, depositions from witnesses, transcriptions of statements by the accused and others. Everything known about the case is studied, analyzed, and reviewed.

"The first thing you do is take all the facts and look for weaknesses in the government's case," explained Debus. "Where are they weak? Where does their evidence fail? Where can it be attacked?

"One side of it is attacking their case. Then, from the other side, you have to get with your client and find out what facts are available from your client's side which refutes their evidence. Demonstrates an alibi in some instances. And in many cases simply shows that your client couldn't have committed the crime, both from a moral point of view and from another point of view."

Sometimes the evidence is negative. There were witnesses who were willing to testify to the angry, violent side of Joyce Lukezic. These included her one-time business partner, Cathy Fox, a witness who seemed likely to testify to Joyce's hatred of her husband and threats against Pat Redmond. It did not matter if she was lying or telling the truth. Her testimony, and the testimony of others who were hostile to Joyce, just might affect the jury.

"Now we chose, in our case, not to call in character witnesses. We chose not to because we were faced with a court determination that her character couldn't be brought into the case unless we opened the door. And we felt that the bad character that would have been brought in, and they had witnesses that would demonstrate certain things that she did in the past and said, would be more detrimental than beneficial. Basically most character witnesses are worthless in most cases. You bring in all the facts, then you bring in a character witness who says, 'Oh, this is a good person.' "

"I guess you could say I was a hard person then," said Joyce. "I had been raised not to show my emotions except at home with family. What you were feeling was no one else's business and I was afraid, afraid that once my reserve was broken all the anger, pain, resentment inside me would pour out. It would never stop."

And it was this reserve, this distant attitude that had won Joyce few friends. She was a private person, ready to laugh, to delight in her children, yet uncomfortable with strangers and seldom close to co-workers. She was respected for her intelligence and her business abilities, though she was not someone who was frequently asked to go to lunch or for a drink after work. What little socializing she did was with her husband, yet she was never comfortable with his friends in the business world.

"The Ice Bitch," she would be called by the media during the trial. "Cold, seemingly heartless." Her appearance would make good copy. This was a period when television shows such as "Dallas" were delighting the nation with stories about people who were rich and greedy, willing to do anything for personal gain. Joyce Lukezic made better copy as a villain than she did as the sympathetic victim of justice gone wrong.

It was the role of Joyce's defense lawyers to try and counter any negative image. They wanted her to understand what she would be facing. They wanted to prepare her for the trial.

"We used a professional jury selector. We used polling. We used our two wives," said Debus. "Kimerer's wife is a psychologist. My wife has a degree in English, a degree in nursing, and a law degree. And we went through Joyce's testimony and they looked at her, and we tried to get colors for her to wear, and we tried to get her to lose weight. In other words, we tried to soften her. She's dark, she had short hair, she was overweight . . . She was a pretty hard-looking woman. That was the very image we tried to play down."

The jury selection process is a difficult one. Some lawyers use professional help. Others go on their own instincts. The number of potential jurors is always fairly large, then reduced to appropriate size through questions asked by the lawyers and/or the judge.

There are frequent attempts to make jury selection a science, the method Joyce's attorneys used. Yet much of the process is logical. If a person has been burglarized, he or she will probably not be sympathetic to someone accused of burglary. If a juror earns $15,000 a year, the individual is not going to look kindly on someone earning $200,000 a year who is accused of embezzling money from the office. If during the course of a trial it becomes known that the defendant evaded the Vietnam War by moving to Canada, the lawyer does not want to see a disabled Vietnam vet on the stand.

There are other methods professionals use, including watching a potential juror's body language during questioning. Sometimes there is a physical reaction to a question that seems to belie the spoken response. Yet most lawyers agree that no matter how they select the jury, most juries come to what the lawyers believe is a fair conclusion based on the evidence presented.

The main concern for Debus was that the jury selected would be sensitive to the issues that might be raised in defending Joyce. As he explained, "If your case is predicated on weaknesses of the government's case, on their witnesses being creeps, on prosecutorial misconduct, which we had a lot of, then you want people who are going to be irate about that. You want nullification jurors. Then even if the government shows something, 'we're not going to convict this woman based on this kind of bullshit! This doesn't happen in America!' That kind of juror.

"There you're maybe talking about minorities. You're talking about less educated people.

"Going beyond this case, let's say you've got an insanity case, and I've done a lot of work with insanity cases, believe it or not you're looking for—sex doesn't make a difference but age does. Twenty-five to forty-year-olds are the people who are going to buy the insanity defense. Better-educated people are going to buy the insanity defense. You might think it's the lower-educated people who are going to buy the 'magic' of psychiatry, but they're not. They're the ones who are generally more skeptical about it.

"So you've got to decide what you're going to do, then select a jury that can relate to what you're going to do.

"We spent a lot of time in the jury selection process."

There was also time spent in role playing. Joyce went to Debus's office to role play what was going to take place in the court. Larry Debus was the defense attorney. Michael Kimerer played the prosecutor. And the wives played the jurors. They worked with Joyce to see how she would answer questions.

The role playing meant little to Joyce. They asked the questions. She answered them truthfully. There were no tricks, no surprises. She had done nothing and had nothing to hide. She was comfortable talking about her estrangement with Ron, her lack of interest in the printing business, her lack of interest in socializing with Ron's friends. She felt no sense of the importance of the impending trial. She simply went along with what the professionals wanted from her.

For Larry Debus, Joyce Lukezic's trial was of greater concern than normal for the very reason that he believed her innocent. "In my practice of law, you very seldom . . . well, let's face it. Ninety-nine percent of the people that get charged are guilty. They may not be guilty of what they're charged with because prosecutors are so inclined to over-charge. And there may be reasons for what they did, so there's all these other factors of defense. But most of them are guilty. The real hard cases are when you defend some-one who is absolutely innocent. Then you don't know what the fuck to do. That's a toughie.

"As far as Joyce was concerned, we pretty much maintaincd a philosophy that Joyce was innocent, number one. And number two, they couldn't prove she was guilty. Even if the evidence that they had was enough to get the case to a jury and enough where reasonable minds can differ, no one was going to impose a first degree murder verdict based on such scuzz ball, scum ball, bad peoples' testimony. You just couldn't predicate the most important judgement you were going to make in your life on an Arnie Merrill. . . . You had to eliminate Arnie Merrill to win this case. He was *the* center of the case."

It was June, 1982 when Joyce Lukezic went on trial. The days were hot, humid for Phoenix. It was a time when the locals stayed inside all day, coming out only after dark when the desert cooled to 95° or 100°, any slight humidity would drop, and the weather would be at its most comfort-able. Many tried to escape to high country, traveling to the White Mountains, Flagstaff, or nearby small towns with quaint names such as Strawberry and Snowflake.

"I didn't have the emotions I experienced when I was arrested and brought before the judge. I had been hand-cuffed, taken away in a police car, put in jail . . . There had never been anything like that in my life. I couldn't comprehend it. I was terrified of what was happening, of feeling so helpless and out of control," Joyce said.

"It wasn't like that at the trial. It wasn't real. It was like back in college when they'd put on plays. You'd sit in the audience and watch *The Crucible* or *Death of a Sales-man* or *A Midsummer Night's Dream*. There was all this drama taking place in front of you and you'd just sit and watch it. You weren't a part of it. The actors were living out their lives on the stage, oblivious to you.

"That's the way it was in the courtroom. There was the seal of the state of Arizona and the judge and the lawyers. Each morning I'd get dressed and drive to the court house. I'd take my place down front, Judge Gerber would come in, we'd all stand up, he'd sit down, we'd sit down, he'd smile and say hello to us. All I could think of was the old television series, 'Perry Mason.' It was like that. I was part of the audience. The jurors were part of the audience, though they got the best seats. And the judge, the lawyers, everyone else was part of the show.

"I never made eye contact with the jurors or the press or anyone. There was no need. It wasn't real life. It was a show.

"Then people like Arnie Merrill got on the stand, telling lies about what had taken place. I thought how ridiculous he sounded. I thought everyone knew the truth: the judge knew that he was lying; the lawyers knew he was lying; the jury knew it; we were all watching him make a fool of himself on the witness stand. I never stopped to think that no one else knew what I knew. I never stopped to think that they didn't share my knowledge, my memory. They didn't know the truth. They were being asked to judge me based on what was being said, and what was being said was lies."

There was more that Joyce did not understand. She may not have been paying attention to the jury, but they were paying close attention to her.

One of the concerns many of the jurors had was the relationship between Joyce and her attorneys. The jury was witnessing a "damsel in distress." A housewife, a mother, a woman much like themselves or their wives was on trial for her life. She had to be frightened. She had to be feeling helpless, sick inside, in need of emotional support.

If she was innocent.

And there were her lawyers, big men, strong men. Larry Debus, the ex-cop, appeared almost double Joyce's height when he stood to speak. He was the kind of man who seemed as though he would be at home in the old West, clearing land, building a cabin, fighting for justice, defending his wife and children from violence. Such a man would be sensitive to the fears and needs of Joyce Lukezic. Such a man would come to her, touch her, lean close and whisper words of encouragement when the person on the witness stand spoke harshly against her.

If she was innocent.

But there was a distance between Joyce and her defense lawyers. It was both emotional and physical. There were times when Joyce wanted to lean over and whisper something to them, to comment on what was happening, to ask a question. To her the moments did not seem particularly important. The questions or comments did not seem to be ones that might affect the course of the trial. They mattered to Joyce, but not enough to risk making a scene by shifting from her seat to be closer to the men who were working together, seemingly ignoring her.

Larry Debus was also insensitive to one of the ways he was being viewed by the jurors. Perhaps this was a factor of his personality. He was not a toucher, not aggressive towards women. He was more the type to sit back and wait for a crying client to compose herself than to come around the desk to provide a box of tissues and an arm around the shoulders. And he followed his natural traits in the courtroom, concentrating on the law, the testimony of the witnesses, the critical matters at hand.

There was other support expected for Joyce. Artie Ross was the closest person in her life after her mother died two years, almost to the day, before the trial started. Her relationship with her brother was a critical part of the trial. Her brother's name was mentioned in connection with Merrill, with Cruz, and others. Yet Artie Ross was not present.

The truth was that Artie Ross was running scared. He felt that he had been harrassed by Dan Ryan when he ran the Gun Trader and was involved with Arnie Merrill. He had learned that in Arizona it was possible for someone to be indicted and, possibly, convicted of a crime based on the testimony of someone known to be guilty of that crime —even if there was no other evidence or witnesses. He saw what was happening to his sister and feared that he could be the next victim of a vendetta.

"I would do anything for Joyce," said Ross. "If she needed money, she'd have it if she asked. But I wasn't about to go to the trial. I left Arizona so I wouldn't be treated the way Joyce was."

Yet the jury only knew what they saw. To them, family rallies around a person in trouble. A brother is supposed to be close to his sister. A brother is supposed to love his sister. A brother is supposed to stand up for his sister.

If she was innocent.

There was also the issue of Ron Lukezic. Joyce thought he would come to the court house. She was also certain that he would testify in court. She felt that her lawyers had given her the understanding that he would appear on her behalf.

But as the trial stretched on Ron Lukezic did not appear. He did not come to the courtroom to give his wife moral support.

Yet to the jury, a loving husband couldn't be kept from his wife's side. A loving husband would be present to hold her hand, if only symbolically by sitting in the courtroom each day. A loving husband would demand to testify, would probably make a scene in the courtroom, challenging those witnesses who would malign his wife's character.

If she was innocent.

And there was Joyce, herself, stoic, seemingly unflappable, dispassionate. She did not laugh. She did not cry. She did not express outrage. She did not react when she was called a killer. She did not challenge witnesses who claimed that she had threatened the life of her husband. She went on the stand and was controlled, unemotional, speaking almost in a monotone.

"I never let myself feel what was happening," Joyce later explained. "It was as though I was in traffic court facing a speeding ticket and I could prove I wasn't driving. I did not let myself feel the truth of what was taking place just as I had withdrawn into a world of fantasy while sitting in jail.

"When I testified, I did what I thought you were supposed to do, what they did on 'Perry Mason'. You're asked questions. You answer the questions. You tell the truth. You step down. The judge and jury thank you, tell you you're innocent, and let you go home. I was going to go home. I just had to sit through the trial and then I was going home."

But the jury, like the press, saw the "Ice Bitch." They could not get inside her mind. They could not understand the way Joyce felt she had to cope with the nightmare she was enduring. All they knew was the image they saw and they felt she was not acting the way she should.

If she was innocent.

And there were side issues taking place, stories within stories that were not fully being revealed. One of the most damning was the testimony of Cathy Fox, Joyce Lukezic's business partner during the period when the murder allegedly was being plotted by Joyce. Fox testified of Joyce's anger toward her husband when he was having an affair. "She said she would have his ass and the business to boot," Fox related, the implication being that Joyce wanted the printing business and might have him hurt. She also claimed that the Ross family was mob-connected and that she was told that if she didn't fulfill certain obligations, she would have to sweep her son off the street.

On June 29, Fox said, "She (Joyce) made statements to the fact that she would take—she wanted her husband—she wanted the business."

The prosecutor asked, "Did she say anything about her husband?"

"Yes."

"What did she say?"

"That she would have her husband taken care of."

Then, since she had said that Robert Cruz and Artie Ross were present, she was asked, "Did Mr. Cruz make any response at this time? Just answer 'yes' or 'no' if you would."

"Yes."

"And did Mr. Ross become involved in the conversation? Just answer 'yes' or 'no,' if you would."

"Yes."

Then Larry Debus, Joyce's defense counsel, began questioning Cathy more closely. "Miss Fox, the time that Joyce talked about her husband, that she had caught him messing around on her; do you remember that?"

"Yes, I do."

"You told that statement to Detective Martinsen at the police department, didn't you?"

"Yes, I did."

"In fact, what you told him was, was it not, that Joyce came in or said she was very upset and angry, that Ron was screwing around on her. Isn't that what she said; weren't those her words?"

"To the best of my knowledge, it was."

"She was mad, she said she was going to have his ass, didn't she?"

"Yes."

"She didn't say she was going to have him taken care of, did she?"

"You are correct," Fox admitted, the first of many conflicting stories she would be forced to admit she told.

"So you said a while ago that she was going to have
him taken care of. That is *not* what Joyce said, is it?"

"No, she said she would have his ass."

"She said something else to the extent that, like some
women do, I will have everything else and his business,
too, didn't she?"

"Yes, she did."

Fox also discussed Robert Cruz, claiming at first that
he was a partner in the business she and Joyce were in.
Later she admitted that that was not the case. She also
admitted that she had dated Artie Ross, been his lover, and
then been dumped by him. She did not discuss their plans,
but others who knew her during that period claimed that
Fox thought she would be marrying Ross, a millionaire
who could keep her comfortable for the rest of her life.
Her testimony, eventually proven to be unstable, apparently came from a desire to strike back at the family that
seemingly had rejected her.

But all that information was to come. With what little
was known during the trial, it was difficult for the jury to
fully discount what Fox was saying. After all, why would
she feel so strongly about her former business partner . . . ?

If Joyce was innocent.

There was also the odd case of Wally Roberts, a brilliant graphic artist, one of the best in the United States,
who was a friend of Ron, Pat, Marilyn, and Joyce. He was
frequently in their homes and claimed to be a witness to
Joyce's plotting to have Pat Redmond killed. The prosecution proudly put Wally Roberts on the witness stand to
have him tell his story to the jury. His words were dramatic. He firmly linked Joyce with the murder plot.

Roberts also admitted to other circumstances that
were rather unsettling. He mentioned that Dan Ryan had

provided him with money and transportation to return to Phoenix after he had left the city. He talked of being with Dan Ryan when the investigator learned that Joyce had been assaulted in the Madison Street jail. He said that Ryan had stated, "Well, Joyce is finally getting started to get what she deserves."

He also said that Ryan told him he would "like to be standing watching this nigger lap her pussy." It was a shocking statement, but it did not alter the damning evidence Roberts provided against Joyce. The fact that Ryan's attitude, as reported by Roberts, was viciously unprofessional had nothing to do with whether Joyce was guilty or innocent. And Roberts was hurting her credibility—until cross-examination by Debus. Then Roberts' drug and alcohol abuse came out.

"Is it fair to say, Mr. Roberts, that for that period of time that we have set the limits at (when he claimed to have heard Joyce say she was having Redmond killed) every single day you were either high on alcohol or high on drugs at some part of the day?"

Roberts answered, "Not every day."

"How many days do you think we could exclude in that year's time? Very many?"

"Probably—I was high most of the time on one thing or another."

Roberts went on to say that the drugs and alcohol affected his memory during the time he had claimed to have heard from Joyce that she wanted Pat killed. He admitted that he would blend stories in his mind, reading something, hearing something, talking with people, then combining everything into what he thought was the truth but perhaps had not occured.

"Would you say that sometimes your recollection was aided by what other people told you?"

"Yes."

"Then that became your recollection, did it not?"

"Correct."

"And when you would repeat it, you would believe as if you had experienced it yourself; is that true?"

"That's true."

"Another factor of your drug use was paranoia, wasn't it?"

"Yes."

"You were afraid of everything?"

"Yes."

"And you in fact would conjure up fears, real or not real; isn't that correct?"

"I had my own monsters."

"Okay, and you still suffer from some of that paranoia, don't you, Mr. Roberts?"

He nodded noncomitally.

"It is true, is it not, that the story you have told the jury about a conversation you had with Joyce Lukezic in October, in your opinion that testimony is unreliable, isn't it?"

"I have stated that; that's correct."

"It's not testimony that you would want someone to believe if you were in Joyce Lukezic's spot, is it?"

"No, I would not want that testimony on me or directed towards me."

"The reason you would not want it is because you know that because of all your problems the testimony is not reliable, is it, Mr. Roberts?"

"That's correct."

Suddenly, Joyce felt relieved. The truth was being heard at last. Wally Roberts was admitting that his insane story of her wanting to kill Pat Redmond was just that, a story, a fabrication, a lie. The jury would surely take notice. The jury would listen more closely to other negative testimony now that the truth was coming forth.

Yet, there was another side. The jury could not see why the prosecution would be so foolish as to use a man like Wally Roberts unless, despite his statements to the contrary, this time he was telling the truth. Roberts was so reprehensible, an admitted alcoholic and drug addict who was destroying his brilliant gift of artistic ability that had made him wealthy, that he never would have been called to the stand.

If Joyce was innocent.

It was in August that the defense rested its case. "I still thought they were going to call Ron to the stand. That was my understanding," said Joyce. "That was what I expected."

But Ron Lukezic was never called. Her attorneys felt his presence was unnecessary. He would be no better than a character witness. He could not help her. He could not hurt her. There was no point.

Except to the jury. In their minds, a husband would want to be present, a husband would want to stand up for his wife.

If Joyce was innocent . . .

The prosecutor made his closing argument against Joyce. He spoke about the killers, about Ed McCall, Murray Hooper, Billy Bracy. He discussed the fact that their actions were not the concerns the jury should have because those men were not on trial.

"The State isn't on trial," said prosecutor Joseph Brownlee, a Deputy County Attorney. "I am not on trial. Dan Ryan isn't on trial. Mr. Jones (the assistant prosecutor) isn't on trial.

"You know what a smoke screen is? A smoke screen is a war term. Smoke screen is something that is laid down across the water so you can't see the other ships, so that one side cannot blast the other ships out of the water."

Brownlee explained that Larry Debus was trying to show the guilt of others instead of defending Joyce. "This is not a novel defense. In a book called *King Of The Courtroom,* Percy Foreman for the defense, Mr. Foreman says at the very beginning of his book, 'You should never allow the Defendant to be tried. Try someone else, the husband, the lover, the police, or if the case has social implications, society generally, but never the Defendant.'

"The State's case presented the evidence to you as far as what the Defendant did and her role and her complicity and her agreement in the conspiracy to execute Pat Redmond. That's the evidence that you have, not the smoke screens, not the subterfuges, not the attempts to get you off the trail of the evidence."

Brownlee continued, mentioning Arnie Merrill's testimony concerning both the New Year's party and the Christmas party at his brother's house. He stressed the confusion about who was and who was not at the Christmas party, reminding the jurors that Joyce admitted to having been at the Christmas party.

The statement was Brownlee's own smokescreen. Some of the more damning evidence presented by Merrill was his lie about Joyce and Ron Lukezic being at the New Year's Eve party at the Kleinfeld home when news of the Redmond murder was announced on television. Merrill had mentioned her coldness, her acceptance of a tragedy that would have been upsetting for someone else. The only problem was that his statement that Joyce had been there was a lie and he was caught in that lie. Yet by switching to mention the Christmas party and reminding the jurors that Joyce had been there, he had a chance to confuse the jurors as to which statements by Merrill were true and which were false.

"In determining whether this Defendant was a member of the conspiracy, you should consider only her individual acts and statements. So you have the conspiracy, you now have to tie the Defendant to that conspiracy. Consider what she did, what she said.

"The Defendant said, 'I have the connections to have Pat Redmond killed.' The Defendant gave a photograph and addresses to Bobby Cruz so Bobby Cruz could try to get Mr. Merrill to kill Pat Redmond for $10,000.

"The Defendant told Bobby Cruz where Mr. Redmond hangs out, 'At Chester's bar, you'll find him there, it's a Saturday night."

The prosecution continued its attack. "The Defendant said, 'When is Redmond going to be taken care of?' Not talking about a party, not talking about selling him something, talking about killing him. 'He will be dead by Christmas,' is the response. But that's a response. You should consider only what she said. Clearly in listening to the response you can get the import of what she said, but for the moment just consider what she said.

"She is clearly a member of the conspiracy. She is conspiring with Bobby Cruz."

The prosecutor pressed the idea that Joyce had wanted Pat Redmond dead for at least two years. He quoted individuals who worked with Joyce, who disliked Joyce, who were willing to testify that she had repeatedly made such statements as "I am going to have him killed. I have the connections to have Pat Redmond killed."

He also explained the nature of a conspiracy, the fact that prior knowledge of a crime, being a part of the planning, all require the Defendant to face the same penalty as they people who actually commit that crime.

". . . this is a contract murder," said Brownlee. "You have evidence of the hit men, somebody sent them someplace. There are actors, that's the perpetrators, there are the planners. By its very definition a contract murder involves people paying other people to do something and obviously the further removed from the actual commission of the crime itself, putting the bullet in the back of the head, the further removed, the less people know.

"You have the evidence that has been established, Joyce Lukezic's connection in this case. She wanted money. She wanted power. She was very greedy. That establishes her motive."

Concerned about the credibility of Arnie Merrill and the other witnesses, Brownlee addressed the issue directly.

"When the State calls witnesses, the State does not choose its witnesses. You don't go out and have some kind of a beauty contest. You take witnesses as you find them, warts and all. You take witnesses with their imperfections, with their liabilities, but with their testimony, whatever that may be.

"And then you, as ladies and gentlemen of the jury, decide: Do I believe this witness? Is this witness telling me the truth or not?

"In providing witnesses such as Mr. Merrill and Mr. Campagnoni, witnesses that do have a felony, they told you how they got that felony. They told you how they got into trouble. The State does not offer them as choir boys or saints."

Brownlee continued, ". . . the fact of the matter remains, while we do not choose our witnesses, the Defendant did. Wally Roberts was a friend of hers. Arnie Merrill was a friend of hers. She tried to isolate herself away from that, but the fact remains. It goes back for years. Parties, bar mitzvahs, on and on, business associates."

Then, moving in for the conviction, Brownlee stated: "This wasn't a robbery or a burglary, not at all. It was a cold, calculated murder. It was planned for a long time and certainly one that Joyce Lukezic had furthered for two years, for two years she wanted Pat Redmond dead.

"Now the theme throughout the defense case was: I'm

rich. I don't need money. This is ridiculous and I didn't have anything to do with it.

"Well, you heard the testimony from some State witnesses that the Defendant was very concerned for money and very concerned that she wasn't being treated according to the way that she perceived herself. She wasn't taken places, she didn't have the material things." He then stressed testimony that indicated Joyce would become rich if Ron Lukezic was dead, despite the fact that Ron's son by a previous marriage would have inherited, not Joyce or her children.

Finally he stated:

"There is one other thing you should consider. You are the jury in this case, you're the jury of Joyce Lukezic. You are also the jury of Pat Redmond and Helen Phelps. They had rights, they had the Fifth Commandment (sic) rights. On the evening of New Year's Eve they didn't have any rights and the gun was put to Mr. Redmond's head. He didn't have any rights. You can see on those photographs the tattooing powder burn from how close that gun was. You can see on Mrs. Phelps' head how close that gun was. They didn't have any rights.

"Remember this, not all crimes are committed equally. Not everyone's roles are the same, not everyone's participation is the same, not everyone's involvement is the same, but every conspirator is accountable for every act of the other, for every statement of the other.

"Remember the justice that Mrs. Phelps got when she tried to remove and hide her wedding ring. She didn't have any. She didn't get any mercy (sic). But they are gone, there is not too much you can do about Mrs. Phelps and Mr. Redmond, but Marilyn Redmond asks for justice.

"You collectively can answer the question that was asked by defense counsel: Who was this a message to? Well, this was a message to all businessmen to stay out of the way of people who think they have power. And you can send the message to those people that the Mafia isn't going to move into this community and it's not going to take over businesses and it's not going to kill people who have been honest, decent citizens, working in their business for twenty years.

"Consider all the evidence. You will find beyond a reasonable doubt that Joyce Lukezic is guilty of all eleven counts. Thank you."

It was over except for the deliberations. Larry Debus had established a defense of innocence, building a case for the murders having been an armed robbery that had gone awry. The prosecution managed to include the Mafia in its summation, to build a case against Joyce by the absence of her husband and brother, and generally create an image of a woman who should die in the gas chamber for her crimes.

"I wasn't worried about the outcome of the trial," said Joyce. "I knew that I was innocent."

There was more stress than Joyce realized, though. She and her brother had inherited the same type of heart condition that had killed their father when he was in his early forties. They were both on medication, both knew that they might face major heart surgery at some time in their lives. But they did not dwell on that fact.

However, the trial had taken its toll on Joyce, who developed severe chest pain. She was rushed to the hospital for treatment of what was believed to be a mild heart attack shortly before the jury returned with its verdict. She was on medication, sedatives, confined to bed, unable to watch television or read the newspapers. It was only when a friend arrived to see her that she knew what had happened. The friend was crying, barely able to get the words from her mouth. Joyce had been found guilty of First Degree murder. Sentencing was being delayed through legal actions being taken by her attorneys. But the penalty for First Degree murder in the state of Arizona was death in the gas chamber.

Chapter 7

DURANGO

"Oh, momma why can't we all wake up and real-
ize that this is all just a nightmare? I miss you so much.
I wish I could hug you right now. The other night I
woke up scared because I had been having a night-
mare. Well I realized then that I had nobody to go tell
and was afraid to in the middle of the night."

Eden Dow, writing to her
mother, Joyce Lukezic.

At first the words were impossible to comprehend.
Joyce stared at her friend, watching the tears, listening to
her barely controlled voice as she explained that the jury
didn't believe Joyce.

Jail. The only jail she had known was Madison Street,
the closest experience to hell on earth Joyce could imagine. The toilet telephone system. The rapes. The endless
obscene chanting of the mentally ill.

Jail.

Joyce looked around the small room where she was
resting. There were monitors, an EKG machine constantly
checking the condition of her heart, intravenous lines
bringing fluids and medication into her body, emergency
oxygen connectors, a paging unit for reaching the nursing
staff. And a guard just outside the door. A uniformed officer with his revolver, extra ammunition, Mace, night-
stick, and handcuffs. A man sworn to uphold the law. To

113

protect the public from the possible escape of the just-sentenced killer resting in bed.

Once again reality was beyond comprehension. First there had been the arrest when she came home from getting doughnuts with her daughter, Eden. Then there was the brutalizing reality of Madison Street. And now a man was armed and ready to shoot her if she tried to escape, to shoot anyone who might try to rescue her.

Ron arrived with Joyce's youngest son. Ron had picked him up at day care so he could visit his mother. The boy did not know what to say or think, the experience too confusing for someone so young.

Ron had been drinking, his breath reeked of alcohol. He acted neither happy nor sad. There was no reaction Joyce could identify. He was just present, his bulk seeming to fill the room, adding to her sense of claustrophobia in the unusually small facility.

"I can't go back to jail," said Joyce. "I just can't do it. I would rather die instead."

Ron was impassive. The boy had left the room, the guard just far enough outside the door so as not to be able to hear their conversation.

The drugs, the pain, all served to erase the exact memory of those few moments. Joyce no longer remembers if Ron greeted her comments with stoicism, with joy, or sorrow. He was not shocked by her words, not hostile to her expressed desires. She wanted to end her life. He felt that there was a way he could help if that was what she wanted. He would be back. She was not to worry. He would help her find the way.

The pills, when they came, were accepted without question. White, slightly smaller than aspirin. Ron used his physical bulk and the fact that he was Joyce's husband in order to get past the guard and the nurse who was in the room.

He stood at such an angle that his ample stomach

blocked Joyce's actions from view. She sipped some water, swallowed a pill, took a little more water, then repeated the process until she had consumed all of the drug.

The reaction, when it came, was intense. First there was cardiac arrest, the heart muscle unable to pump blood throughout the body. At one time this would have meant death despite the fact that the body can survive for a brief period of time without the heart pushing blood throughout the body. So long as the brain is functioning properly, and Joyce's EEG, the measurement of her brain wave, was normal, resuscitation is possible.

The nurses and doctors raced into the room, alerted by an alarm within the EKG monitor to heart failure. Their actions were a blur, erased from memory. A blow to the chest, cries for various drugs, an injection, preparations for the defibrillation paddles to be readied in case a massive jolt of electricity was needed to get the heart beating again.

"All I remember was feeling my heart racing. It was doing at least 150 beats a minute, more than two-and-a-half times normal. I felt it was though it was outside my chest, the sound of it filling the room.

"There was an IV of Valium, but they didn't pump my stomach. I never told them about the pills. I never asked Ron what they were or where he got them. I just knew that they hadn't worked the way I hoped," said Joyce.

Eden was in the room when Joyce was recovering from the suicide attempt. She was unaware of her mother's request, her step-father's actions. All she knew was that her mother was near death and that thought terrified her.

"I talked with her," said Joyce. "Eden was always more mature than her age. She was the one who came to Madison Street jail as often as she could. She was the one who coped by writing about what it was like to visit her mother in jail, turning in the paper to her English teacher as part of a class writing assignment. I knew I could share anything with her and she would understand.

"I told Eden about the pills I had taken. I explained that I didn't want to go back to jail. I would rather die."

Eden looked at her mother, more hurt than surprised. Her words, when they came, were soft, questioning, demanding an honest answer. "Mom, don't you love me enough to stay with me?"

"And then I was crying," said Joyce. "Crying hysterically. I cried and I cried, and we cried together.

"I loved my daughter. I loved all my children, but right then my daughter was something special. She had become the mother to the frightened child inside of me. I put my head against her and she comforted me as I cried. It was all I could do just then, and I knew I would never again try to take my own life. Whatever I would have to face, I would do it because, eventually, I would be reunited with my children and that was worth the effort to survive."

Dan Ryan had been correct. Had everything gone the way he hoped, Joyce Lukezic would have been sent to the gas chamber. She was an accessory to a murder. She had planned the deaths of her husband's business partner and all other witnesses to that crime. She had paid to have the crimes committed. Or so the jury had determined, and under Arizona law, Joyce deserved the same penalty as the men who pulled the trigger and slashed the throats.

But something was wrong with this case. Statements were contradictory. The jury had found Joyce guilty, yet her attorney, Larry Debus, had made enough telling points that the judge knew there would be appeals, knew there was a chance something might change. Instead of getting the death penalty, Joyce was ordered to spend the rest of her natural life in jail.

In Arizona, life in prison for a woman meant a trip to

the Perryville State Penitentiary. Joyce should have been held in the Durango Detention Center, actually the Maricopa County Jail, until such time as transfer arrangements could be made. However, an exception was made for Joyce. Since there was an active appeal and she would have to be returned to the county jail each time her case was heard, it would be easier just to leave her in Durango for the first few months of her sentence.

The transfer should have been a simple matter. Joyce normally would have been taken from the hospital as soon as she was healthy enough to travel. She would be handcuffed, placed in a car, a van, or an ambulance, depending upon her doctor's orders, and driven to the entrance of the county jail. There she would be photographed, fingerprinted, strip searched, go through a delousing process, showered, and given her prison issue clothing. It was all supposed to be routine, all handled by minimal personnel.

"The first thing I knew was that there were policemen everywhere," said Joyce. "They were wearing their guns, checking the halls, the windows, the roof. They seemed to be sealing off my floor, but I couldn't tell very much from my bed and no one came in to see me."

An apparently anonymous caller had alerted the police that Artie Ross had obtained a helicopter and was going to free Joyce Lukezic from jail. The details were vague. No one knew if he was acting alone or coming with a team of professional Mafia escape artists. It was known that Artie was a private pilot and, with his wealth, would have access to any type of aircraft he desired. It was also known that he had been accused of being a tough guy, a man who might benefit from the deaths of others, a man who was willing to bend the law for his own ends. What no one bothered to note was the fact that he had left Arizona prior to the trial and was too frightened of the justice system to return.

"I had to laugh," said Joyce. "All I could think of was

Bonnie and Clyde. Artie and I were going to break out of the hospital and go on the lam together. The whole idea was funny. How would he do it? Where would we go?"

They came for Joyce early in the morning, much earlier than normal. Their orders were: take no chances. Protect all lives.

Armed men were everywhere, in constant radio communication, eyes sweeping the streets, the buildings, the skies. Joyce was placed on a wheelchair, drugged, weak, the excitement and the fear so overwhelming that she drifted in and out of consciousness. Down the corridor, into the elevator, downstairs, out to the vehicles.

Everything became a blur. There was an unmarked van, ambulances, and various cars in a large outside area. She drifted out when they wheeled her toward one of them, unable to recall which vehicle actually drove her to the jail. Then she was out, going into the jail, and she realized she had been followed by at least one other vehicle containing well-armed officers.

The jarring drive, the rush, the medication, and her weakened condition caused her to forget the entry procedures. She had to have been processed, her possessions and clothing taken, but the routine was forgotten. Her first memory was of being in an isolation cell, wearing prison clothing, the only diversion being a fourteen page form entitled "Inmate Rules And Regulations Maricopa County —Jail Regulations."

"I wasn't scared," said Joyce. "I don't know why. I guess it was because Durango was different, cleaner. I had heard that Durango was safe, not like Madison, and even though I was in isolation right then, it seemed an easier place to be."

Then there were the rules. "1. Inmates are responsible for their own behavior and are expected to be courteous and respectful toward other inmates and the facility staff.

"2. Inmates shall address all staff personnel by either their rank title or as 'Mister', 'Miss', or 'Officer'.

"3. One box is provided for storage of writing material, magazines, and all other personal property. Excessive amounts of books, paper, etc., will be removed from your cell and placed into your property lockers."

"It was like being back in a college dormitory," said Joyce, and her attitude was confirmed when she was placed in the general inmate population area after a couple of days in solitary. The jail was arranged in pods, clusters of rooms, each with their own doors, which were sealed off from a large common area by another door that could be locked. The common area had a gym, areas for eating, for meeting with attorneys. Families were allowed in for visits. People could touch one another instead of being separated by thick glass walls and telephones for communication. To Joyce, who had gone to school in the 1960s, all that seemed missing was Elvis Presley, the Beatles, and pajama parties. The rules were not much different from those expected of any student during the time when the sexual revolution was still in the planning stages and everyone was shocked by the idea of co-ed dormitories.

"Abusive and profane language and gestures will not be tolerated."

"Meals will be served three times a day."

"Conduct will be orderly and courteous at all times during all meals. There will be no loud talking or disruptive behavior."

"Gambling in any manner is strictly prohibited."

"No writing, drawing, or the hanging of pictures on walls or equipment will be tolerated, nor will the defacing of any items within the facility be tolerated at any time."

The rules went on and on, an endless litany of demands for courtesy, respect for others, and respect for the facility. "I decided right then that I would not let myself think about the fact that I was in jail. I would not let myself be exposed to anything that would remind me that my freedom was being denied. I took my shower (Rule 7 of section L, Personal Appearance And Hygiene— "Inmates will shower at least once a day.") during the hour when everyone was allowed out into the exercise yard. It was safer then, of course. If there were going to be problems with some of the inmates, it usually wasn't then because the troublemakers liked to go out like everyone else. But that wasn't the real reason.

"I couldn't go outside because then I would hear the birds. I would see the blue sky. And I would see the concrete, the fence, the barbed wire and razor wire. I would know I was in jail, have a constant reminder of freedom denied, and I couldn't stand that. I couldn't let myself think about the fact that I could never leave the jail. So long as I was inside, I could make believe I was in a college dormitory. Only outside was the truth obvious. Only outside would I truly know the pain and I didn't think I could ever handle that."

There were other reminders of where she was, included within the list of jail regulations, and they had nothing to do with the idyllic life of a college student. For example, there was a list of 133 Prohibited Acts. Some seemed almost humorous, the types of offenses for which you might get demerits or be forced to stay after school and sit in the study hall. There was no sleeping on the job (Rule 120), nor was it permitted to be untidy (Rule 125). Goofing off on the job was not permitted (Rule 110), and being insolent towards the staff (Rule 112) would get you in trouble.

It was so easy to laugh, so easy to make believe, until Joyce saw, in the midst of all the innocuous rules, that she was not permitted to kill. It was a rule. It had to be stated. The implication was that without the rule, the inmates would assume that taking a life was okay.

She couldn't kill.

And there were others. There were rules about extortion, about protection rackets, about sexual proposals and threats.

Memories. "Central Avenue bitch!" Being pulled down from the upper bunk. One woman grabbed her hair. Another woman grabbed her arms. And the third woman straddled her legs, fondling her, using her hands, her tongue . . .

And her attorney's voice saying, "Don't worry, Joyce. If they give you one day of time, I'll do it for you myself." But Larry Debus, her attorney, was not in Durango. He was free making his appeals on her behalf but also able to walk down the street, go to a restaurant, listen to music, lead a normal life. Still, Durango was different. The place was cleaner, the layout seemingly safer. Yet it was not a college dormitory.

And then Joyce realized what she was facing. These walls, these women, the rules, the guards, the constant fear would be her companions for the rest of her natural life. Each day would be the same. She could never fully relax, never spend meaningful time with her family (Section K, Visitation, Rule 2: "Inmates are limited to three visits of thirty minutes duration during a seven-day period.").

"I sat there in the cell and I cried, and I cried, and I cried . . ."

"Dear Mom,

"Hi! How's it going? I hope that Durango is better than Madison Street Jail. Is it? I really don't know what to write except that I love you and miss you more than you can imagine.

"If you don't want to stay alive for yourself, than

stay alive for us (Eric, Ron, Jason, me) (especially me) because we need you very much. You may think, like you said the other night, that you've 'done your job' as our mother, but you haven't. To be a mother you don't just give your children a sense of security or even teach them to take care of themselves (which Jason and Eric still can't do). You still need to be around to love your children, or help them if they have a problem, or teach them what's right when they do something wrong or just be around when they need you. Your job isn't done, these circumstances will occur again and again and you need to be around and your children need to know you're around.

"So you see mom your job is far from done; your not getting out of it now.

"And what about Ron? Who's going to yell at him every night about his drinking? Who's going to be there for him?

"And what about all these other people who love you and care about you? Some of those people need you very badly also. We may all be acting selfish, but the truth is that we need you and you can't quit now. You have to be strong. You *have* to be!

"I know your probably thinking 'I've been strong through this whole thing! I can't do it anymore!' Well, your thinking wrong. You've come this far you *can* make it a little longer.

"Boy, for a person who didn't know what to say, I sure said alot! That's about all for now. I love you and miss you so much.

"My Love Always and Forever,"

> Letter from Eden Dow to her mother, Joyce Lukezic, in the Durango Detention Center.

The Durango Detention Center was a huge gymnasium with housing sections off each of the four corners. The housing units, called pods, were labeled by letters. A Pod was for special short-term people, such as those on work/furlough programs. C Pod was the misdemeanor pod where most of the women were serving terms of a few days or a few weeks. B Pod was the section where the felony cases were held. And D Pod was the isolation unit.

Each pod held between eight and sixteen cells. Joyce was first placed in an isolation cell, an extremely tiny holding area where movement was almost impossible. She was able to only take two steps in one direction, perhaps five steps in the other. A steel bed was built into the wall and a one-inch mattress pad rested on the frame. She was issued one sheet and a hospital type thermal blanket for sleeping.

The isolation cell also contained a steel toilet without a seat. Next to it was a tiny sink, perhaps two hand widths across, with a push button for water.

In isolation there was no contact with outsiders except when food or medication had to be provided. The door would open and shut five times a day. First it would open long enough for food to be passed in. Then it would be opened for medication. There would be lunch, dinner, and a second round of medication.

Everything was provided by trustees, but conversation was kept to a minimum. There was no way to ask why she was in solitary. There was no way to get to one of the telephones available throughout Durango from which inmates could call friends, relatives, attorneys or anyone else, provided they called collect.

Larry Debus arrived at Durango to see Joyce the second day she was in isolation. He was shocked to find her where she was. Isolation was uncalled for and against all rulings related to her case. She had not been involved with violence, had not encountered the regular inmates. The court had not ordered such treatment, and her health was such that the isolation might be dangerous.

Debus had other worries as well. Joyce had confessed to him while in the hospital that she had asked Ron to bring her something to help her commit suicide. The attorney was shocked not only by the depth of her depression but also by the fact that her husband obtained some sort of drug for her. There had been no tearful discussions between husband and wife, no attempt by Ron to talk Joyce out of the suicide attempt. She had asked, he had agreed, and she had almost died. To have her in so depressed a mental state and also faced with isolation was both cruel and dangerous. Debus had not told the authorities about the suicide attempt because Joyce refused to allow the information to be made public. But he was not about to let his client remain in isolation. She was immediately moved to C Pod, the misdemeanor unit. Sentencing had yet to officially take place, though it was understood that she would be moved to a higher security unit when the judge passed sentence.

"It was like being in a small town in the country," Joyce said. "Most of the girls seemed to know each other and many of them had been in Durango before. They seemed out of their element in the city, unable to cope.

"They were nice girls, most of them. Not bright or maybe just not educated.

"They came from poverty. For some of them, the jail was just like home. Others were enjoying a nicer, cleaner place than they would return to when they left.

"The meals were awful. We'd have oatmeal at breakfast, but it was thick, like library paste. And we had toast, maybe a cup of coffee, and 'juice.' What they called juice. It was something like Kool-Aid.

"Lunch and dinner were the same. We almost always had what they called chicken. It was one of those soy patties. I don't know if it had any meat in it at all. And they'd cover it with some kind of sauce, like maybe a raw can of tomato paste one time, some sort of lumpy gravy another. If you were very lucky, maybe once a week, maybe less, you'd get a piece of cheese.

"We had what they called mashed potatoes and some vegetable. Usually it was from one of those cans where you get a lot of corn, some beans, and whatever else. None of it had much taste. They'd fix it one way for lunch. Another way for dinner.

"There would be one cup of weak coffee. Sometimes a carton of milk. We'd get an egg for breakfast maybe once a week. And sometimes someone would donate real fruit to the jail so we'd get an orange or something. But you couldn't count on that. It depended on what they got. We got real meat maybe once a week, sometimes less.

"It was all terrible, but many of these girls were eating better in jail than they had ever eaten in their lives. My teeth began to rot from the malnutrition. And this was the best some of them had ever eaten.

"They seemed to take a liking to me. I think they saw me as being a little dumb. They were doing things I had never known about and I guess I was fascinated with their lives.

"There were prostitutes who had been given forty-five days or whatever and they saw it as a vacation. There were illegal aliens waiting for the 'Federales' to come and take them back across the border. There were parking ticket violators who had run up fines so great that the judge sentenced them to forty-five days in jail. And there were those who were arrested because they were inside a building when they had no business being there. It was obvious they were going to burglarize the place, but for whatever reason, the court plea-bargained the arrest to a misdemeanor Criminal Trespass charge which got them very short time.

"Frequently they were laying around, sleeping, watching the soap operas on television, listening to the news. That was one of the things that surprised me. They were all interested in the news. They'd watch it when it came on, keeping up with what was happening. I guess they were more interested in the local news than the national news, but they kept up on what was happening. Of course, they listened most closely to things that affected one of their cases.

"The rooms were a little larger than they had been in the isolation cell. There were the beds coming out of the wall, the toilet, and the sink. But the difference was not that great. If you sat on the edge of the bed and got up, you could take one step to the wall. However, the doors to each room were open, only the pod itself being locked.

"Each pod was L-shaped with sixteen rooms and a bathroom. The bathroom had two steel sinks, two steel showers without curtains or any means for privacy, and two steel toilets just past the showers. The openness was not to harrass the inmates. It was meant to keep the women from using the privacy for sex, drugs, or beatings.

"There were three large, barred windows on one side of the communal area of the pod, a locked back door, and the door that led to the gym. Each pod was allowed outside for an hour a day but the gym was used for getting food, for greeting visitors, and for going to medical.

"The common area of the pod had Biblical books, religious magazines, and some incomplete checker sets. There were two steel tables with eight steel stools, all of them bolted down. This made 16 seats with a population in the pod of thirty-two people. There was also a television set that went on around 10:30 in the morning and was shut off at 9 P.M. The set was black-and-white, but it provided a distraction.

"You had to sit on the floor to watch the television, though that was no deterrent to its use. The shows were familiar, comfortable, distracting for many of the women.

Weekdays meant soap operas which some of the women had watched for years. Saturday night, the show 'Star Search' drew almost everyone. I don't know if it was their intelligence level or just the desire to see something consistent with what they knew on the outside, but the set was the focal point for many of their lives.

"All of us had cleaning detail in the pod. Two cells at a time would handle the chore, switching after each meal so that we were cleaning once roughly every third day. The cleaning meant sweeping and washing the floors after every meal, something that often did little to get anything clean. In D Pod there was an indoor/outdoor carpet and the inmates were given one of those Navy string mops. They'd mop that thing three times a day and that carpet was filthy. The floor was disgusting because the carpet was not meant for mopping in order to get clean.

"Then, every week or two, they came around with a push-type cart of old magazines for additional reading material. You could also go to commissary once a week for candy, cookies, writing paper, and other items.

"The guards walked the pods, checking on the inmates, following a regular routine that took twenty-eight minutes to complete. There were also times when we were expected to stop everything we were doing and stand by our pods for a body count. Sometimes this would be at random. Most of the time they would follow a fixed schedule. But what was most important to the women was that twenty-eight minutes it would take them to make the rounds of the different pods.

"Every twenty-eight minutes the women were on their own. It was a time when they could talk without being overheard. They could have sex or make bootleg liquor from fruit stolen from the meals. Some of them would use the time to hone a blade on a spoon or other piece of metal. Some would fight and others would rape. And all of us knew that for twenty-eight minutes it took the guards to circle the other pods and the gymnasium floor, none of the guards would hear you scream."

The misdemeanor women were fascinated by Joyce's naiveté about the streets. She quickly learned that, in their eyes, she had been working too hard, paying too much for the items she purchased, not understanding the ways of the world.

One woman owned a VCR she had purchased for $25. Another woman told of expensive appliances and stereos she had purchased for no more than ten percent of the lowest advertised prices. "They'd get them in the projects. Trucks would pull up and they'd buy them new, still in the original cartons," said Joyce.

"I was still thinking like the practical suburban house-wife. 'What about the warranty?' I asked them. 'How do you get them repaired by the store if something goes wrong with them.'

"The women looked at me like I was the dumbest thing going. And that's when I realized that everything they bought was stolen."

The women explained how they would get free meals in restaurants. A group of them would go in and sit near people who looked like they might belong together. Then, when the meal was over, they'd leave the table one at a time. There would be five or six of them, the last person to go explaining to the waiter that the person at the next table was paying the tab. By the time the waiter realized that that person had never heard of the others, the women would be gone.

"I learned that the best way to pick pockets was at race tracks. They're crowded, and if you use your middle and index fingers, you can lift a wallet from someone's back pocket without their feeling it. Everyone is bumping everyone else because of all the people and that's all it takes to distract someone.

"They taught me about using credit cards to slip locks. And I learned how to make alcohol.

"The women also taught me how to work the system in the jail. They showed me how to steal a plastic trash bag during clean-up, then make it into a shower curtain. The guards would tear it down if they caught you with it, but you could usually use it a few days before you got caught.

"The shower curtain gave you privacy. It wasn't just for modesty. Even with the non-violent women in the misdemeanor section, you always had your weirdos. They would walk by and make comments. Sometimes they'd just camp outside the shower and talk to you.

"One of the women in the day room, the common area in each pod, showed me how to take the elastic bands used to hold legal mail and use them for the shower curtain. There were screws coming out of the shower. You'd loop the elastic through itself with a corner of the plastic bag trapped when it was pulled taut. Then you'd take the other end of the elastic and hook it over the screw. You'd do the same with the other side and you'd have the privacy you wanted.

"I learned how to get extra clothing from the trustees. They would sneak blouses and slacks, giving us a chance to trade them until we found the ones that fit the best. The clothing would be taken from us when they made their periodic searches of our cells, but then we'd just arrange to have more smuggled to us. No one ever went into solitary for getting extra clothes. It was part of the system, winning some and losing some."

While Joyce was adjusting to the jail, Larry Debus was fighting for her life. She had talked her husband into helping her kill herself, a fact that made Debus wonder if she would either try again or deteriorate emotionally.

Jail was a culture shock for those who had never done

time. Joyce had already been to hell in the Madison Street jail. She had been raped and emotionally battered. Debus knew she had a tendency to withdraw and there was a chance she would take such an attitude to enough of an extreme that he would lose her entirely.

All criminal defense attorneys, given enough time in the profession, had seen the nightmare results of imprisonment on people to whom the idea of jail was foreign. Some became angry, violent, inviting assault by other prisoners and the guards. Others became withdrawn, seemingly to the point of autism where they would sleep, eat, and perform essential bodily functions, but do nothing else. They might sit and stare for hours at the wall, the television set, or the passing parade of inmates. Or they might find themselves sleeping more and more throughout the day until their waking hours became a minimum, their bodies became obese and flabby from lack of use, and eventually they suffered heart attacks or other stress related illnesses.

Joyce had a weak heart. She had also become emotionally withdrawn. Larry Debus was convinced of her innocence, determined to prove that she should not be in jail, and concerned with her emotional stability. He arranged for a therapist to visit her in the hospital and teach her methods for coping.

The therapist provided relief for Joyce. He got her away from the main population when he came to visit. He talked with her, listened to her, helped her through the transition.

"He taught me how to leave the jail in my mind," Joyce explained. "It was like what I tried to do in Madison.

"He had me close my eyes and go to some place quiet, peaceful, where I was safe and free and could breathe clean air. I went to the woods one day. I walked through the tall grass, looked up at the blue sky, the passing clouds. I stooped to look closely at the wild flowers, delighting in their fragrance. There were no people around, no distractions. Everything was calm, relaxed, the only sounds being the rustling of leaves in the wind, the songs of the birds, my own feet moving through the meadow. I could feel the sun on my face and bask in its warmth.

"And I was safe. Most of all, I was safe."

Visit after visit, the therapist worked with Joyce. The techniques were standard procedures for self-hypnosis and she learned to do them on her own. Eventually he would stop visiting her, his work completed, Joyce being left with the means to emotionally protect herself from the extreme depression she had felt.

"I learned to live inside my head. I learned to sit for hours, saying nothing, having conversations with myself. I led an active life, though not on the outside. It was a way of getting through the days without having to be pressured by everything going on all around me."

Arthur Ross also reached out to Joyce during this time. He still would not return to Arizona, still too frightened of what might happen to himself. But he arranged for a mutual friend to deliver a letter to Joyce. It was a note of support, short, written on a piece of paper that was torn from a Chicago Title Insurance Company scratch pad. Yet the words were important to her. The words told her she was not abandoned by the closest person in her family.

"Dear Joyce,

"I will never in my life forsake you. I will not leave you in there. Overnight you won't get out. If you can just hold on mentally, I have spoken with many people. They say it will just take time.

"I know I can not put myself in your place, but we come from strong stock. We are survivors. I am trying to sell whatever I can to raise some cash for you right this second. But I will have money for your appeal no matter what it takes.

"I am okay, staying together with Max (Max Kugler, a business partner), but he also has a problem and so we're stuck together for a little longer.

"I pray for you every day. We'll win.

"You only read about miscarriage of justice being so tiny. But unfortunately you more than I are living it.

"I will take care of you and the kids until my last breath. Todd (a friend) told me that you still want to work with Debus and that is your choice. I think that he can't handle your appeal. He really fucked up the trial from what I heard. Also the comments Gerber (the judge) made after the trial was the reason he didn't throw out the case or (illegible) the judgement from public pressure. He's a pussy, but he knows the judgement will not prevail. I hope Ryan will get his and also Brownlee.

"I will keep in touch. I love you, and all I can say is you have to psyche yourself out mentally knowing that you will get out. It is up to you, physically and mentally. Don't let them wear you down. That's what they tell me.

"All of our prayers are with you.

"Your loving brother, Arthur."

PART TWO

ARIZONA JUSTICE

Chapter 8

INMATE GAMES

Arizona law allows a lawyer to request a new trial between the time someone is convicted and when they are sentenced. Regardless of the allegations of competence concerning the handling of the first trial, Larry Debus and his partner in the case were determined to see justice done. And justice, in their minds, was not railroading Joyce to death row, the only sentence likely for the crimes of which she was accused.

Under Arizona law, the motion for a new trial is based on Rules for Criminal Procedure, #2401. These state:

"1. The verdict is contrary to the law or the weight of the evidence.

"2. The prosecutor has been guilty of misconduct.

"3. A juror or jurors has been guilty of misconduct by receiving evidence not entered properly in the trial, deciding the verdict by lot, perjuring himself or failing to respond totally to a direct question, seeking a bribe, becoming intoxicated during the course of deliberations, conversing before the verdict.

"4. The court has erred in the decision of any matter of law or in the instruction of the jury on a matter of law."

There were others, but all essentially stated that the defendant must have not received a fair and impartial trial for matters over which he or she had no control.

"We had a number of those things," Larry Debus explained. "Primarily we had prosecutorial misconduct. And we had a hearing. We subpoenaed the telephone records of the county attorney's office.

"When we wanted to call their investigator, they said they didn't know where he was, that he was out of town. We proved that he had been calling in and that they had been lying. And we had all kinds of shit.

"We proved that the investigator had arranged for their main witness to get drugs in jail."

Debus explained that while some of the information came out during the trial, especially the perjured testimony of Arnie Merrill, they did not give up after the trial was over. "We knew that they were bad apples and just kept digging. And as we dug, we found more, and we found more, and we found more. By the time we got to our motion for a new trial, we had a bunch of shit. It was so bad, you know, that the judge cited them all for contempt."

The action brought the new trial, though there was no way that Joyce was going to be released before it was held. She also was aware that if the new trial was lost, she would be sentenced to death. Only then would someone file an appeal.

The knowledge that a new trial would be allowed was not comforting for Joyce. She was in jail, isolated from her children, her friends, the freedoms she had known all her life. She was also completely innocent, so that she had been certain there was no way a jury would believe the lies that had been told about her.

But the jury believed the testimony they had heard. They accepted her guilt. She feared that a new jury would not behave any differently. The new trial might only be a way of delaying the inevitable.

Joyce entered jail with the knowledge that she would be behind bars for weeks, months, years. There was no way of knowing when, if ever, she would be free. As frightened and sick as she was, she would have to adjust. She would have to become an observer, more keenly aware of the people all around her than she had been when first arrested. To do less meant to die.

Rosemary was one of the first inmates Joyce noticed, perhaps because of Rosemary's age—nineteen, not much different from Joyce's older children. The girl was clean cut, 5'5", lean and wiry. She seemed to have come from a better background than the other inmates. She did not seem to have worked the streets, to have been hardened by life. She was lazy and self-indulgent, the kind of girl Joyce had seen in Eden's high school, the type whose parents thought that spoiling a child with material goods and no responsibilities was a way of showing love. She probably did not even exercise, especially since she was so comfortable lounging about the cell, her perfect figure the result of genetic good fortune.

Rosemary had obviously never been in jail before. At least not in long-term detention. She was too much of a hostile loner, her attitude one that more experienced inmates knew could get you in trouble.

"The first time I saw her she was smoking a cigarette," said Joyce. "Cigarettes are treasured in jail. They're used as money even by those who don't smoke. Cigarettes buy sex or protect you from assault. Cigarettes can be used to neutralize a vendetta or hire someone to kill another inmate. Cigarettes are gold and their possession or lack of them can be part of the constant power struggle that is an underlying aspect of prison life.

"A black woman, big, rough, yet somehow defeated by life and old before her time, saw that Rosemary had a pack of cigarettes and asked to borrow one. All indigent inmates are provided with tobacco and papers for rolling their own, but they tasted terrible. Women who had enough money for commissary privileges bought packs of cigarettes and shared them with those who couldn't afford them. Almost no one abused the privilege, some of the women going so far as to only ask for partially smoked butts left in ashtrays.

"Rosemary looked at the black woman with disdain. 'Fuck you, bitch. Get your own cigarettes.' Then, to show how superior she was, Rosemary took the few remaining cigarettes from the pack and proceeded to crush them, destroying tobacco, paper, and filters so that there was no way to salvage any of them. It was an action little different than if a beggar had asked a millionaire for pocket change for food, the millionaire not only refusing but then proceeding to burn a wad of $100 bills in front of the starving man."

Joyce was shocked, partly as a mother who was witnessing a spoiled brat whose parents had failed to discipline her, partially as a fellow inmate who felt that Rosemary was playing a deadly game. She began watching the girl, observing the way she interacted with the other inmates. She sensed that there would be an explosive reaction to what was taking place, though she had no idea where, when, or how.

"Later I saw Rosemary out by the telephone while someone else was using it. The telephones were a blessing and a luxury, our link with the outside world, with loved ones whose presence we were deprived for all but ninety minutes a week. You had unlimited calls so long as you called collect and so long as no one was waiting to use the telephone. The time was precious and we each respected the others, keeping our conversations brief when someone else wanted to use the phone. Yet we knew not to interrupt, to demand. We stayed far enough back to not be able to readily listen to what was being said, much like the unspoken, unwritten etiquette surrounding the use of automatic teller machines. No matter how many people want to withdraw money or make a deposit, the line always starts at enough distance from the person using the machine so that the transaction can be conducted in private. The jail telephone etiquette was equally understood, everyone except Rosemary following the system.

"Give me the fucking telephone," she demanded, cutting off the call. "I need to use it."

"The inmate who had been so rudely interrupted was in shock. I could not tell if she was going to burst into tears from the abrupt loss of her connection with the outside world or if she was going to become angry, striking Rosemary with the receiver still in her hand. She did neither. After the brief flash of emotion in her eyes, she dropped the receiver so it dangled towards the floor and walked away. Rosemary, triumphant, punched '0' and then her number, placing whatever call she wanted to make.

"I was repulsed by her actions. She had no compassion for anyone. She was selfish and lazy.

"Most of us ignored Rosemary, letting her go her own way. You couldn't help but overhear her, of course. We were in the same pod together and we all ate in the same room. She would get into arguments, running off at the mouth, letting everyone know that she felt herself superior to them.

"It would seem that someone would have told off Rosemary. For example, each time it was her turn to help mop the floors after eating, she would take the mop, make a couple of half-hearted passes at the floor, then set the mop back in the container. The floor would be filthy, and her share of the bathroom cleaning would go undone also.

"This meant more than it might seem at first. The room where we ate was the largest area for recreation. We'd lay on the floor to watch television, talk, and even play cards. The chairs were never adequate for the number of women using the room each day, the floor the only place to relax. The mop water was never that clean to begin with. Not making any effort to clean the place left it filthy until the next pod's turn to disinfect the place.

"Some of the women had newer and better clothing in jail than they did on the streets. Others, like myself, had plenty of nice clothing on the outside, but were stuck with the prison clothing on the inside. Either way, the number of changes were limited and all of us were a little grimy at best. We did everything we could to keep our clothing reasonably clean between the changes we were allowed, and resented Rosemary's unwillingness to help.

"There were other rules of etiquette Rosemary refused to follow. Food was shared. Some of the women could not get enough with the skimpy meals that were served. Sometimes they were big eaters with the bodies to show it. Other times their life on the street had brought them near to starvation. Frequently they were caught committing violent crimes to get money for food. The jail, as bad as it was, provided better nutrition than they had known most of their adult lives. We made certain nothing was wasted. Everything was shared, even special diets. No one was overly greedy, trying to eat at the expense of someone else, yet those who did not share were physically threatened until they did.

"Except Rosemary. What she didn't eat, she would trash. She did not contribute fruit to either the pod bootleg operation or the women who wanted to eat it. She chose to destroy whatever she did not keep for herself.

"I may have been rather arrogant on the outside myself, but everyone coming to Durango quickly understood the unspoken rules of behavior. For example, I could order my favorite foods from the commissary, Grandma's Oat Meal Cookies and Mars candy bars. I had $20 a week to spend on such things, the maximum allowed, and I frequently brought things back for others. Sometimes they could reimburse me; sometimes they couldn't. It didn't matter. The cookies would be divided among those who asked, the Mars bar carefully sliced in even sections for sharing.

"When I began losing my teeth from the poor diet, the dentist arranged for me to have special food. My tray would have celery, peanut butter, and cottage cheese, luxuries the others were denied. I would eat maybe three-fourths of the peanut butter, a real luxury, then give the rest to anyone who wanted it. I loved the cottage cheese and needed the calcium for the teeth I had left. But I would share that, too. That was why everyone left me alone.

"Perhaps the final problem with Rosemary resulted from her adolescent whining. She was like a little kid having a fight with an older brother or sister who was breaking family rules. She would see some infraction of the rules by someone she did not like and she would start saying, 'I'm going to tell the guards. I'm going to tell.'

"I don't know if Rosemary was a snitch, the lowest form of life inside the closed society of a jail. The idea was to hear nothing, see nothing, and say nothing. Beatings, murders, drug deals . . . On the outside you would be a hero for reporting the crimes so that the streets would be safe from violence. Inside the jail, violence was a normal part of daily life, a way for inmates to settle differences with each other instead of randomly coming after others who were locked inside with them. Everything was the mirror image of freedom, the guards the enemy and a snitch the lowest form of humanity.

"The trouble with Rosemary was her timing. We had real chicken perhaps eight or ten times a year. This was meat on the bone, not the chicken flavored soy bean patties that were our daily sustenance. And the chicken was a double treat, a fact of which the guards were aware.

"First there was the taste. It is hard to destroy the taste of real chicken. No matter how it is prepared, the meat is distinctive enough that it was radically different from the usual food and that made it a treat.

"There was a second appeal to the chicken. Chicken bones can be honed to sharp edges. They are brittle, splintering easily, so when they are used as knives, they will shatter inside the body. Even if they are not long enough to kill when rammed into the chest, they will cause great pain and infection, often requiring surgical removal of some of the shards.

"The guards had seen enough chicken bone knives to know that whenever we had a meal like that, it might be necessary to conduct a search of the cells. We had chicken one day when Rosemary was in the pod. She watched one of the women slip a bone under her clothing, obviously planning to make it into a weapon. 'I'm going to tell,' she whined. 'I'm going to tell.'

"There were no guards around at the time, no one to overhear her comments except those of us who had to live with her. We had all seen the stealing of the chicken bone, but we also knew to say nothing. We pretended it had not happened, nor would we admit to seeing anything if we spotted the inmate fashioning her weapon back in the cell area.

"That night there was a shakedown. The cells were searched, personal possessions strewn about, everything checked for contraband. The chicken bone knife was found carefully hidden in the mattress of the inmate's cell and she was placed in solitary confinement. Rosemary's cell was also searched and she was as angry about the intrusion as the rest of us.

"None of us ever knew if Rosemary had snitched to the guards the way she threatened. I don't even think it mattered. We all knew that cell checks after chicken dinners were likely to occur because of past experience. Yet in the past there had been no one foolish enough to keep saying, 'I'm going to tell. I'm going to tell.'

"That Tuesday everything changed. It may have been related to the search for the home-made knife or it may have resulted from other actions. None of us ever asked the women involved. None of us wanted to know.

"The timing for the search was what it always was in jail. The guards had just finished checking B Pod, an indicator that for the next twenty-eight minutes no one in an official capacity would be aware of anything that might take place in our pod. The lesbians could have sex. The bootleggers could add to their fermenting fruit hoard. And Rosemary could go into her room, sit on the bed, and read.

"I don't remember if I saw the women go into Rosemary's room and close the door. I don't want to remember. To this day I still fear that to admit to seeing too much can mean your death and I have forced the identities of the attackers from my memory if, indeed, I ever did see them.

"First there was the thud of a body. Involuntarily I winced, stifling a scream that rose in my throat as I remembered the last time I had heard that sound. It had seemed to be coming from a distance that first time, but that was only because of the emotional cushioning effect of my shock and terror. It was the sound of a body being pulled from an upper bunk and smashed against the wall, just as I had been during my rape. This time it was Rosemary who was being attacked.

"There was another sound, like the wail of a giant animal still strong enough to roar with anger in the midst of pain. I heard a thud, a scream, and saw a head appearing at the glass of the door to the cell.

"The pods were designed in such a way that we could lock our cell doors and the door leading into each pod could be secured. The doors to the cells were solid, though, with a large window about two-thirds of the way up. The solidness assured a degree of privacy. The windows allowed the guards to enter each pod and view what was taking place in the rooms. That partial privacy was still greater than what was offered by the cells in the Madison Street jail, and we truly appreciated that fact. Except when there was violence.

"Rosemary had run to the door in order to escape her attackers, her face pressed against the glass as she desperately tried to get someone's attention. Her nose was bleeding and there was a cut on the side of her mouth. More blood drooled from her lip and it appeared that some of her teeth had been chipped or broken. But there were no guards to help her, no inmates who would admit to seeing anything, then or ever.

"Suddenly Rosemary's head was jerked back as though someone had simultaneously grabbed her hair and kneed her in the kidney. She disappeared from view, only the bloody smudges on the glass a reminder of what was taking place.

"The sounds were intense. Short screams were gradually replaced with sharp cries of pain followed by moaning.

"I forced myself not to think about what was taking place.

"I could have intervened. I could have gone in and tried to stop it. I could have seen if someone else wanted to help me. I even could have gone to the guards, though that would ultimately have resulted in my being battered or killed unless I voluntarily put myself in solitary confinement.

"I did nothing. I knew what she might be enduring, yet I had no compassion. Later I would wonder about myself and my inaction. Later I would wonder if I had become as much a street animal as some of the women with whom I was caged. Later I would wonder about the depths to which we will sink in order to save our lives and our sanity. Right then I pretended I did not hear, did not know what was taking place.

"Suddenly the cell door opened and shut, the attackers slipping out and hurrying to the bathroom to clean the blood from their clothes. Again I either missed seeing their faces or deliberately put them out of my mind.

"And then I saw the hands. Bloody. Like something from a slasher movie. Two hands pressed against the glass and, for a moment, it looked as though they had been severed, then placed in position with Super Glue.

"Rosemary's face appeared for an instant. There were gaps where teeth had been. Her hair was straggly, her face smashed and bloody, her eyes damaged, the skin starting to swell. I thought for a moment she was going to scream, but her face had gone almost lifeless. Her mouth was open, the jaw slack, her look vacant, as though she was no longer seeing what was taking place around her.

"And then her head dropped, followed a moment later by her hands sliding down the glass. All that was left were two slightly blurred, bloody handprints and the tracings of Rosemary's face against the glass."

Rosemary was found by the guards during their next check of Joyce's pod, twenty-eight minutes after the beating began. Physically she would recover. No one had wanted to kill her. No one had wanted to do permanent physical injury. All they wanted was for her to know pain hour after hour, day after day, for weeks. She had been a tough bitch to everyone and someone decided she needed a lesson in how to behave.

What no one expected and, perhaps, no one cared, was what might happen with her mind. Rosemary was not streetwise. She was angry, perhaps from an abusive home-life where she learned that a chip on the shoulder prevented people from looking too closely at her pain. She was child-like, throwing temper tantrums, demanding her way. Her actions had been those of someone desperate to be in control of as much of her life as possible, even though she was in jail. And the beating showed her she was not in control, helpless, at the mercy of women who were delighted by her battering.

The guards said nothing when they found Rosemary on the floor of her cell. She was weeping, babbling, spitting up blood. Her eyes were wild, darting about even as she was carried from the building. She looked and sounded like she was insane.

Eventually Joyce heard that Rosemary had been transfered to a psychiatric hospital. Rumors abounded that she was quite mad and would never be able to leave the hospital. But that may have been prison bravado talking because everyone knew that no matter what happened to Rosemary, she would not be returned to Durango. Crazy or sane, Joyce never heard of Rosemary again.

But Rosemary stayed in the back of Joyce's mind. The beating was deserved by the standards of Durango and its inmates. Joyce knew that to survive she had to accept that fact, accept her own inaction, so she could endure and return to her children. She was determined not to try to commit suicide again. She would do what was necessary to keep her heart as strong as possible. But she had to get out.

Perhaps the adjustment would have been easier if she was guilty. Then she could accept the cause and effect of taking a life.

Innocent, she was in hell. She lived only for her children and for word from her attorney that he would be obtaining a new trial.

Joyce was trying to adjust to the reality she was facing when she was shattered once again. Larry Debus was pulling out of the case. He had taken her through the first trial. He had won a second trial. She would remain housed in the county jail instead of being sent to the penitentiary, a fact that ensured her ability to see her family. But she was suddenly alone, without a lawyer, seemingly without anyone to argue her side. And she was alone in a society where no one cared if you lived or died.

For the first time Joyce realized that she was literally fighting for her life and that she would have to do it alone. So long as Larry Debus was her attorney, she felt that she had an advocate, a father figure who was all-caring, all-powerful, who would rescue her from her nightmare. She had not thought about the fact that her only connection with him was an attorney/client contract from which he was free to withdraw. He was free to take another case. He was free to never again accept her calls or come to see her in jail. He was free.

Joyce tried to focus on getting out of jail, repressing the memory of Rosemary, the ongoing tension, the fact that life in jail was one of constant danger. Larry Debus had uncovered evidence of prosecutorial misconduct. Larry Debus had arranged for her to have a new trial. But no one believed what amounted to a convicted felon even if the sentencing had not yet taken place. She had to find a way to be able to again present her side of what had taken place in court. She needed a new attorney and she needed one immediately.

Ron. Joyce wanted to go to Ron. He knew the city, the lawyers. He could find someone to help her. He could . . . But increasingly she was coming to the realization that their marriage was over. He rarely came to see her; his excuse was that he was a busy man. He had a print shop that he was single-handedly running now that his partner was dead. He was hustling new business. But she knew he was drinking and perhaps worse . . .

Her head and heart ached. There were three children, hurting, in need of love and guidance. They weren't Ron's children but he had accepted them when he married her. He didn't have to love them. He just had to act responsibly. They were just children. They might be older, having matured to a level where they needed more freedom, less discipline, but they could not be on their own. They needed a father figure. They needed Ron.

Joyce needed Ron as well, yet he wasn't there for her either. She could not tell him of Rosemary. She could not tell him of the horrors she was witnessing, the fear that had become an integral part of her daily life. What she did not know was that Ron would not have cared. He was seeing other women, taking them home, planning to leave Arizona.

Eden was the one who had to endure the humiliation of Ron's womanizing. She could not tell her mother what was happening, could not risk the results of the emotional impact such a disclosure might cause. Instead she had to experience the sounds of noisy lovemaking taking place in her mother's bed, her bedroom wall acting as a loud-speaker, broadcasting the passion occurring on the other side, in the room her parents once had shared. And in the morning she watched the woman, a stranger, prancing about in Joyce's clothing. The two women being a similar size and build, the girl friend was delighting in the dresses like a child released in a toy store. It was another heart-ache for Eden, another pressure she could not reveal to anyone.

In December Ron told Joyce and the children that he had to go to California for two or three days on a business trip, like numerous others he had taken over the years. What he didn't say was that he would never return to his family.

Meanwhile Joyce tried to adjust to being in jail, to not living in fear. She was determined to survive any way she could. While she wrestled with the question of how to find legal counsel and the daily question of how to stay alive in the volatile atmosphere of the pod, she also created her own diversions. Among these was what came to be known as the "Great American Bowling Tournament."

Joyce's action was not so unusual. When life is hell,

there is a tendency to embrace the things that might give a moment's pleasure. Jail had an atmosphere of hopelessness so that it is the ultimate but perhaps not surprising result that Joyce who had been committed to such a hell learned not only to survive but to accept, to adapt and to make the best of her confinement, which is one of the reasons that Joyce developed the great American bowling tournament.

"Save your paper cups," Joyce whispered, making certain the guards did not know. "Clean them out and dry them. And save one of the oranges. We're going bowling."

The cups were carefully arranged like bowling pins at one end of a long corridor, at least 30 feet in length. Then the inmates in her pod lined up at the other end, using an orange that was unusually hard. Not only would it roll, but the game would soften the orange, allowing them to use it in the fermenting bootleg mix they were preparing. They used the fruit skin and all, though they had to pound the hard ones to get them soft enough for use. Repeated rolling of the orange during the bowling tournament nicely accomplished the same goal.

"Each one of us took two turns, one of the inmates acting as 'pin spotter' to reset the cups each time they were knocked over. There was carpeting that was uneven and even the straightest rolled orange had a tendency to veer toward the wall, careening from side to side before it finally reached the cups. I had always been a terrible bowler; my score with the cups was bad as it had been in real life. Some of the other women were quite accurate, figuring out the defects in the carpet and using them to their advantage.

"The game lasted about an hour, not counting the breaks every twenty-eight minutes so the guards would not catch us. An hour was a long time in jail and we all delighted in the diversion. We bowled again and again in the months ahead, and I suspect the guards knew what we were doing. But even the worst among the guards recognized the need for non-destructive diversion. They said nothing."

There were other motives for bowling and ignoring such horrors as the attack on Rosemary. Joyce was gaining the confidence of the other inmates, learning to trust their experience in the legal system. Their backgrounds, their crimes, their innate sense of people often made them excellent judges of others. They may have repeatedly made bad decisions concerning their own lives, but they had learned their way around the courts. They understood the players, the cons, the good guys among both the criminal defense lawyers and the judges. Joyce knew that their experiences could help her.

Chapter 9

NEW COUNSEL

Joyce went to the telephone book and began listing criminal defense attorneys. Some had names she knew from various trials written about in the newspapers. Others were unfamiliar to her. She also added names of Tucson attorneys she knew about, since many Tucson lawyers traveled to Phoenix for cases. In addition, she added a national legal expert who was frequently in the news, his name linked with cases of injustice he was trying to correct.

Feeling terrified, Joyce began making collect calls, the only ones allowed, to the criminal defense attorneys she had placed on her list. She also contacted attorneys by mail, including one of the most prominent in the nation at his office in Harvard University. He replied, requesting that she send information about the case for him to review, and promising to immediately get back to her. She complied with his request, but never heard from him again despite repeated attempts to reach him.

Most of the attorneys were local or from Tucson, approximately 125 miles distant. She made appointments for them to drive to Durango to see her, scheduling one right after the other to discuss her case to see who might be willing to handle it.

Then she began giving the lawyers' names to the inmates, letting them provide a rating system for her. What she learned was discouraging.

The bulk of the criminal defense attorneys she named was said to be greedy, corrupt or immoral. Although several of the attorneys were known for their stiff legal fees, something Joyce had already encountered, more common were the ones who were willing to accept more than money in exchange for their services. Sex was a common instrument of barter, and not just from the prostitutes. The level and quality of representation sometimes depended upon not only a woman's willingness to go to bed with an attorney, but also her acceptance of whatever kinky variation he might desire.

Then there were the lawyers who handled drug dealers and users in exchange for a quantity of cocaine or other illegal stimulant. Sometimes the lawyers were users. Other times they enjoyed having it available at parties. Occasionally there were rumors that the drugs were used to bribe judges into making favorable rulings. No one was certain how the drugs were used, but the lawyers looked upon them as a proper fee for services rendered.

There were lawyers considered incompetent and lawyers who would "beat your check to the bank." Some were dandies, more interested in the fashionable clothes on their backs than their clients in the jails. Others were proud of a down-home, rumpled look, a Jimmy Stewart "Aw, shucks, ma'am" image that they thought impressed the jury despite the fact that they drove to the court house in Mercedes, Jaguars, or Ferraris.

One of the attorneys who arrived was nationally known for his flamboyance in the courtroom and his willingness to take unpopular causes. He delighted in a succession of young women and cheating wives to fill his leisure time schedule. In his most unusual case, he defended a man guilty of stabbing his wife to death in bed by putting the woman on trial. He convinced the jury that the late wife spent her days endlessly shopping, an activity that bordered on the obsessive and eventually caused him to murder her. The action seemed almost justifiable by the time the defense was complete, a case that left some witnesses looking upon him with awe, and others, horrified and disgusted.

The lawyer was also known for his willingness to defend individuals harrassed for protecting illegal aliens fleeing oppressive nations. Joyce felt that it was the compassionate, caring side that would cause him to want to help her.

" 'Pay me $15,000 up front and I'll take your trial transcripts to the beach to read over the weekend,' he had the nerve to tell me," said Joyce. " 'If I'm interested, I'll come back and we can discuss my fee.'

"There was another man, quiet, slightly rumpled in appearance, soft spoken, and extremely comforting. I liked him more than anyone, but I didn't think he could handle my case in court. He didn't seem tough enough for what I was facing."

Joyce's days were filled with a steady stream of attorneys, yet the meetings in the small room over the large gym area did little to alter the misery of life in jail. Her bathroom was positioned in such a way that anyone using it could hear the sounds coming from the isolation area nearby where she had spent her first couple of days. It was also the area where they kept the crazies, both those who were dangerous and those whose actions were harmless yet unpleasant to be around.

The guards seemed less concerned about the crazies because they were in a secure area. Anything that might be used as a weapon for self-destruction had been removed. The sounds that came from the section were often the screams of the damned, yet they were coming from internal torment, not something that was happening to them. As a result, the guards learned to ignore them most of the time. Some might try to quiet someone who was in terror over monsters of her own sick fantasies. Others treated the screamers like babies who cry for no apparent reason other than the fact that they seem to just want to cry themselves to sleep. Leave them alone and eventually they'll be quiet.

One afternoon the screaming began in a slightly different way. At first the woman's voice seemed to be filled with anger. Then there was the sound of fear. And then a more rhythmic pattern, the screams suddenly becoming stronger every few minutes.

Time passed and many of the inmates became uneasy. Even though the crazies were a world unto themselves, they were hesitant to push the issue with the guards. "They heard just as much as we did," said Joyce, a trace of bitterness in her voice as she remembered the incident. "And there was no reason for them to respect us enough to want to give us peace by trying to calm some nut case who was perfectly safe."

An hour went by. Then two. By the end of the third hour, the screamer was going hoarse yet seemed to make no effort to slow or stop.

Finally the guards checked on her and suddenly there was a flurry of activity. Security people. Medical personnel. Phoenix patrolmen. Sheriff's deputies.

There was also activity outside, which Joyce and the other inmates in her pod could witness through the windows. Lights flashing. An ambulance.

And then they learned the truth. The woman had been pregnant and gave birth in the toilet. No one was aware of the pregnancy, nor did they learn if she had gotten pregnant before or after she was jailed. The screams were from labor, the rhythmic contractions of the mother giving birth.

Both mother and child were rushed to the hospital,

but it was too late for the newborn infant. It had drowned in the toilet.

"And that night, like all the other nights, I sat on my bunk, tears flowing down my cheeks. I cried, not in great gulps of air, noisy wailing, my nose running uncontrollably, but in silence."

Interviewing the attorneys helped Joyce keep somewhat of a perspective, though. She needed her day planned in much the same manner as she might schedule her time if she was working in the "free" world.

The most important question Joyce needed answered was whether or not the attorney believed in her innocence. She could not work with an attorney who believed she was guilty, regardless of his skill or determination to free her based on some technicality. She wanted her freedom, but she wanted vindication from the charges leveled against her. To her delight, she felt that every attorney familiar with the case was also convinced that she was not guilty. Many of the attorneys did not meet her standards for personal representation, though all of them shared the belief that a new trial was winnable.

Joyce Lukezic was frightened, angry and desperate when she had her first meeting with Thomas Thinnes and his partner, Craig Mehrens. Her first attorney had told her to trust him, had told her that she would not serve a day in jail, had said that he would serve her time for her. Her husband had told her that he was by her side, then ran off with a woman with whom he had been having sex in Joyce's bed. Her brother had pledged his support, yet fled the state and never visited her. Even her beloved daughter was planning to go to Boston for a year, too pressured by Joyce's life to continue living the way she had been. She felt deserted on all sides, and reluctant to trust anyone.

But finally she settled on Thinnes and Mehrens. She

only wanted Thinnes to represent her, but he came with a partner or not at all. The fact that the partner was a sharp dresser who seemed more concerned with his appearance than her predicament, upset her. But she found Thinnes to her liking and later found despite his upscale clothes that his partner was quite competent. She felt she had found her lawyer, though Thinnes insisted upon reviewing the material before making his decision.

Thinnes' early impressions of Joyce were equally hesitent. "At the first trial, Joyce looked like . . . I think Frank Sinatra used to describe (columnist) Dorothy Kilgallen, 'She had a mouth like a ripped pocket,'" said Thomas Thinnes, describing his first meeting with Joyce Lukezic in the jail.

"I remember Joyce. She had her hair pulled back so damned tight, it's a wonder she didn't have gangrene of the nose. And her face was always so cold. And the jury, the first jury, noticed this. In the newspaper, one of them said it seemed as if the attorneys weren't concerned with their client. I mean, I'll touch my client. I'll put my hand on my client. I'll put my arm around my client. I'll shake hands with my client. I make contact with my client so the jury doesn't look at him as some sort of leper.

"They, at the first trial, whenever they showed outtakes on TV, they would circle her. I mean, they looked like the Indians around the settlers. You know, that just gives the jury the impression that this son of a bitch must be guilty.

"She was out of custody at the first trial. She was out on bond. I don't know who the hell . . . Bela Lugosi may have been in charge of her make-up the first time and she looked hideous. She looked guilty. And that was the one thing we wanted to change.

"When we saw her in jail, she sure as hell didn't look hard. She looked beaten. She looked defeated. And she knew she was going to get sentenced to death."

Being in jail had proven a shock to Joyce. There was an utter helplessness to her situation, a condition outside her experience. Her movement was limited to the confines of the pod, the gym floor, and the areas used for visitors, attorneys, and religious services. Her only escape was in her mind, doing the exercises the psychiatrist had taught her. And such freedom was illusory, easily shattered by the brutality of a guard, the vicious touch of an angry inmate, an unexpected scream.

"I wanted to be in control of my court case. I had listened to everyone else before and it resulted in my going to jail. I wanted to be in control this time, to remind the lawyer that he was working for me.

"Thomas would hear none of it, but he understood. I was going to have to follow his guidance, his strategy. I think he was a little angry with my attitude, though he knew where I was coming from," said Joyce.

"Joyce told us that she had been promised all along that she would not spend one day in jail," said Thinnes. "This is what Debus had told her. And I said, where are you now? And she said, obviously I'm in jail and, obviously, that wasn't true.

"I didn't draw any conclusions having met with her. I never do. But after she told me some of the representations made to her, that she wouldn't spend one day in jail and that he would serve her time for her, that concerned me from a professional standpoint. But it was nothing so far as evidence. It wasn't admissible evidence anyway."

"Thomas did what I asked," said Joyce. "He told me in advance who he was going to talk to. He told me how he would put witnesses on the stand and what the reason for their order of appearance would be. He gave me copies of the trial transcript to read and asked me to look for things that weren't there, things that I could counter or add. He also kept giving me dates when things would happen. In three weeks we file this motion. In five weeks, the court will make this decision.

"I don't know if he needed to do that or if he just did it for me. I needed it. I needed to be looking forward to something. To know that there was something happening all the time. That was how I kept going. Always having a purpose, a date when something was going to happen."

Joyce felt admiring but a little intimidated by Thinnes when she first met him. He seemed a little distant yet honest, well-dressed, though in a slightly rumpled, casual kind of way that she liked. Craig Mehrens, Thinnes' partner, was perfectly dressed and obviously clothes-conscious. He seemed more concerned with the cut of his three-piece suit and the position of his pressed handkerchief at that first meeting than he did about her. Still, both men had good reputations among the inmates.

Thinnes felt Joyce was innocent from the start because of what he had read in the newspapers and had seen on television. He became convinced of that fact after reading the trial transcripts.

At the same time, there were other factors seemingly weighing on Thomas Thinnes' mind. Part of it was competition.

The Phoenix, Arizona, legal fraternity is like a closed society. There are those who are considered part of the establishment and those who are seen as rebels. Often the attorneys will protect one another, whether the protection is in the form of dismissing complaints against a lawyer with less than a thorough investigation or in the form of assuring a successful practice by making referrals to a legal specialist as much as possible.

Criminal defense lawyers fall into a special category within the fraternity because of their egos. These are the surgeons of the legal profession, the men and women who take the greatest chances. Their clients may literally live or die based on their skills. A mistake in real estate law, for example, may cost a client property and money. A mistake in a felony case may cost a client the next thirty years of life. As a result, these lawyers have tremendous self-confidence and attitudes which can be abrasive.

Larry Debus was an oddity among the criminal defense attorneys. He was a quiet man, withdrawn, seemingly uncomfortable with strangers. It is doubtful that most other criminal defense attorneys could handle the isolation he enjoyed when sailing with his wife during their year-long sabbatical. They would go "stir crazy" from being too far away from the action. As a result, Debus was a more popular member of the Phoenix legal society than were most other specialists in his field. He did not need to dominate the room. He was not antagonistic. He was content with being quiet at a gathering, either interested in what was taking place or escaping in his mind while seemingly attentive.

Sometimes Debus' subdued attitude worked against him. Eden Dow, Joyce's daughter, saw the lawyer as "slimy, cold, unfeeling." The jury seemed to take his lack of contact with Joyce as being a rejection of his client, not the natural condition of an introverted man. But despite these seeming shortcomings, he remained popular with other lawyers.

Thinnes was more aggressive, self-assured, abrasive. He also hated Larry Debus, considering the man incompetent at best. He frequently made angry statements about Debus to Joyce and the trial transcripts he reviewed have occasional angry margin notes ridiculing a statement or conclusion Debus made in court. "I didn't know if Thomas was determined to win because he wanted to do something Larry Debus hadn't done or if it was because he believed in my innocence. I like to think it was because of both things, but I think that his beating Debus was a little more important than I was," Joyce later stated.

Yet there was a compassionate side of Thinnes. Eden

felt that Thinnes was caring where Debus had been cold. She sensed that he was genuinely concerned about her mother and the case. He wanted the family to be reunited and she felt confident in his potential for freeing her mother.

More than the pressure of wanting to best a long-time rival was a race against time to free Joyce. There had been another case lurking in the background, a case he did not discuss. This was the case of Jean Holsinger, a former English teacher at Arizona State University, a case heard by Maricopa County Superior Court Judge Sandra Day O'Connor (later elevated to the United States Supreme Court.)

There were interesting similarities between the Holsinger case and the murder of the Redmonds. She was charged with plotting to kill Dr. Henry Schornick because of a potential inheritance. Ultimately the doctor was shot and wounded, his eighty-one-year-old housekeeper murdered. The plot centered around her husband, W.G. "Buster" Holsinger and two hired assassins, Gary Cagnina and James Arnold. The two convicted killers were sentenced to twenty-five years to life and "Buster" Holsinger was given the death penalty. Jean Holsinger was given the same sentence as the killers, despite the fact that she was innocent.

The case was similar to that of Joyce's, since Holsinger was a respectable, well-educated woman thrown into circumstances totally foreign to anything she had known. Prosecutorial misconduct was felt in the trial. The allegation was that a Deputy County Attorney had withheld a portion of a witness' testimony from the defense counsel so that certain statements would not be known until they were in court. Such an action was not only in violation of the law, it prevented Thinnes from being prepared with witnesses or other evidence that would counter what had been said.

Thinnes was able to gain Holsinger's freedom until she could face what he felt would be a fair trial. But Holsinger was deeply hurt, emotionally shattered, and unable to cope with the possibility of a return to prison. She also became involved with another woman who had a credit card scam meant to make them desperately needed money. Holsinger's career had been ruined and her defense expenses were extremely high. When she was arrested for the credit card scam, the idea of returning to prison under any conditions overwhelmed her. Before she could get emotional help, Jean Holsinger committed suicide, a fact that Thinnes was unable to forget. He did not want to see Joyce become another Jean Holsinger.

It was with the subconscious pressures of a seemingly innocent client, competitive anger towards Larry Debus, and the memory of the late Jean Holsinger that Thinnes went to work. Yet it was from the facts in the case that he began to develop new approaches. As he explained:

"When Debus and Kimerer were making their motion for a directed verdict (acquittal) to (Judge) Gerber, they were so cock-sure that they had it won that they were up at Durant's (a restaurant/bar) having a beer at lunchtime. This is while they were in trial.

"Debus is not one to be very neat. He was shooting his mouth off as to how Gerber had no alternative and no choice but to grant the directed verdict. Actually Gerber didn't, and the jury found her (Joyce) guilty. This was in the press."

Thinnes continued: "There were interviews with the jurors after they returned the verdict of guilty, and the jurors said that if they were ever charged with as serious a crime, they would want to have attorneys who seemed more interested in their client. And these attorneys were more concerned with obtaining a mistrial than with getting to the actual facts of the case. Something to that effect."

Discussing how he got started, Thinnes explained that his initial background came from the newspaper accounts of Joyce's first trial. "After we agreed to represent her, we went through the trial transcripts. Craig Mehrens and I picked up all of the files, at least that which was represented to be all of the files, from Debus. And, at the time, we asked him what his feelings were about the case. He said he felt that she may have known something about it, but did not actually participate. In other words, she had some knowledge, but knowledge alone does not make one an accomplice, nor does it make one a co-conspirator."

Thinnes continued: "We reviewed the trial transcripts and it was obvious to us that the people who had, for lack of a better term, represented her in the first trial had completely missed the obvious defendant, and that was Ron Lukezic. They had overlooked him, and I thought that it was intentional because it was so obvious.

"What was most telling in this case, not only was she not the likely suspect and her husband was the likely suspect, but it turns out that Debus also represented the husband, Ron Lukezic. He represented both of them.

"I don't know what the hell he (Debus) was doing, but I remember at the first trial, in going through the transcript, when one of the fellows from Graphic Dimensions was testifying . . . He's got the white, curly hair with the real red face. He drinks quite a bit. I've seen him quite often at Durant's . . . He said, at the funeral of Redmond, that Ron Lukezic came up to him, threw his arms around him, and said, 'Oh, my God, what have I done.'

"Debus spent his whole cross-examination of that witness trying to convince the jury that Ron wasn't serious about it. Nothing to do with Joyce. Not pointing out that, hey, Joyce never said that. Joyce didn't do this. Joyce didn't do that. But that Ron wasn't serious about it. And that bothered me when I was reading it.

"Then we later found out that Debus had been a witness in a case involving McCall—He had been called by Ron Henzie, that's another defense attorney—as early as December of 1981. I think that's when the case went to trial. McCall and Cruz went to trial.

"Henzie called Debus as a witness, and Debus testified under oath that he represented both Joyce and Ron Lukezic. He said, 'yeah,' under oath, that 'we represent them.' The 'we,' I assume, meaning he and Kimerer.

"So when we were reading the transcripts of the trial and putting that together, we looked at it and said, "Well, wait a minute. Who the hell has the best motive in this case? The obvious one is the surviving partner, which is Ron Lukezic. That coupled with the fact, and I know at the first trial they, meaning Debus and Kimerer, had information concerning the set-up and that if, in fact, Ron died Joyce wouldn't inherit the business, that told us—that told Craig and me—that she has absolutely no motive to want Redmond out of the way. So it's got to be somebody else.

"So our defense in this case was structured to showing the jury just who the guilty people were, and who the individuals who, circumstantially, may have looked like they were involved, but who had nothing to do with it. In fact, one of the instructions given to the jury was that knowledge of a crime does not make one a participant or a co-conspirator. And that, in fact, it is a viable defense that some other third party is responsible for the act. That was one of the other instructions that we had.

"After going through the transcripts of the trial and the departmental reports, I arrived at the conclusion that this gal had been sold down the river by her previous defense lawyers and that's what I told the jury in the second trial. And when we met with the jury after the second trial, one of the questions they asked was, are these two characters still practicing law? And we said, unfortunately yes. And Judge Gerber interjected and said, 'Oh, these two are very respected members of the profession.'

False Arrest

"A bar complaint was then made against us by Debus for saying that he would sell his client down the river. It was subsequently dismissed by the bar, but it led to a lot of hard feelings, that defense. And I was told by other defense attorneys in the community that no one would have mounted that defense for her. If we hadn't mounted that defense for her, she'd be on death row right now because Debus tried to sell the jury, the first time around, that this was a robbery gone awry.

"Those were his words in his closing argument to the jury. But this case was not a robbery gone awry. This case was exactly what it was. It was a murder for hire. And my only question is why to this day does the county attorney insist that Ron Lukezic had nothing to do with it? I would have been willing to prosecute Ron Lukezic."

While Thinnes was looking through the case, coming to an understanding of how he wanted to defend Joyce, where the weaknesses were, and venting his anger over the previous attorney, she was being forced to face herself. Joyce was given transcripts of the trial and asked to study them, to see where she could challenge statements made, elaborate on matters hinted at but never explained.

Thomas Thinnes was sympathetic to calming Joyce's fears in jail but there was no direct line between prisoners and their attorneys. The lawyers would call the jail, then a message would be given to Joyce to call them back. She would then have to use a pay telephone to call collect. However, when she had concerns, even if it was only learning how things were going, she could reach them and the secretary would put her through if at all possible. "I was billed for every minute we talked, but I didn't care. I had to know what was happening, had to know things were moving forward," said Joyce.

For most people, the fact that Joyce was charged at all

added credibility to the allegations that she was a criminal. However, the justice system often took the simplest way out. Thinnes later commented:

"The mentality of the prosecutors here has always been, since I've been practicing from 1966 until now, once they get an individual charged with the commission of an offense, and they feel that that individual is responsible, dynamite won't blow them off of that position. And they'll ride that thing to hell.

"The best example is out of the attitude toward Ron Lukezic. In fact, even looking into it, investigating it, they offered the guy blanket immunity in exchange for anything he's got to testify about because they assumed that he'll testify that Joyce was responsible. I think that's crazy. I think that's investigation of the worst kind."

The County Attorney had their own investigative staff. "The blue coats are called to the scene," Thinnes said. "Then they call the detectives in. Now Larry Martinsen investigated this case. He's a highly qualified detective, a bright guy, a damned thorough investigator.

"Once it gets to the County Attorney's office, which is in a matter of days, they have their own investigative staff, in this case, Dan Ryan. So Dan Ryan gets the case and he's working with (deputy prosecutors) Brownlee and Jones, two individuals with whom I have had exposure in other cases, but have never had a trial with either of them. Once they get the case, then the detectives from the city sometimes will do some follow-up stuff, but the primary investigator is then the County Attorney's office. And in this case, Ryan went hook, line, and sinker for Merrill, and they're off to the races.

"Merrill told them 'what happened,' and that's their theory and they're going to ride that to Hell.

"There were so many times in our case that he (Ryan) was discredited that it's obvious the guy works in investigation the way I used to do algebra. Go to the back of the book, get the answer, and then work back to the problem. And that's basically the way he investigates. He gets that call from Arnie Merrill. Arnie Merrill feeds him a pile of crap a mile long. He makes a deal with Merrill, meets him back in New York, they have a potato knish, and the whole thing's off to the races. And that's how this started.

"Then they start carving the pieces of the puzzle to make this thing fit. And what they wind up with is a portrait of Dorian Grey in its latter stages. It's a hideous God damned thing that's transparent to any jury."

Except that it wasn't. Joyce was in jail and the problem was going to be to free her.

There was no way of knowing what Thinnes might do. There was no way to know what he might say. All she knew was that she had made a tentative decision, the first one she had made on her own. For better or worse, wherever possible, she was determined to take control of her future.

Yet, with all that she was facing, her first concern was survival and her second, because of her history of heart disease, was keeping healthy.

Chapter 10

SURVIVAL

There are few recreational activities in jail. Durango had the large floor area, but, because the inmates were doing short time, either being released or sent on to the penitentiary, no one bothered to establish an exercise program for the inmates. They would eat the food, eat whatever snacks were obtained from the commissary, and generally sit around doing very little.

Joyce began taking to her bed for a major part of her day once the lawyers stopped coming for interviews. Thinnes was immersed in the reading that had to be done before he could do more with the case. Joyce and the other women would be awakened early for breakfast, sometimes finishing before 6:00 A.M. Then there was nothing to do until they ate again at 11:30. Dinner was five hours later.

Some of the women adapted comfortably, playing cards or watching television for hours. Joyce needed more stimulation than that, or she needed to completely escape. Eventually she found herself escaping by taking a two-hour nap after breakfast and another two-hour nap after lunch. Part of the sleep she needed, not resting well at night because she had too much time to lie in bed, listening to the sounds of the jail, thinking, crying. But most of her nap time was used as a way of escaping the jail, the thoughts about the trial, the helpless feeling she had concerning her children whose living conditions fluctuated constantly.

When Joyce finally realized that it was dangerous to become so depressed and sedentary, she decided, at least, she had to improve her physical condition if she was to survive, a belief shared by several other women in the pod. It was then they decided to have an exercise class.

"Each morning, for at least forty-five minutes, we'd go out on the floor for our workout," said Joyce. "I was the leader at first because it was my idea. Later there would be an inmate from another jail who was transferred and looked the part. She was tall, thin, and in good shape. Looking at her I felt a little like a squat midget standing next to Jane Fonda. But I was the one who planned everything.

"The first thing we needed was music, a luxury we were denied in the jail. No one had a radio or a tape player. However, despite different backgrounds and different tastes in music, we found that we all were familiar with a total of 81 songs, a rather remarkable discovery, at least in our minds. All we had to do was pick one, then everyone would hum the music as I led the group.

"Later, after the transferred inmate took over as leader, the others came to regret the change because I had to sing along with the others, something they had not heard me do before. I've always wanted to be a singer and I have great enthusiasm. I also have to agree with my daughter who commented, upon hearing me play the piano and sing to my own accompaniment, "Mom, you're really great. You play in one tune and sing in another."

"The women who were exercising, and there usually were about a half dozen of us, would start to hum the agreed-upon song. Then I would tell them what to do. 'Bend to the left and bob and bob. Now bend to the right and bob some more. Now straighten your body, hands over your heads, and arch your back. Then touch your

toes.' And on and on, several different songs from our rep-
ertoire were used during each session. Everything was designed to get our bodies stretched and limber, what would
probably be called low impact aerobics in a health club.

"Many of the women watched us, refusing to sweat
though delighting in our actions. Probably a few were lesbians who just liked to watch other women's bodies. Others were curious for any diversion and we looked like we
were engaged in a musical (?) version of the child's game,
Simon Says. Still, it kept me from trying to sleep my life
away and helped to restore my health."

During the first trial Joyce had existed in a state of
shock. She had not been an active participant in her own
case. Now she had the opportunity to help with her defense, reviewing the records and trying to learn the truth
about what had taken place. Thomas Thinnes and Craig
Mehrens began supplying her with documents; the information she read stunned her. On May 20, 1983, statements
filed before the Arizona Supreme Court had already shown
how outrageous the prosecution of Joyce Lukezic had
been. While the statements had not kept her from jail, they
revealed the nightmare reality of lies and innuendo, of
bribes and coercion that resulted in an innocent woman
going to prison. The report, accompanied by specific refer-
ences to existing documents and court testimony, stated,
in part:

"1. Investigator Ryan admitted during testimony that
he had made 'loans' to State's witness Wally Roberts. These
payments, according to Ryan, were, at least in one instance, made by way of a money order. This is the same
manner of payment used in making the Merrill car payments.

"2. Investigator Ryan admitted during testimony that
he had contacted members of Arnold Merrill's family and

informed them that if Merrill did not cooperate with the State either he or his family would, in all likelihood, be killed by the Mafia.

"3. Investigator Ryan admitted in testimony that he removed Arnold Merrill from incarceration and took him for visits at his wife's home, visits where Investigator Ryan waited outside the home which would enable Merrill to have personal contact with his wife.

"4. Investigator Ryan admitted in testimony that he had provided State's witness Wally Roberts, a known drug addict with schyzophrenic (sic) tendencies, with a firearm to carry concealed during a meeting in a public restaurant with one of the defendant's witnesses.

"5. Investigator Ryan also admitted that he told the witness Wally Roberts that he was being followed. This was an obvious attempt to frighten and intimidate Roberts, a man with paranoid tendencies. Ryan knew Roberts was not being followed and knew that the person who had previously been in the restaurant with Roberts was a licensed private investigator and a retired Federal Bureau of Investigation agent.

"6. When asked whether or not he threatened two potential State witnesses in an attempt to obtain their cooperation Ryan denied such threats. In answer to allegations that Ryan had told Raymond Kleinfeldt that he would break his legs if he didn't cooperate, Ryan testified that what he told Raymond Kleinfeldt was, 'I won't break your legs if you don't cooperate'. In answer to an allegation that he threatened to take Mrs. Kleinfeldt's children away and put them in a home, Ryan responded that he told Mrs. Kleinfeldt, 'I won't take your children away if you don't cooperate'.

"7. Investigator Ryan and Deputy County Attorney Joseph Brownless, both testified at the Motion for New Trial that the payments made on behalf of the Merrills were not handled through, or as a part of, the Witness Protection Program.

"8. Deputy County Attorney Joseph Brownlee testified that he was unaware of any 'loans' or other payments made by Investigator Ryan.

"It was in this context that the trial court heard testimony relating to the GMAC payments made by Ryan on behalf of Arnold and Cathy Merrill.

"The State's memorandum indicates that Mr. and Mrs. Merrill made their car payments through Investigator Ryan beginning at the time that they became protective witnesses. The contrary is indicated by the records of General Motors Acceptance Corporation.

"These records reflect that Mrs. Merrill made car payments in various names, long before Investigator Ryan became involved. In fact, the GMAC records contain photocopies of checks written by Mrs. Merrill in her new name, with her new address and phone number in Las Vegas. It is obvious that no attempt was being made to conceal her new identity and whereabouts from officials at General Motors Acceptance Corporation.

"Apparently Mrs. Merrill was short of money from time to time and unable to make car payments. It was at these times that Investigator Ryan would make the payments for her. This fact is best demonstrated by a check in the amount of $408.00, written by Mrs. Merrill in the name of Rhonda Montana with her Las Vegas address, which did not clear because of insufficient funds. She apparently telephoned Investigator Ryan informing him that she did not have the money to make her car payment. Investigator Ryan immediately made this payment with his own funds.

"At the hearing on the Motion for New Trial, Investigator Ryan was unable to produce any loan agreements, writing or other documentation that the monies advanced on behalf of the witness Wally Roberts and the witnesses Arnold and Cathy Merrill, were in fact 'loans'."

The charges continued:

"In each instance where the State was discovered to have paid monies to witnesses or conferred some other benefit on their behalf, the State attempts to hide behind the Witness Protection Program. Yet, there is not a single document, record, or other piece of evidence which demonstrates that any of this conduct was in any way related to, or a part of the Witness Protection Program. As indicated, Deputy County Attorney Brownlee testified that he did not know of these acts."

There were other statements, including discussions of the volume of Valium and Seconal, a sleeping medication, provided to Arnie Merrill, an addict, while in jail. There were also details of the deliberate misrepresentation of Merrill by some members of law enforcement.

"It was demonstrated during the trial that Arnold Merrill planned numerous burglaries and robberies, including burglaries of people with whom he was acquainted or had worked. He also fenced the property from these burglaries, some of which involved injury to elderly victims. He was also involved as a principal in the planning and casing of the Redmond murders. He admitted that in the year preceding the Redmond homicides, he made a living primarily by selling drugs and committing burglaries. His plea agreement enabled him to avoid several hundred years of incarceration, and two death sentences. As a direct result of the falsified presentence investigation report, Arnold Merrill received a sentence enabling him to be parole eligible in four years."

The details continued for almost thirty pages, the documentation taking far more. The issue of another suspect was not raised. The issues of Joyce's lack of motivation and the potential motivation of others were not covered. But there were enough facts concerning misrepresentation, improper acts, and similar details that the horrible injustice of the first trial was evident. Also, many of the issues which the new defense attorneys would have to raise had been established. The tragedy was that Joyce was confined to jail, facing the very real possibility that she might never again be free.

And in this literal and figurative trap, her life went on.

The jail was a unique society, a subculture that could not be defined, that had to be experienced, endured, never conquered, ever with the potential of destroying those within its confines. But even within this strange and violent world there were moments that mimicked normality, when relationships seemed a perverted parody of what was enjoyed by those who were free.

"I had a reputation in jail that, for a number of reasons, was becoming more positive among the other prisoners," Joyce explained. "I was no longer the Central Avenue Bitch because no one cared about my past. I was one of the inmates, my education, friendships, or past of no concern to anyone.

"There was only one time anyone challenged me in a way that I knew could lead to violence. What the woman did not realize was that I am both a coward and know nothing about fighting. I have a quick temper with words. Every time my kids would act up, I would rant and rave. I would shout, "If you don't stop, I'll kill you," but it meant nothing. Even my kids would laugh. I cowered any time anyone threatened me. I did not know how to fight, did not care to learn. All I knew was that if a fight broke out, I could get hurt and I had endured enough pain in jail.

"Yet when the woman threatened me I did not act as I normally would. I was terrified but managed not to show it. Instead, I glowered at her and said, 'I'm here for two murders. A third doesn't matter at all to me.'

"The woman believed me, backing off. I don't know if

she told anyone else what happened, but I wasn't bothered again.

"Perhaps it was the threat. Perhaps it was the publicity my case had received in the newspapers and on television. All I know is that my name was known, a fact that became clear when I developed a "relationship" with a man.

Chapter 11

MEN, WOMEN AND SEX

"There was some man working in the kitchen. I never saw him. I have no idea why he was in jail. All I know is that he decided to send mc gifts of a type that only inmates can fully appreciate.

"The situation began after the dentist insisted upon my having a special diet while in jail. Most of my food was like everyone else's, though I also was to get cottage cheese and celery. As a result, I had a tray clearly labeled 'Lukezic' sent up to me each meal.

"One day I noticed that there was something attached to the bottom of the tray. I didn't know what it might be, whether it was just dirty or if something was there, but I had been in jail long enough to know that you never called attention to anything out of the ordinary. I carefully slipped my hand underneath until I felt what turned out to be a note attached to the underside. I removed it, palmed it, and read it later. It was from the kitchen worker, a man named Fred, wishing me well.

"A few days later another item appeared underneath a tray. This time it was real coffee, packaged in a plastic bag, taped to the underside of the tray. There wasn't much coffee, but there was enough so that I could use a smuggled cup, hot water, and several matches to heat what was truly a luxury in jail.

"The notes were called 'kites,' a term used for any prison communication. A grievance filed with the administration, a love letter, or anything else that went through the prison, legally or illegally, was a kite.

"Fred and I began corresponding through the tray 'mail' system. I had no idea who he was, nor did I care. All of us were desperate for any sort of support, no matter the source, and when it came from a man, even a fellow inmate, we delighted in it. The only problem was that Fred's love offerings led me to get into trouble.

"The guards kept track of everyone in the pods, their routines, and anything that varied from those routines. Any inmate who suddenly acted differently than she had been acting was immediately suspect.

"Most of the women were street smart and knew how to handle themselves. I was naive, never having had to think like a criminal.

"It was on a Friday when I received a special kite from Fred. He told me that he had a surprise for me out in the yard. The men and women both used the exercise yard, though never at the same time. Both groups of cells had access to the exercise area and it was possible for the men and women to hide notes or gifts for each other, carrying on a romance from afar. Fred had taken the opportunity of his exercise period to bury a present for me.

"My kite gave me very explicit directions where to go in the yard in order to find my surprise. The map was extremely detailed and I carefully memorized every move I would have to make. Psychologically the idea of going into the yard for anything was frightening, but I felt that if I just went out, found what was left for me, then went back inside, I would be all right. I would not have to focus on the birds, the sun, the sky, and the high fence that spoke of freedom's denial.

"I told my roommate what I was going to do and she thought that I was crazy. She explained to me that each time she went out in the yard, her name was noted and reported to guards who were positioned overlooking the exercise area. They would know my name, know that I had never gone outside before, and be watching for my actions. There was no way I could beat the system. However, when I insisted upon doing things my way, she agreed to go with me.

"I went out into the yard, glanced around to get my bearings, then walked immediately to the patch of ground where Fred had buried my present. The soil was loose and I began moving it with my foot. When I started to uncover some plastic wrapped packages, I stooped down and nonchalantly began picking them up. Two of the packets contained coffee; two Kool-Aid. Because of the way the drinks were rationed, the present was more precious than gold. These were items to be savored. These were items to be shared. This was contraband for which inmates could be beaten or killed, so precious were such commodities.

"I slipped one package to Sandra, my roommate, who hid it on her person. Then I placed one package inside my clothing, a second package between my legs, and the third package behind my back. Thrilled with my brilliance as a smuggler, I started back to the entrance to the cell area.

"Walking was extremely difficult because I had to keep my thighs close together, moving stiff legged towards the door. I was clutching one of the packages in such a way that all movement was hobbled as though I was wearing one of those ultra-tight skirts we sometimes wore back in the 1950s. I had to take mincing little steps quite in contrast to the longer stride I had used when going into the yard. I also clutched both hands together behind my back in order to keep the package of coffee concealed. I looked like an oversized bird with clipped wings who was unable either to walk or fly.

"As I entered the pod area, I was greeted by one of the security guards. 'Let's have it, Joyce.'

" 'Have what?' I asked, smiling nervously. My body was unnaturally positioned as I fought to keep the packet between my legs. My hands locked behind my back were equally uncomfortable.

" 'Whatever you picked up out there.'

" 'Me?' I asked, my voice cracking.

" 'Hand it over, Joyce.'

"I smiled weakly, bringing the package from behind my back. Then I relaxed my legs, letting the second package drop. I possibly could have brazened out the third, but I realized that I was never meant to be a criminal. I handed over everything. Only Sandra was able to smuggle her package back to our cell.

"There were other men in my life as well. Every week there was a counter-culture newspaper, The New Times, delivered to the jails without charge. Along with various articles and columns, the classified ads were a place where prisoners looked for pen pals. I never wrote to anyone, but if one of the other women did and mentioned my name, either the man writing to her would write to me as well, or one of his friends might write.

"Most of us led active fantasy lives while in jail. It was something to do, something to plan, even though it meant nothing.

"For example, there was Ben. He was related to one of the women in jail and I agreed to write to him in the state penitentiary in Florence, Arizona, where he was doing time. None of the women knew honest men or, if they did, they never provided any of us with a way to contact them. We were limited to the male version of our own closed society, though it was far more bigoted and violent than Durango.

"People tend to adjust to their surroundings. You see this fact in prison more than anywhere else. Phoenix, Arizona, like everywhere else in the country, has strong racial prejudice. There are whites, blacks, Hispanics, and Indians all struggling to have a piece of the American dream. People are vying for the same jobs, looking to achieve the same types of future for their children. Most are hard working and just want to be allowed to achieve whatever their abilities might allow.

"One of the problems with society at large, though, is that people vying for the same employment, the same advancement, often become insecure. Some are fearful that they won't get promoted because they're not as good as a co-worker also in line for the job. Some are concerned about discrimination, having a minority advanced over them, even when they're more qualified, because quotas have to be met. Many are so insecure that when they hear people laughing and talking in a foreign language, they think that they are being ridiculed.

"Most people in jail are either not very intelligent or not well educated. They have been put down, usually holding only menial jobs during their periods of legitimate employment. They are behind bars, unable to control their own destinies, and desperate for some sense of personal power.

"In larger prisons, the inmates gain power by joining gangs. The gangs may be white versus black or Hispanic. They may be divided among ethnic rather than racial lines. There were such groups as the Aryan Nation, the Black Guerrilla Family, the Crips, and others. They have wars and vendettas. They will kill each other, given the chance, regardless of what that will do to their sentence. In some instances, jail is so much a way of life that a young person takes pride in being old enough to go to the penitentiary where he can become a part of one of the adult gangs.

"Usually the guards are helpless. They are always outnumbered. They are always considered the enemy or are used for various smuggling and communication needs. Either way they get little respect and recognize that they must overlook much criminal and violent behavior in order to keep the prison from exploding. It is better for the inmates to establish the rules within their confines than for the guards to be constantly at war with all of them. So long as they are killing each other, the guards are a little safer.

"In the lower jail system, life is a little different. There are too few women in too close quarters for hatred to matter. Whites, blacks, mulattoes, Hispanics, and Indians are all thrown together in the same pods. The racial backgrounds are well mixed to reduce the chance of gangs being formed, and the approach works. During the time I was in Durango, only once did I encounter intense racial hatred. This was from a white woman who would go into a rage each time she saw a black. She would attack both verbally and physically, screaming racial epithets such as 'nigger' and worse at any black who came near her. She had to be kept separate from the blacks, though no one, white or black, seemed to like her. She was the oddity in the county jail. Once a woman went on to the penitentiary, she would likely be absorbed into a gang, expressing racial violence she had not shown in Durango.

"Knowing all this, I was not surprised by Ben's foul language. He talked about the pigs, the niggers, the spics, and other groups he hated. He was a part of one of the white supremacist groups and quite proud of a 'white power' tattoo that he wore.

"Ben had a romantic ideal of women. We were helpless creatures to be protected from the harsh realities of life. As I received letters from more and more men over the months to come, I realized that we were a fantasy for most of them. They fantasized that we were virgins or had been properly married so that we could still be considered virtuous. We tended to fall in love at first sight (or first letter, to be more exact), and immediately made a commitment to one another that was as sacred as wedding vows. The fact that the women, like the men, were liars, thieves, burglars, stick-up artists, prostitutes, swindlers, embezzlers, or had engaged in numerous other less-than-respectable activities meant nothing. We were special, to be cared for and protected, even if a pen pal's crimes included mass murder and dismemberment.

"Ben used to write to me about the drug business he was running in prison. Drugs were smuggled in and out seemingly at leisure. Deals were made and those who did not fulfill their obligation were beaten, disfigured, and/or murdered. Ben talked about setting up beatings and killings from the inside. His language was crude, his descriptions shockingly vivid, and I was naive enough to think he was just trying to impress me.

"I came to like Ben, with all his crude macho posturing in his letters. I became like a first grader feeling the muscle of the self-proclaimed strongest boy in class. I expressed suitable emotions of surprise, delight, and awe at his stories of smuggling, bribery, drugs, and mayhem behind bars. If he wrote that he arranged to have some 'motherfucker's head bashed in,' I sympathized with the problems that made such an action 'necessary.' If he claimed to have moved a load of heroin through the system, I expressed amazement because I knew how hard smuggling could be.

"It was all a game and a fantasy, yet there was something about Ben that defied the image he tried to project, some inherent goodness despite the seeming lies with which he filled his letters. That was why, I decided to visit him after I was released from jail.

"Visiting Ben was a mistake. The truth is that the vast majority of people who go to jail deserve to be in jail. In fact, if you met many of them you would hope and pray that most of them would never be released. Their actions make your worst nightmares come to life.

"So it was with Ben. All he did was lift weights, pumping iron hour after hour so that his body had the same sculpted appearance as a mountain. He was massive, and with his temper he reminded me of a volcano capable of erupting at any moment.

"Ben's face and upper body were covered with scars. He had obviously been knived, clubbed, and beaten with fists at various times. One look at the marks on his knuckles and it became obvious that he gave perhaps better than he received when it came to fights. His posture, his attitude, his voice . . . I realized that this man hadn't been trying to impress me. He liked to hurt people. He liked to kill people. He would have enjoyed killing a guard just because the guard had more freedom than he did.

"But that meeting would be many months in the future. It was all fantasy at the start. I was innocent, a mother, trying to be a good person, and I was in jail. Why shouldn't my pen pals also be the exceptions?

"They weren't, of course, and the more you wrote to different men in jail, the more they would become jealous and possessive. These were men who had never met you, who usually did not know what you looked like. Yet you were theirs.

"For example, there was William, an adolescent in a grown man's body. Typical of his writing were such statements as:

" 'I haven't been thinking about anything but you and the Love that I have for you, and then I wonder what I should expect from you. What I mean is this, Love is sharing, giving and most of all caring for one another, Love is to unite and become one in all things good and bad, and that's the kind of Love that I have for you.

" 'And I am expecting the same from you, But then when I don't get it Im angry with you and I think that its wrong to be that way, because as you said I should be more understanding with you, and I really try to be and when Im pissed at you I keep it to myself because I dont want to have you thinking that Im some kind of animal, can you understand that.'

"The endings of his letters were filled with the type of sayings that are found in high school yearbooks. Frequently the last page of his letters would have such things as:

" 'Your My Everything
        And So Much More
Im Forever And Always
        Loving You
Im Totally Yours
        Once Again Your Ole'Man
                William'

"And then he would add:

" 'You-N-Me
        Bill-N-Joyce
                Tarzan-N-Jane
For Life. . . .'

"And also:

" 'I-need-want-care-crave-cherish-admire-adore-and-Love-You-and Only-You!
For Real'

"And:

" 'Be-Good- -Be There
        -And-

-Most of All-
-Be Mine-'

"Some of the inmates liked to talk about sex. Most were just trying to maintain some contact, some love interest. They would be jealous ('. . . but after I wrote to you for about a week I didnt receive an answer and then when I did you were telling me about some asshole that you were writing and that tended to piss me of just alittle.') of other men even though all of them were strangers to each other. It was a way of surviving for all of us; a way for getting from day to day in a society where we were out of control.

"Oddly there were conflicting rules about writing to other inmates. Anyone in the state penitentiaries could write to us with no problem. The men wrote so freely about their on-going crimes that either their letters weren't censored or it was an indication of the foolishness that had gotten them caught in the first place.

"The women in Durango could not write directly to the men's penitentiary. We had to send the letters to someone on the outside who would remail them to the prison. Everyone knew we were doing this and no one minded our writing. We just couldn't do it directly.

"I joke about the relationships now, but it is impossible to say enough concerning their importance at the time. Here were adults reaching out to each other, telling me to be strong. Some one believed in me. A stranger who knew little about my case accepted me as innocent, was concerned about my welfare, believed in my future. I was offered hope, emotional support, a sense of human dignity that was almost completely destroyed by the circumstances in which I was living.

"The men were adolescent in their maturity. Many of them had served most of their adult lives in jail. They were a part of a closed society where, no matter how much power you obtained through beatings, bribery, and murder, you were still in captivity. Your position inside the walls might be that of a king, yet outside you were a cockroach waiting to be crushed. Despite knowing and having to live with this day-to-day awareness, the men were able to give in the only way they knew how. It was corny, childish, and a fantasy I can no longer imagine ever having nursed. But in many ways, my 'boy friends' aided my emotional life and, I suspect, the relationships other women had with other men within the system gave them similarly essential reinforcement."

As Joyce teetered between fantasy and reality trying to maintain some emotional balance, her new lawyers were working on her case. The psychologist Larry Debus provided had taught her to escape in her mind from the surroundings that, at times, overwhelmed her. Yet there was no true escape from the jail. This was her home. This would continue to be her home. She was no longer a wife. Ron had seen to that. She was no longer a mother, though her children, now scattered about the country, were the most precious aspects of her existence. All around her were violence, madness, anger, and pain.

Yet there was a certain comfort about the jail. The routine was established. There were limits to personal responsibility. There was nothing she could do about her family. There seemed nothing she could do about her future. There were no demands on her other than to conform to the few simple rules that were required of all the inmates in Durango. It would be easy to give up, to become institutionalized, to stop fighting, perhaps to let herself die. And all around there were people who, for a price, would supply the substances she needed to take her own life.

It was probably easier to get drugs in jail than on the

streets. Not crack and the other recreational drugs that are discussed in newspapers and magazines, but hard drugs—like heroin.

Joyce never learned all the ways they were smuggled into the building. The guards had to be involved to some degree, but it was not healthy to ask questions.

The women had an easier time. Joyce never knew how much could be stored in a woman's body. Inmates would put their "fits" (an outfit which consisted of a syringe and needle for injecting heroin) either in their vagina or up their anus. The heroin itself would be smuggled inside the same body cavities or in their mouths. Men and women could swallow balloons or condoms filled with drugs, then fish them from their waste before flushing the toilet.

Visitors would also pass drugs. "We had visits where we could sit with family members and friends. Typically someone would place the heroin in a plastic bag or similar container, then store it in the mouth. They would slip it from their mouth to their hand, then hold hands with the inmate, passing the drug in that manner," said Joyce.

The inmates were supposed to be searched after being out in the exercise yard and after each visit. The search following the trip to the yard was a casual one, a pat-down above the waist and a check for anything obvious. Obviously, it was possible to smuggle contraband into the yard, as Fred proved. Men could pass weapons to women the same way.

By contrast, there were always supposed to be thorough searches after visits. The guards would put on rubber gloves and use their hands to explore all body parts. It was humiliating, disgusting, and painful. There was also no way that they could avoid finding any drugs that were being smuggled. Yet heroin was constantly available to the inmates.

"I never used drugs, never wanted to use them, and

that made me quite popular with the women. The guards knew the users and made periodic searches of their cells. The users relied on people like me to hold the drugs for them, knowing that it was unlikely anyone would check me.

"There was one woman, Liz, who was being sent to Perryville, the women's prison. She was a major drug dealer and planned to be involved with drugs at the state penitentiary. However, she also knew that she had only limited contacts in Perryville and she would need a quantity of drugs for both use and sale until she could establish her prison business. As a result, she arranged for her family to smuggle in a packet of heroin that was the size of an egg. It was large enough and pure enough that it would last the average junkie several weeks.

"Liz was afraid of being searched and asked me to hold the heroin for her. Sometimes I hid it in my pants. Sometimes I hid it in my bra. Sometimes I hid it in my room. I kept it three or four days before she took it back, during which time her cell area was checked by the guards.

"My lawyer was angry with me when he discovered what I had done. He reminded me that such an incident would be terrible for my record and would possibly hinder my appeal. I did not care, though. The alternative to being helpful, including hiding drugs or looking the other way when crimes were going down, was to risk a beating or worse. Tolerating the actions was the only way to survive.

"The part that bothered me about the drug users, most of whom were hard-core addicts, was the way they would do anything to get the heroin into their bodies. Sometimes, in the evenings, I would go into one of the cells of our pod with some of the other women. We would sit on the bunks and on the floor, talking, while they injected themselves and each other with heroin.

"The 'fits' were limited. Often only one or two out of

several users had one, and the needles were dull and blunt. Nothing was clean and no one cared. There was no way to sterilize a fit without the guards getting wise. All that mattered to the users was escaping into the drug.

"I sat in a cell one night, watching a large woman who was a heavy user become increasingly frustrated because she could find no way to inject herself. Most of her veins had collapsed. The ones that were still useable and reachable were not responding to her repeated attempts to plunge the dull needle into them. Finally, frustrated, she handed the loaded syringe to one of the other users and had that woman jam it into her neck. It was a horrible sight to witness.

"There was also a night when I witnessed what the addicts call 'nodding.' I was talking with a woman when the drug took effect. One moment she was awake, alert, and talking animatedly. The next moment she stopped, her face looking as though she was seeing something thousands of miles away. No sound came from her lips. It was as though she had been struck mute.

"Seconds passed by, then minutes. Suddenly the effects were reduced and she began talking again, picking up the conversation from the middle of the sentence where she had stopped when the heroin was injected. She hadn't lost her train of thought or of the conversation. For a few minutes she simply seemed to have lost all life from her body."

There were milder forms of intoxicants in Durango, some of which delighted Joyce because making them was more like a high school prank than an action that was both criminal and destructive. When Joyce was going to school in the late 1950s and early 1960s, the girls used to think they were clever if they convinced a diabetic to contribute a needle and syringe to the cause of trying to get high in the cafeteria. They would fill the syringe with vodka stolen from their parents, then inject oranges with the alcohol so they could try to get drunk during lunch time by peeling the fruit and sucking on the juice. Those who could not obtain such sophisticated paraphenalia would add vodka to milk in their Thermos. But those were kid pranks. In Durango the women made their own bootleg alcohol, a treat to which even Joyce looked forward.

There were definite rules to the making of bootleg alcohol. Each person who was given a share to drink—and they all received equal shares—had to contribute something to the cause. The primary ingredients were fresh fruit, that would be chopped or torn into pieces as best they could with the limited tools they would make or steal, bread, liquid Kool-Aid, baby powder, matches, and plastic bags.

First, they would put the plastic bags together, one inside another. Then they would fill the center bag with the torn apart fruit, bread (for the yeast it contained), and the Kool-Aid which provided necessary liquid and sugar. Once the bag was full, they would tie off the end to make an air-tight, leak-proof seal. Then they would set it inside more bags and fill them with the powder to absorb the odors that would otherwise seep from the bag. As the liquid was fermenting, the smell was about as pleasant as the odor arising from a dead goat rotting on the pavement of a highway in the 110-degree summer heat after having been struck by a Mack truck three days earlier.

This rather foul mixture was supposed to ferment from seven to ten days or longer in order to have the most effective potency. Each 24-hour period, the bag would be sneaked into the bathroom and "burped" to remove some of the gasses that had been building inside the sealed container.

Burping was an elaborate procedure. One or two of the women would stand guard, watching for the authorities. If it looked as though they would be caught, the bag was tossed into the trash and they would all deny knowing who was involved. Otherwise one woman would carefully unseal the bag while the other would begin lighting match after match. This would continue the entire time the bag was open, the matches helping to hide the odor coming from the bag.

After burping, the bags would again be sealed and taken back to one of the cells. Each participant in the making of the alcohol would keep the bag, usually about the size of a basketball, in her room for a 24-hour period. In that way the risk of discovery and lock-down was shared equally.

Because they all feared the guards, and because they all wanted a taste of the liquid as soon as possible, they seldom waited more than the three days they considered the minimum necessary for the alcohol to form. They didn't know if it was ready to drink or they just fantasized that it was, but they were convinced that they got high from whatever they had.

"The liquid smelled and tasted terrible, of course. And it burned going down our throats the way good (bad?) whiskey is supposed to do. But we felt that we had gotten away with something naughty. We felt that we had created a taste of the outside world, assuming any of us had the bad taste to go to a bar that was so cheap they would have the nerve to serve such foul liquid. And we felt we were bucking the system just a little.

"The truth was that the administration knew we made the bootleg hootch and they always caught us. We didn't have fresh fruit all that often in the jail, and the guards knew that we only made alcohol when we had the fresh fruit. Invariably they would conduct a search within a couple of days following our getting the fruit. As a result, we frequently lost the hootch we were making," Joyce explained.

The only reason the inmates sometimes beat the system was through the guards stopping their search with the first bag of hootch they found. Often several different groups within the pod would make the alcohol. They would all follow the same procedures, each woman in a particular group sleeping with the bag as though protecting a baby. The rest of the time the bag would be hidden in the room until it was time to pass it on to the next person. They risked lock-down if they were holding the bag, but if it was just in their room, the inmate would lie and say she didn't know how it got there. The other women involved with the bootleg operation would back up the story, everyone feigning innocence and "angry" over the "planted" alcohol. The guards knew they were lying but couldn't prove it and couldn't order punishment for the suspected offender.

"I suppose our actions were childish, but in the closed society of Durango, we took great delight in what we were doing. And again I was able to fantasize that somehow I was in a school sorority, that perhaps the guards were house mothers, that life wasn't the nightmare of violence and death that wrapped itself around the pods like a black, suffocating cocoon."

The problem was that Joyce could never escape the fact that the bootleg operation was just another aspect of the constant effort to get high, to escape through whatever chemistry was available. Joyce was controlled, playing the game of being a bootlegger. But most of what took place was neither innocent nor healthy nor safe.

"The worst part of the drug use was the fact that there was nothing that could be done. There was no way for someone like myself to avoid being in the midst of it. There was no way to avoid holding the drugs when someone wanted you to do so. Accepting the lifestyle they had chosen without participating in the use was all right. Anything else could mean as much trouble as if you were a snitch."

All jails and prisons have their standards for determining someone's worth. Bank robbers and people who deliberately murder police officers are among those who are most respected. Child molesters and rapists are among the least respected. Yet no matter what the crime, the lowest form of humanity in the eyes of the prisoners is the person who tells the guards about crimes others have committed. Such an individual—the snitch—will be given a life of hell within the prison system.

"My lawyers always wondered why I took chances doing things like holding someone's drug stash. They wondered how I could witness a beating and never say anything. I knew what happened when a mulatto, a black, and a white woman left Rosemary's cell just before Rosemary was found on the floor, battered. But when I was interviewed about the battering, I claimed to know nothing. I claimed to accept the story that Rosemary must have fallen because there was certainly no one near her cell at any time that day.

"Staying loyal to the other inmates was difficult, especially for me. They had little or no education. Their interests were often limited to those things which gave them personal pleasure—sex, drugs, eating. They watched the television news, but they seldom read books, magazines, or newspapers, and some of them were incapable of doing such reading.

"The guards, on the other hand, were from all walks of life. Some were little different from the women they guarded, the main difference being the fact that they were either honest or at least had yet to be caught committing a crime. Others were college graduates, working their way up in the corrections system or using the job for experience before going into psychology, social work, or some other field. Their interests included art, music, and other activities. They read both fiction and non-fiction. They traveled. They knew what was taking place in the world and enjoyed talking about the greater significance of what was in the news. They were people with whom I could easily relate.

"I longed to get involved with the guards on a more personal level. I wanted to talk with them, to find a way to walk that line between being friendly with the inmates and enjoying the conversations of the guards. But if I ever became friendly, the inmates would assume that I was also a snitch. And I learned early on what happened to snitches.

"Karen's circumstances were typical of what I would see week after week and month after month whenever someone decided to snitch. Karen had witnessed a fight between two of the women in which one was badly stabbed. Everyone claimed to have been somewhere else at the time. Everyone, that is, except Karen.

"Normally when there are no witnesses to a fight, one of two things happened. If the fight was not stopped by the guards, only the victim discovered battered and bloody, the official report would show that she had fallen. Rosemary was noted as having fallen in her room. Numerous women would be listed as having fallen in the shower where most beatings took place.

"If both parties involved with a fight were discovered, then they would be considered to be equally guilty for what had happened. They would both be sent to solitary as a punishment, neither one of them blaming the other for what had taken place.

"Karen broke the code, however, identifying the assailant. There was no special reward for her. She received no special privileges. The guards thanked her and punished the woman who started the fight. They also arranged medical treatment for the victim, letting her return to the general population as soon as she was released from the medical facility. And Karen was labeled a snitch.

"The punishment for Karen came from all the women

in the pod. Many participated. Others, like myself, watched but said nothing about what was taking place.

"First there was dinner. Karen was walking with her tray when someone bumped it, spilling the contents. There were no seconds in the jail, no replacement trays if you dropped your food. Karen had the choice of picking it up from the floor and eating it or going hungry. She went hungry.

"The next meal the same thing occurred. This time Karen picked up the food, setting the tray on the table, only to have one of the other women nudge it back onto the floor.

"Karen brushed off the food, then ate it slowly, hating what was taking place and being too hungry to do anything about it. She was certain the harrassment would continue and she apparently was steeling herself for the inevitable situation of being forced to eat dirty food each and every day.

"Then came the times when Karen went to the bathroom. She hung her shower curtain like everyone else did, only to have it ripped down. She sat on the toilet and three or four women walked over to her, staring intensely at her as she was on the pot.

"Karen had enough money to order some food from commissary, but it never came. She paid for it, then her commissary items were stolen from the cart.

"The sheet and blanket on Karen's bed were wet with urine when she tried to go to sleep. Later other bed clothes would be torn or soiled for her. Personal belongings would be broken or taken.

"There was no peace for Karen. No one talked with her. No one wanted anything to do with her. Even her roommate was blind, deaf, and dumb when it came to what was taking place. If Karen wanted to know who had gone into the room and damaged her things, the roommate saw and heard nothing, even though there was no way she could avoid seeing what was taking place.

"Occasionally there would be beatings as well. Karen would be grabbed and pulled into the shower room during the twenty-eight minutes when the guards were making their rounds. The beating would not be severe. A few blows to the face, the stomach, the breasts. Just enough to be so quick and painful that Karen was constantly reminded she would always be vulnerable to assault and injury. There was no place to run, no place to hide, no way to get help. If she went to the guards, she would be placed in solitary confinement because that was the only way they could protect her. And solitary confinement meant listening to the screams of the crazies, witnessing the occasional suicide, and being deprived of others, of the sights and sounds that helped us survive the time in jail.

"Later I learned that Karen's actions would stay with her. She was eventually transferred to a correctional institution meant for long term, non-violent criminals, a place where most of the women in B Pod would not go. Yet, through friends, the women at that location would know Karen was a snitch. Their actions would not be so personal or vicious as they had been at Durango. They would have no direct score to settle with her. But they would treat her with silence and contempt. She would lack trust, lack friends.

"Oddly, I also came to see that the guards did not appreciate snitches, even though they relied upon them. A snitch was treated with the same contempt as someone in business who tries to get ahead by sucking up to the boss. They are tolerated because they serve a purpose. They are used because they let themselves be used. But they are not respected and not trusted. They are the deviants of the system, destined to be outcasts with both sides."

In the midst of such a system, loneliness is intense and painful. It is a circumstance which led Joyce to believe that anyone, given enough time in jail, is likely to be vulnerable to a same-sex relationship. "I know that I was," Joyce admitted, "a confession that will probably shock my children.

"My situation began with the feeling of helplessness I had after being placed in jail. For months I had been feeling like a puppet on a string. Ron pulled my string and I denied that he could be the lying, vicious, womanizing, hard drinking deceiver. Larry Debus pulled my string and I danced into the courtroom, accepting everything that was said and done, even when I disagreed with his handling of the case. The doctors concerned with my rotting teeth and my weak heart pulled my string and I changed my lifestyle as much as I could behind bars. The guards pulled my string and I would stand at attention while searched, allow them to smash my possessions in the name of hunting for contraband, permit them to put on their disgusting surgical gloves, then probe my body cavities in search of hidden drugs. I was polite. I was cooperative. I was misled, lied to, manipulated and abused. And I lost everything that was precious to me.

"My home was gone. My inheritance was gone. Most of my valuables were gone. My older son seemed to hate me. My younger son was confused and feeling abandoned. Eden was being forced to keep her feelings hidden. And Ron ran off with another woman.

"Then I became angry, determined to fight. I obtained a new attorney. I feared and admired his strength, yet resented his having such complete control over my life even though there was no alternative. I made demands to which he often agreed, giving me the illusion of power. And I gained the respect of some of the inmates who did not know me after I made the comment that an additional death would not bother me after being sent to jail for two killings.

"Yet all the courage, the strength, and the willingness to fight were not genuine. I was trapped, alternately fueled by the desire to win my freedom and the desire to give up, to accept my surroundings and let myself die. I laugh about some of what I saw. I remember some only in darkness, when the memory of the damned filters up to conscious awareness. And some I have repressed, knowing that the sights and sounds remain too terrifying for me to allow myself to relive them. Yet I vividly remember that each night, whether sitting alone or while talking with the other women, I would cry. Tears would fill my eyes and tumble down my face, the day's sadness overwhelming all my efforts to retain control.

"I could not stand the role of being tough and in control. I fought with Eden, making demands from jail, trying to play mother to a child who was on her own in ways neither one of us wanted. I wrote to my sons, wanting to shape their lives in the positive ways every parent desires. And always I knew that my current life was a fight I was not winning yet was trapped on the battlefield by insurmountable walls.

"Women were not taught to be strong in the 1960s when I was coming of age. We were at the start of the period of bra-burning rebelliousness, yet our role models were mired in the thinking of the post-World War II years. June Cleaver, the housewife/mother of "Leave It To Beaver;" Robert Young's role on "Father Knows Best;" even Lucy's, her antics always made right by her husband, Ricky Ricardo, on the "I Love Lucy Show," these were the people we emulated. Girls went to college and had careers, but we were taught that no matter what other degree we might seek, the most important one was the MRS. Even graduate schools were filled with women saying that they didn't know if they wanted to go for their MA or for their MAMA.

"I was of that last generation of women for whom being a wife and mother were the ultimate calling. We were supposed to be slightly subservient, not so much addle-brained as less capable of handling the traumas of life than a man. We did not question why so many of our friends' fathers died young from the stress of life, stress that could not be shared with anyone because to do so was not manly. We did not question the tragedy of so many of our mothers being forced to work in often menial positions because they had neglected to develop skills outside of the bedroom, the kitchen, and the laundry. We watched women burn bras and talk of gaining new rights and responsibilities, yet even the most militant ended up taking notes, working the mimeograph machines, and being available to the male leaders for any type of pleasure they sought.

"I was a product of my culture, a product of my times. No matter what I had achieved on the outside, no matter how much I had handled just by surviving in life, I wanted to go back into a familiar role. I wanted to turn my cares over to someone strong, capable, willing to place a shield between myself and the turmoil raging all around me. I wanted a husband.

"There was a second pressure working on me, a pressure that is a part of being human. I wanted to be loved, touched, nurtured, and cared about. Prison was an area of isolation from all the sensory experiences humans need to thrive. We are emotionally unable to live in isolation. We can talk about survival without others. Certainly I had learned to go inside myself, to engage in memories and internal dialogues for hours at a time. Yet such abilities do not alter the inherent nature of humans. Without the caring of another human being, without periodic reinforcement concerning their love, we wither and die. Even in my fantasies, I was remembering happier times with my mother and others, having a relationship through memory that I was denied in person.

"My children were not visiting me. My friends were not coming to the jail. My uncle came to see me a couple of times, but he was old and the trip was physically too taxing. And Arthur was still in hiding, justifiably frightened, yet also depriving me of much-needed companionship.

"In the real world I would have been able to be with my children, to love and be loved in turn. I would have dated, gaining comfort in the courtship and the touching that are preliminary to establishing a more committed relationship. Even if I did not find the right man for my life right away, even if I went for years seeking the personal involvement we all need, I would be comforted by the fact that I was moving forward.

"In jail there are no such opportunities. In jail there is no past, no future, only survival in the present. Yet our needs do not change in such circumstances.

"My emotions were torn in many ways because of this. I wanted companionship, loving, support. I wanted a husband, a protector, a friend.

"Nadine came into my life at the right time and in the right way to show me one reason women in prison so frequently develop a same sex relationship. She was tall, attractive, physically and emotionally strong. She was staying in Durango only four months before going on to the state penitentiary to serve a five-to-seven year sentence for embezzlement. She had deliberately stolen money from the business where she worked and had the maturity to accept the punishment she knew she risked from the moment she started committing the crime.

"Nadine was an intelligent woman who kept herself abreast of world affairs. She had many interests, a good sense of humor, and the ability to accept life for what it was. She was also as much at peace with herself as you can be in jail because she knew she had "earned" her time, knew that she would justly be serving it.

"We became friends immediately because we were each so different from the other women in Durango. We were both educated, both comfortable with a certain amount of luxury, both out of place compared with our pasts.

"It is a cliche that everyone in jail is innocent, yet Nadine knew that I was, knew that I should not have been serving time. She had compassion, again a trait quite different from the self-serving attitudes of most of the inmates. She was genuinely happy that I was facing a new trial, hopeful that I would triumph. She even offered to help me, reading through the thousands of pages of transcripts at the same time I was having to review them.

"Eventually Nadine became a part of my preparations for my second trial. Thomas Thinnes had underlined sections of the transcripts where he needed more information, my comments, my counters to what was stated, or my agreement as to the accuracy of what had proceeded in court. I was expected to review those passages, to remember the facts as I knew them and/or lead him to people who could corroborate whatever the truth might be.

"Nadine would quiz me on those underlined passages. I had blocked so many memories, and she worked to get me to recall what I did not want to think about. She pushed, she prodded, she backed off, then brought the questions up to me again at a later time. We worked constantly together, something no one else would even consider doing, helping me to help my lawyer and myself.

"I began looking forward to my time with Nadine. Previously I had sought escape through sleeping and internal dialogues. I had taken my 'mind trips' to forests filled with birds and trees and flowers, forests that existed only in my imagination as the psychiatrist Larry Debus sent me had taught me to find. But once Nadine was in my life, the world of live people became more important. Given a choice between going to bed and sleeping away the day or talking with Nadine, I would talk with her. We ate our meals together. We worked on my trial together. We shared information about our pasts, our families, our lives. We were best friends."

Chapter 12

INTROSPECTION

"I began to see myself in ways I had never thought about," Joyce explained, talking of the reading of the transcripts and the sharing of her thoughts with Nadine. "The two testimonies against me that made the least sense were those of Cathy Fox and Sandy Perez. They viciously lied or exaggerated what I was saying and I didn't know why they would hate me so much.

"Cathy Fox I came to understand. At first I thought that she was getting back at Arthur and me because he dumped her. I never did ask him the circumstances of their affair. I know they were going together, sleeping together, that she thought she was going to be the next Mrs. Arthur Ross, and so did I. Then suddenly it was over and she was angry, hurt. Her lashing out at me made sense knowing that.

"Later I learned more. The investigator Thinnes hired, Mary Durand, discovered that Cathy frequently lied about her background. She was not trained for the job she held. She was a great sales person but she did not have the technical background she claimed. She had not graduated from the college she listed on her background sheet. She had not graduated from any college.

"Sandy Perez was something else. She was a hard worker, desperate for a job, and I had given her work. I thought she would be grateful. I never thought her testimony would be against me.

"Then I began thinking about myself, who I was, how I had acted. I realized that I had been an arrogant snob, a bigot, a bitch.

"Sandy Perez was a girl down on her luck who had gotten into trouble as a kid. She was from a white, Anglo-Saxon, Protestant heritage, the kind of background that normally lets you get through life without problems. Yet when she was a teenager she took up with a Mexican/ American boy and got pregnant, having a baby at fifteen, then marrying the boy.

"Mexicans are hated in Arizona. There is a distrust of anyone who is different, who speaks a language that Americans can't understand. There was even a move in the state legislature to declare English the official language of the state and the nation, making it more difficult for bilingual children to get an education.

"The general attitude towards Mexicans was that they were dirty, stupid, uneducated, and worthless because they took menial jobs when they were offered. The truth was that the best and the brightest of the people in Mexico were frequently the ones that went across the border. They took whatever jobs they could get while learning English and bettering themselves, making certain that their children would have the same opportunities as Americans. They were escaping grinding poverty and areas where the only jobs often were involved with the drug trade, the growing of marijuana and other illegal substances having supplanted production of fruits and vegetables because they were greater cash crops. They took any jobs they could get, moving in together to save money so they could support families back home. But the reality had nothing to do with the myth of bigots such as I had been.

"I made it very clear to Sandy Perez that I thought she was a jerk. The idea that someone with her potential would let herself get pregnant as a teenager, and by a Mexican at that, was disgusting to me. I had no respect for her, no compassion for a child trying to raise a child. I felt she had compounded her felony by marrying the man, and I generally made her life miserable. That she worked with me at all was surprising. That she hated me enough to twist my words to help send me to jail was understandable.

"I began to see myself and my life in ways I had never looked at before. I was shocked by how many people I had alienated. I was even more surprised to realize that I was not finding myself a very nice person. The trial transcript, coupled with the horrors of jail, was acting as a mirror; I did not like the reflection.

"I also began remembering other details about the case, some of which were quite important. Wally Roberts had always been my friend. I admired his brilliance as an artist and he knew he had my respect. We spent many hours talking and I found him good company when he was sober. The idea that he would turn against me in court made no sense to me, even though he later stated that he was someone whose word should not be believed.

"Then I began remembering things I had forgotten. Wally was supportive of me after my arrest, even after he was involved with giving statements to Dan Ryan. I learned that Wally wanted to disappear for a while; so Ron arranged for him to go to his father's place, a secluded location where he could hide. I also remembered Ron surreptiously lifting the trunk lid on the car Wally was going to drive. Craning my neck I glimpsed at Ron holding up hundred-dollar bills. Only in hindsight did I come to recognize the fact that this was probably a pay-off for Wally.

"I came to grips with the fact that Ron was a severely troubled man. I thought about the volume of alcohol he consumed. I remembered him sleeping late in the morning so that, by the time he was shaving, it was almost noon and he could justify having a drink while he shaved. His liver became damaged and the doctor wanted him to cut liquor out but all Ron did was change to the seemingly less potent use of vodka mixed with a soft drink. Ron only ate one good meal a day, the evening meal, the rest of the time substituting alcohol for nutrition. After drinking he had no appetite. At dinner time he would begin smoking joints in order to make himself hungry enough for food.

"I also remember the quantity of marijuana Ron would buy. He had bricks, though I don't recall the weight. I think it was at least five pounds at a time, and I remember him hiding the marijuana in the yard. He would use it, share it with friends. I don't know if he sold any. I doubt it. I think he just liked having it, liked using it, liked being the source for friends such as Wally Roberts.

"I had never let myself think about such things before. Part of me was too angry, too embarrassed, too self-centered. I was married to the man but emotionally estranged from him. And where there were substance problems, I avoided facing them.

"Part of me was too frightened to face them. Moreover there were even more serious problems than Ron's drinking or drugging. Ron seemed sexually attracted to my daughter. I didn't know it but I sensed it. I tried to push the odious thought away, pretend it didn't exist, too insecure to seek out the truth and deal with it. There was no way I could have anticipated that I would be facing death in the gas chamber before I began to understand myself and the world in which I had lived. I was shocked, saddened, yet helpless to change the past."

It was this intense introspection of her life that seemed to bring about the change in Joyce that would help a jury see a different side of her. It also strengthened her relationship with Nadine with whom she shared her self-examinations and suffering. Yet while Joyce became emotionally closer to Nadine than she had with any adult in recent years, "Nothing happened between Nadine and me.

We did not become lovers playing in the showers like so many of the women there. But, God help me, we might have become lovers given more time together, not because I was drawn to women, an idea I found repugnant before I went to jail and one I cannot imagine today. I was drawn to her because she fulfilled an overwhelming human need that could not be fulfilled in any other manner in that abnormal society. It was a relationship borne of emotional desperation, a relationship I did not want and would have found repulsive given other circumstances. Yet just as a starving man adrift on the high seas will catch a fish, kill it by smashing its head on the side of the life raft, then eat it raw, so the isolation of prison can cause you to act in a way that would otherwise be inconceivable. I did not cross the line, but I was more vulnerable than anyone should ever have to be.

"I don't know about the sexual part. That was still so foreign to me that I don't know if I would have wanted it, could have handled it. Perhaps, being honest, I would have allowed it if she wanted it just to be able to give her pleasure since she was so important in my life. I don't know and am glad I never had to find out. All I know for certain is that we were as close as you could get without physical touching and I am certain that sexual closeness would have been the next step had she stayed in Durango or had we both gone to the penitentiary.

"This is not to say that prison was turning me into a lesbian. Nor is it a case where she was 'more man than the men in my life.' Had I someone I loved and who was standing by me, visiting me regularly, writing to me, the incident never would have been possible. Nadine and I still would have been best friends. We could relate to each other far easier than prostitutes, drug abusers, and violent, homeless women whose total existence outside of jail was as foreign to me as a remote village in China would have been. But I would not have considered turning to her for love, for intimate emotional support.

"What Nadine did was to give me an understanding of how women and, I assume, men adapt to the abnormal. We are all human. We all reach out to fill certain needs. Through Nadine I came to understand why lesbian behavior is a reality of prison life. It is not the sex. It is not the result of male battering. It is not because the women are filled with sin and evil. If anything, there are more instances than we want to admit where lesbianism is the only conceivable way to achieve a closeness we all so desperately crave. The fact that the women can still love, can still reach out to another person is to me a triumph of the spirit. Certainly it should not be praised, but I also learned that it should not be condemned by those who create the surroundings where the only alternative may be emotional death."

Time passed, day after day. The lawyers were reading the trial transcripts and reviewing the work Larry Debus had left behind. Joyce and Nadine were reviewing the same materials, adding side comments that might help the attorneys or any investigator trying to determine the truth. There was a sameness to the days and nights, a sameness punctuated with the screams and violence that were always just beneath the veneer of seeming calm in Durango. And always there was thought of escape, of freedom, of life outside the pods and gymnasium.

"There were times in Durango when I thought that having a chance to be away from the confinement of the pod, to eat better food, to see different faces, would be a wonderful escape. I wanted my freedom. I wanted to be home with my family. But if that was to be denied, then getting away to somewhere else seemed as though it would be a touch of heaven.

"My opportunity came under rather unpleasant circumstances. I fell on a wet floor, landing on my back, then developing great pain from what later proved to be a relatively minor, though extremely uncomfortable injury. Another occurred when I experienced an angina attack and needed to have my heart monitored. Both times I was taken to the Maricopa County Hospital, a facility that is respected for quality care despite the huge number of patients they handle each day.

"I don't know what I thought when I was told that I was going to the hospital. I had worked in hospitals. I had been in the hospital when the verdict for conviction was heard in the courtroom. I respected the doctors and nurses. And I knew that there would probably be a certain amount of peace in the hospital setting compared with what I experienced in the pod.

"I was apprehensive about being transported from the jail only because of the way I was surviving. I was not certain that I could handle being reminded too often that I was in jail. The idea of seeing the outside, of seeing people walking freely, of being in a facility where the typical patient could check in and out at will without worrying about someone shooting them, then having to return to the fortress that was my prison home, made me uneasy. Yet hospitals upheld human dignity. Hospitals were places where patients were not degraded. If I could not go home to my family, perhaps the hospital would be a place where I could get some rest. Or so I thought.

"They came for me with chains. When you are arrested, your hands are cuffed behind your back, an uncomfortable position, awkward, designed to hinder your mobility and ability to resist. For a prisoner convicted of a major felony, they used restraints meant for a violent animal whose every movement might bring about an innocent's death.

"My hands were in front, close together, a chain wrapped around my waist so that I could not separate wrists, raise them, or even use them to support myself. Other cuffs were used on my ankles, more chains tethering me more securely than the old hobble skirts women had sometimes worn when I was young. I had to take what looked like mincing little steps, shuffling my way to the van. I was slightly off balance, unable to use my hands to counter the awkwardness.

"The guards told me to climb in the back. I thought they were joking. I thought they would help me up or free my legs. Instead they stood waiting.

"I shuffled to the van, turned, and tried to sit down on the edge of the vehicle. My movements were awkward and I was frightened of falling onto the pavement. I braced myself, kept my knees together, then raised them towards my chest until I could get my feet inside. Then I half rolled, half fell inside, slamming my elbows and scraping my knees until I could wedge myself up and onto a seat.

"No one reached out to help me. No one expressed concern.

"It was easier getting down from the vehicle when we reached the hospital. I could sit, scoot along, and then slide over the side until my feet touched the ground.

"At first I assumed that we would be going through some special security entrance since prisoners from the jail routinely are taken to the county hospital. Then, when I realized that we were going through the standard emergency entrance, I assumed that they would at least remove the leg restraints. But none of my hopes materialized. I was going to have to walk in chains through the hospital, to the elevator, then up to the room where I would be staying.

"All of us have our memories of emotional pain and humiliation. Frequently these happen in elementary school, such as when you are in a play and forget your lines or you're called to the blackboard and have to admit that you don't know the answer to the teacher's question. We hear the laughter of those all around, including those who are inwardly thanking God that they were not placed in the same position, for their experience would have been identical. There is embarrassment, shame, and an indelible memory that fades from consciousness, yet remains a scar we are surprised is still tender when touched many years later.

"None of the memories I carried were as humiliating as what I faced when walking through the hospital corridors. I passed children and tried to act nonchalant, forcing a smile to my face. I remember one little girl who shyly smiled back, then raised her hand as if to wave to me.

"Suddenly her mother grabbed the child's wrist, jerking her back, enveloping the girl in her protective arms. The look on the mother's face was like that of someone in a horror movie staring in shock as the kindly nun from the convent next door suddenly turns into a maniacal vampire about to bite her baby's neck.

"Then I noticed other children being pulled back by their parents, and adults moving as close to the wall as they could. Occasionally someone would stare at me, as though trying to penetrate my soul in order to determine what type of evil person I was.

"I wanted to shout at them that the chains weren't necessary. That I was a victim, trapped in circumstances I did not fully comprehend. I'm harmless, I wanted to scream. I'm like you are. I love my children. I want them protected from evil. I'm a good person, not a monster. Can't you understand? Can't you see?

"But of course they could see only too well. I was in chains, accompanied by guards. Thank God I wasn't on the street where perhaps I would be molesting children, mugging old ladies, or torturing other innocents.

"The room they gave me for my hospital stays was almost worse than isolation. The walls were brick and the door was solid. A guard was on duty outside my room twenty-four hours a day. Sometimes the door would remain open. At other times it would be shut, perhaps locked. There was a bed and the essential monitoring equipment. No radio. No television. No reading material. Nothing except a window looking out over the city of Phoenix.

"The guard came over and attached an ankle cuff to my leg so it would be secured against the bed frame. I was capable of walking to the bathroom, capable of caring for myself within the confines of the room, but such a simple task was to be denied me. I could only use a bed pan that would be brought to me after I rang for assistance. And even then the assistance was often long in coming. There was nothing critical about my condition during the stays so hospital employees saw no need to hurry. I could hold it or I could soil my bed. It didn't matter to them. I wasn't going anywhere.

"The staff entered the room from time to time, checking vital signs, giving me medicine, monitoring the changes in my condition. I was brought my food and it was better than the jail meals. During one of my stays, my lawyer even came by, bringing me a box of See's Candy which I tried to share with the staff. But no one was friendly. No one spoke more than the minimum necessary to complete their tasks.

"The only blessing was the location of the room. The security area in which I was placed was on an upper floor. The bed was raised and there was a window overlooking the city. The first night I was in the room I did not try to sleep. I looked out at the lights, the buildings, the stars. I tried to make myself a part of a world from which I had been separated for far too long.

"Humiliated, cuffed to the bed, unable to perform the most basic of bodily functions without someone else's approval, that view still gave me a touch of freedom.

"Yet as the minutes turned into hours and the hours into days, the loneliness, the pain, the isolation all overwhelmed me. For the first time since my arrest, I lost all control. I called out to my mother, my voice raised in anguish. I needed her, wanted her to come to me, comfort me. I yelled her name in terror, a lost child seeking the only person who could make things right.

"But my mother was dead. She had died a few weeks before I was arrested for the first time. I was in a high-security room of a prison wing of a county hospital. I was alone. I might be alone for eternity. And again, I cried."

"I would like to say that the opportunity for self realization totally changed me, but it did not. There was only one person left on whom I could depend—my daughter. In my desperation I continued to lean on Eden, to demand that she help me. I was in jail. She was free. Each day in prison was a day without sunshine, without birds, without laughter, good food, a safe place to sleep. Nothing was more important than my wishes. Nothing mattered except as it moved me closer to leaving the jail. Not Eden's school work. Not Eden's hobbies and extra-curricular interests. Not Eden's dreams of womanhood, the type of dreams that are a part of every teenaged girl as she comes of age. Not her hopes, her fears, or almost anything else. She could go to school. That was her job. She could take care of her brothers when they were together. But the rest of the time was mine. She was my liaison with the attorneys, the courts, the investigators. She was the only one I could trust. It was unrealistic, unfair, self-centered, and cruel.

Yet Eden did as I asked, my life hanging on her actions and those of my new lawyers."

The mother/adolescent daughter relationship is one of the most difficult to handle effectively. So often your child comes of age looking like you looked when you were younger. Her personality might be different, her interests, her values. Yet it is still a mirror of a past you will never have again and which most women remember as a time of excitement but deep turmoil.

Daughters seem more vulnerable in society. They face sexual assault by both strangers and the men with whom they go to school, share office space on the job, even from men within their own family. They face discrimination in the marketplace and carry the more difficult life choices when considering parenthood since, no matter how helpful the father may be, careers must be interrupted during pregnancy. And women on the fast track in law, business, and other professions may not be able to stop for a few months if they want to meet their goals.

Women understand these problems better than men because they have experienced them, faced the decisions, lived with the choices they made. "My relationship with Eden developed, in part, because of these things but also by chance," said Joyce. "My sons, one older and one younger than Eden, were undergoing emotional stresses of their own when my crises hit our family.

"Part of the problem was my divorce from their natural father, though all of them came to understand why I left him. He was a man who delighted in sons but not in their nurturing. Gradually they recognized this trait, learning to accept the divorce and be comfortable with my retaining their custody. I'm certain that, like all kids, they must have felt more than once that they were the cause of the divorce. They may have thought that if they had only been better somehow, made different choices, that we would have stayed together. Such feelings, no matter how incorrect, are a natural psychological consequence of divorce.

"However, having a mother thrown into jail for murder, seeing the family name in headlines and discussed on television, and facing abandonment by my second husband were crises far worse than the divorce. My children were angry, scared, determined to survive, yet wondering if anyone ever cared for them. And each had to respond in his or her own way.

"My oldest boy showed the anger. Although he is making his career in science, he also is a competent musician who had his own band. He was sixteen when I went to jail, a critical time of discovery concerning relationships, sexuality, and the testing of more adult limits. He was also a song writer and he began channeling his energy into his music. Much of it was violent, hate filled, reflecting the inner turmoil he felt.

"When I was in jail, he sent me a flyer for his band, a group ironically called 'Terminal Justice' whose logo was a capital 'J' crossed by a pointed sword. Among the songs they played were 'Too Real,' 'Kill Preppies,' 'Young Militants,' 'Family Problems,' 'Silent Pay,' 'Terminal Justice,' 'Killing Ground,' 'Search & Destroy,' 'Cruel World,' and 'I Hate Authority.' The music he created, both titles and words, reflected my child's pain.

"Even now that I am out, now that I am able to talk with him, to try and help him, there is still tension. The strain has lessened, but there is enough that I know many years will pass before he resolves his inner conflicts.

At ten, my younger son was little more than a child. He was completely overwhelmed by what was taking place. His world was filled with confusion and fear. He withdrew emotionally, regressing in his actions, his needs and demands. He seemed to feel betrayed, though he has had an easier time talking about his feelings than his older brother.

"The most stable of the three was Eden, a child who never got to enjoy her teenage years because of me.

"There is a maturity about Eden that both unnerves and delights me. She has always had greater understanding about life and emotions than her age would indicate. Even as a young child, when she was enraged at someone she was able to separate what a person does from who they are rather than seeing life in pure black-and-white like most young people.

"Also Eden instinctively grasped things better than her brothers. She was able to keep the majority of her school friends, only one girl dumping her because of the notoriety. She sensed that her role had to change, that she had to become the nurturing caretaker within the family since I could not be there. She took responsibility during the crisis without feeling that she was responsible. And Eden became my best friend, my confidante, and my whipping post, a combination that eventually forced her to flee Phoenix, going to live with her natural father during that year, the worst year of her life.

"I first began to realize my daughter's strength when Ron abandoned the family and it was necessary to obtain money to pay the lawyers. My legal fees were higher than anything I ever could have imagined. It became necessary to sell everything I owned. Just paying my first lawyer Larry Debus's fees ultimately took my home and much of my cash. To pay my second, Thomas Thinnes, I sold my share of the family holdings in Manhattan, jewelry, and also used the remaining cash. The total defense cost me at least $750,000.

"That was the price for my life.

"Sometimes I am proud of the fact that my parents instilled the work ethic in us kids despite the fact that we had enough money so that working was not necessary. I have always loved work, gained part of my identity from work. Not being productive was one of the harder parts of being in jail, and I would work no matter how much money I had. Thus the financial pressures I am under now, with everything taken from me, are not the strain they might have been.

"At the same time, I am bitter. It is as though even my defenders have drained me.

"I also keep thinking of the people who have no money. Who takes care of them when they are innocent? I almost went to death row defended by one of the best defense lawyers in Phoenix, according to reputation. What happens to the people who must rely on some kid just out of law school who is working in a public defender's office? Or to the person who can not pay for an investigator? Or to the person who lucks into a good attorney within the public defender system, but where the funds are too limited for an adequate defense? Must they have their lives destroyed because they were not born with my advantages?

"It is an issue that leaves me bitter, angry, and frustrated. Yet I realize that I was lucky to be financially able to afford a strong defense. But it took everything I had and put great strain on Eden.

" 'Sell everything,' I told Eden. She was sixteen years old. We had a large house filled with extremely valuable items, from crystal to furniture. There were some possessions that held sentimental value. There were others whose beauty and value were such that they should have been kept. But whatever the case, they all had to go and Eden was the one who had to sort out everything, call the various dealers, and try to get the best price.

"I'm certain some dealers took advantage of her. She was a kid working with people who often take advantage of unknowledgeable adults. There was no reason they should look kindly upon her. Others probably gave her a fair price. It was unfair to expect Eden to take on so much responsibility. Yet I had no one else to whom to turn and sometimes in my fear and desperation I raged at her but Eden never said anything.

"Most of what I said to her I have forgotten, yet my actions are vividly reflected in her letters to me. For example, after one of our telephone conversations, Eden wrote:

" 'What did you mean on the phone the other night when you said that you hoped I wouldn't turn out like another Uncle Arty or Ron? Did you mean as far as leaving you and not caring what happens to you? Is that what you think I'm doing here? That kind of hurt me mom, for you to say that to me. For you to think that I would just forget about you, stop caring about you, stop worrying about you, and stop loving you. Is that what you think of me? I love you very much. How many times do I have to say that to you before you realize that?

" 'I thought you realized how much I loved you as I realized how much you love me; I guess I was wrong.'

"I was acting like a jealous bitch, but what I was jealous of was Eden's freedom. I couldn't stop my desolate feeling; I have never taken someone's life, never been violent, never considered violence. Yet I know that I would kill to save her from the hell I was enduring in jail. But despite the fact that I loved her so intensely, I was jealous of her ability to live a normal life and resented any moment when she was not trying to help me gain my release.

"It was an irrational attitude and somehow she had wisdom enough to be aware of that fact. She accepted the adolescent responses of the woman who was her mother, who should have been the more mature in a crisis. Only her handwriting revealed her intense feelings during this time, as I later learned from an expert. Whenever I hurt Eden deeply, when she was trying to make sense from my inexcusable attitude, the writing reflected a desperate attempt to control her emotions. Only later, when she obtained hours of counseling from a psychologist, did her writing return to the natural slant of the emotionally healthy. I was destroying my child with my mix of love and desperation, yet somehow she had the maturity to accept me for what I was and not to hold it against me.

"Although Eden was probably more of a mother to me than I was to her during this period, she was sensitive enough to make me feel a part of her life. There was a period when I was not eating, my life too frenzied as I waited to hear decisions concerning my second trial. Eden, worried about me, wrote:

" 'If you don't stay strong, who will I have to depend on? You can't just let me fall! Without your strength that's just what I'd do—fall. I bet you that even when I marry and have children I'll be calling you all the time for help, advice, or even just because I need someone to talk to. I may be independent in many ways, but when it comes to you, I'm very dependent. Without you I'd be lost. So no starving to death.'

'Eden's sensitivity to my feelings during this period was my one joy. I would meet people in jail and talk about my wonderful daughter. I would tell them to contact her if they needed help. Hardly a week went by without some stranger stopping by my home to get help from Eden. Some were criminals and vagrants. She tried to help them all, never knowing quite what was right nor what I wanted her to do. I was overburdening her and there was no way she could make me understand the problem.

"Finally though she became overwhelmed and decided to spend a year with her natural father in Massachusetts. She would go to high school there and also have some surgery for a medical problem she had developed. He was a doctor, knew the medical community, and I knew she would have excellent care. There would be fewer pressures on her, especially since she would be able to escape the newspaper headlines which were bound to begin when the new trial date was set.

"It was all very logical, very rational, very healthy. And I hated her decision. All I could see was the final abandonment. Ron had left me. Arthur was in touch but not physically available to see me. And now Eden, my only daughter, my major link to the outside world, was abandoning me.

"I wept. I wallowed in self-pity, fear, and anger. Yet I could not deny her, knew it would do no good to deny her since she had to do what she felt was best. Even worse, I could not give her rational arguments for any alternative. She had been living with a friend, no longer having a home to call her own.

"I did worry about how she would get along with her father. My ex-husband was a man who had a difficult time making emotional commitments. He had been having an affair with a woman for the previous nine years, though they never moved in together, nor did they marry. He doted on our younger son, taking great pride in him, yet sometimes acting hostilely towards him. The two of them fought constantly.

"I had no way of knowing all that happened between Eden and her father during the time she stayed there. He was wonderful about letting me call collect every couple of days to talk with our daughter. At the same time, he was frequently in the same room with her and his presence had an intimidating effect on Eden. She resented that, resented the year that she lived in Massachusetts. She tried immersing herself in school work and extracurricular activities. She dated boys. She made girl friends. She wrote constantly to me. But she felt that her father was verbally abusive to her and physically abusive towards her brother. She hated being there, though she still felt that the escape was necessary.

"I wanted to blame her father for all Eden's problems. That's only natural for someone who is divorced. In my case I had a more intense reason for wanting to blame him for I knew that much of Eden's present turmoil was occurring because her mother was in jail, separated from her, and though I was innocent I was helpless to change either her predicament or mine.

"Being objective I know that the year was rough for my ex-husband. I had taken the children when they were small, raising them, being responsible twenty-four hours a day. He saw them, seemed to love them as much as he could, but he lacked the same sense of commitment I had, if only because for so long he lacked the same degree of responsibility. Now he was suddenly faced with two hurting, vulnerable, mildly rebellious teenagers trying to maintain a fragile shell around their emotions. His ex-wife was sitting in jail for murder. His girl friend could no longer spend time with him in the manner she once had. Everything was new, different, unwanted, yet unchangeable.

"Recognizing all this, I know he did his best. Yet it was a difficult period for us all.

"At first I tried to maintain a fantasy relationship with my daughter. Sometimes she was my little girl and I proudly talked about the grades she received on her tests in school, her triumphs in extracurricular activities, and her on-going emotional support of her mother. Sometimes she was my friend, the one person to whom I could tell anything and who, I fantasized, could tell me anything. And sometimes she was my employee, my "go-fer," the person I ordered to handle aspects of my appeal even though she was living more than 2,000 miles away and my demands were unrealistic. All three roles were essential for me so I overlooked another fact. My little girl was becoming a woman.

"I should have seen the changes that were taking place in Eden. She was a normal, healthy adolescent with a normal, healthy sex drive. But she did not act like one of the stereotypical, giggling, boy-crazy teenaged girls and I still saw her as a child.

"Yet Eden was open and honest with me. Her first month in school in Massachusetts she wrote: "I even have a new guy to talk about this week. Bruce was last week's news and now Michel is this week's. He's tall, has dark hair and dark eyes and the best personality as far as girls are concerned. He's exactly the opposite from Bruce. Bruce is a super-ego girl user while Mike is shy and treats girls with respect. I haven't talked to him that much (actually hardly at all), but he seems awfully nice and people who I've talked to who know him say the same."

"It was a nice letter and I smiled as I read about the boy friend. It was a typical adolescent crush from afar, more fantasy than reality because my little girl was afraid to approach him.

"In October Eden went to a dance at a prep school. She went with some friends, met yet another boy, and suffered the pain of all teenagers. 'We were slow dancing and I danced terrible! He was holding me in a wierd (sic) position or something because it was very difficult to dance. Afterwards he said, "that was too short a dance." I felt like saying, "Ya, I bet you're glad to get away from me!" but I didn't. It was so embarrassing.'

"Later that month the letters discussed Bruce and Mike again. Bruce, the 'total girl-user,' had become unusually friendly, something Eden did not understand. At the same time, she decided that Mike was not shy, he was a snob and she had become terrified of talking with him. However, she felt that some of her problems might be resolved through magic.

" 'Remember how I told you I bought that love potion stuff from that Witche's (sic) store in Salem? Well, I've been doing all the stuff that the directions say and nothing happened yet. I hope it works. I need all the help I can get!'

"I laughed and I cried, sharing some of what she had said with the others. No matter what an inmate's background, there was something universal about a teenager coming of age. We all remembered the intensity of emotions as we experienced first loves or the feeling that we were too unattractive to ever find someone who would care about us.

"I ached with longing to be with Eden as I read the letters. I wanted to comfort her when she was in pain, knowing that there was no way she could understand that there would be many boy friends, many joys, and many rejections before she found the right man for herself. I wanted to tell her the stories of my own dating, my own sense of humiliation. I wanted to share girl talk, letting her universal experience be a bridge across the age and role gaps to help us begin the adult friendship that is the ideal to which every mother strives with her daughter. I wanted . . . But all I could do was read the letters, ache with her, long for her, and imagine her growing up so far away.

" 'I'm not in love with anyone at the moment. Forget about Bruce. He's really cute and everything, but I'm too scared to get to know him better because of what a user I've heard he was. I just don't need a guy to use me than blow me off right now. Unfortunately Bruce doesn't get the message. He flirts with me alot, but I only try to stay friendly but reserved . . .

" 'That guy Mike doesn't want to have anything to do with me. He's such a snob! He's in the "popular group" and I'm not, so he won't even say a word to me! . . .

" 'There's this one guy who I wouldn't mind going out with and he's in that same "popular group," but he talks to me in class and says hi to me in the halls all the time. He tickles me and flirts with me in class also. I hope he asks me out. But I can wait—I'm in no hurry. (Not until the prom at least.)'

By December there was Jay and also Eric. The latter

went to St. John's Prep School and took her to their semi-formal dance. By January, Eric became the 'Mr. Right' of the month, as Eden wrote to me:

"'I'm so happy I met Eric (my boyfriend). He's so nice. I wish you could meet him. I know you would like him. He's also a real cutie! And he cares about me alot. He always tells me how much he cares about me and never will hurt me. And do you know what he tells me alot? It's so cmbarassing! He tells me that I'm beautiful and special! I never know what to say when he says that, so I just say "thank you, but I'm not."'

"Then came Gary and a litany of others, though none serious enough for the 'big dance,' the senior prom. 'I'm still searching for a prom date. I keep hesitating from asking this guy Ed who sits next to me in Accounting. I think it's because I'm not really sure whether I would have fun going with him. He's so shy and quiet, so we'd probably sit saying nothing to each other all night.'

"'Our Senior Prom is coming up soon! I can't wait! I'm going to ask this guy named Ed Burke to go with me if I can get up the guts. He's really shy, but he's nice and cute too. He has blond hair, blue eyes, long eyelashes and a really nice smile. I'm so scared he's going to say no! And if he does it will be terrible because I sit right next to him in Accounting class. So if he says no I'll feel so uncomfortable seeing him everyday. If he says yes and we do go I won't have to buy a dress because this girl I know has this gorgeous dress that she says she'll let me wear, and we're about the same size. She wore it last year to her junior prom, so if I wear it this year than no one else will have the same dress. The prom is going to be at the Sheradon (sic) in Boston. It's going to be great! Sue and I are going to rent a limousine for the night also. I can't wait. I hope Ed says yes.'

"And in May: 'Yes, you heard right on the phone I actually asked this guy Lincoln to my Prom. He's supposed to tell me his answer tomorrow. I hope he says yes. He's really cute and I'd love to go with him.'

"One month later: 'I've been seeing this guy Mike for a few weeks now. I know I told you about him. He's so nice. It's going to be sad leaving him. I tried not to date him too much, so I wouldn't like him alot, but I think it's too late for that. I already like him too much. And I know that as soon as I leave he's going to find someone else and that's going to be the end of it. That's a fact I'm just going to have to face.'

"They were bittersweet times for Eden and the hardest times for me. A mother should not witness her daughter's becoming a woman from a distance reinforced by prison walls. A mother should not share in the pleasure and the pain by letter only. I envied my ex-husband's physical closeness to our daughter and hated the circumstances that allowed him to be with her when I knew he would not, could not fully appreciate what she was experiencing. Yet the full reality did not strike me until Eden asked me about birth control. The letter was too mature and it was obvious what had happened. The night, the boy, and all the sexual yearnings so intense at that age had combined in such a way that she was no longer a virgin. It had been a surprise for them both, yet they must have been gentle with each other for Eden instantly realized that it would not be her last time, nor would she necessarily be lucky enough to avoid pregnancy. She was in love and wanted to be responsible, so she turned to her mother for advice.

"I was not naive. No one with two marriages, three children, and convicted felons for roommates is naive.

"I knew that Eden was of age. I knew that Eden was anxious for a relationship. I had read about her love life for months. I had laughed at her antics, cried for her pain, and remembered my own adolescent romances with the same ache that I knew my daughter was experiencing for the first time.

"BUT MY DAUGHTER WAS ASKING ABOUT BIRTH CONTROL.

"All right. It was wonderful. My daughter trusted me. My daughter was in a mature relationship, determined to act responsibly. And she turned to me, her mother, her friend.

"I was so proud. I told my roommate. I sent Eden the information she needed, proud of our relationship. I. . . .

"BUT MY DAUGHTER WAS ASKING ABOUT BIRTH CONTROL.

"And again I was struck by how much I was missing. I was not pleased that my daughter had sex. There is something uncomfortable about knowing your child has gotten involved in that way, even if your child is thirty. Yet it was another sign that Eden had partially attained womanhood, that she was wrestling with emotions and issues that were firmly entrenched in the adult world. And I was not a part of those experiences. I felt that if we had been together talking before her dates, perhaps she would have waited longer. I also knew that my presence might have changed nothing, but I resented the fact that I was denied an important part in my daughter's life because of the vicious actions of others.

"And again, that night I cried."

Chapter 13

THE "BORN AGAIN" CULT

Once Eden had left for Massachusetts, the loneliness and isolation of Joyce's predicament fell like a widow's veil about her face—further cutting her off from the outside world, from her future, from hope. There was no way to know what would happen to the appeal. There was more than a chance she would be sentenced to death, that Thomas Thinnes would be no more successful in freeing her than Larry Debus had been with her original defense.

Cut off from all she had ever known or believed in, she grasped at the only community to which she had a connection, the society of Durango.

"Jail is not always the lonely nightmare it was for me. There are some women who find jail a refuge—women who lived on the streets, doing anything that was necessary for survival. They would steal, or sell their bodies to any man who wanted them. Some had no permanent home, stashing their few possessions with a friend, picking up men for a night, a weekend, or even several weeks, moving from place to place. Others lived in apartments that not even building inspectors wanted to admit existed. These were hell holes with shared, filthy toilets, plumbing that rarely worked, a hot plate for cooking and, if they were lucky, an aged, battered refrigerator that either froze everything placed inside or was not quite cool enough to prevent rapid spoilage.

"For women who knew only poverty, jail was a place of shelter. One, or more, of their friends was usually inside, giving them companionship. They had food delivered to them each day, plumbing that worked, and a regular bed. Some of them saw their time in jail the way others view two weeks at Club Med.

"Life was different for me. My struggles had been emotional ones. The deaths of parents, the pain of divorce, the heartache, the laughter, and the turmoil caused by three children whom I adored, all of these were part of my background. I had never known deprivation. I had never known physical isolation. I had never been forced to adjust to a life of survival.

In my world, friendships end when you're in jail. It was bad enough when I was arrested. Our judicial system is based on the idea that a person is innocent until proven guilty. Yet our faith in justice in this country is such that everyone believes that no one is arrested for a crime unless they are guilty. Good guys don't get arrested. That is the myth to which most of us subscribe, even myself after all I've been through.

Throughout my trial I expected the people who witnessed the court in action or read about it in the papers to be shocked along with me. Of course they wouldn't believe the lies of people like Arnie Merrill. Of course they would know better. No one approaches middle age and suddenly decides to become a murderer. No one has three decent, wonderful children, often raising them alone, unless there is love in her heart. Everyone would understand that and commiserate with my suffering. But it did not happen.

My children wrote and visited, yet life was a strain for them. They felt abandoned, ashamed, frightened. Most of Eden's friends stood by her. They had always come to me with their concerns. I had been a surrogate mother for them. I was available to hear their problems, their hopes, and their dreams. They did not understand the crimes, nor were they certain about what I had or had not done. But they did not blame my daughter for her mother's problems.

Yet even Eden suffered. One of her friends stopped speaking to her, a girl so close that Eden was certain she would understand. Perhaps the action was the result of a lecture by a well-meaning but misguided parent. I don't know. Eden didn't know. The unwarranted break was a shattering blow for a teenaged girl to face.

It was far worse for me. My husband was gone. My brother had left the state. My mother and father were dead. And most of my former friends were so confused about what to do that they did nothing, furthering my isolation.

Every large city has certain areas that have names like "the combat zone." These are places that combine apartments, houses, disreputable bars, drug dealers, pornography and/or prostitution, and random violence. The people who live there become accustomed to the sound of gun fire, screams in the night, the wail of sirens, and the sight and smell of dried blood, urine, and vomit in the hallways and on the street.

Most of us don't live that way, though. Whether low income or wealthy, our lives are mostly quiet. We read in the news about rapes, robberies, and other crimes because they are "news." They are different from what we experience in our daily lives. All we want is to live in peace the same as our neighbors. Since most of us achieve that goal, no matter what personal difficulties we may have, we avidly read about the nightmares of the world because they are different. They are "news."

In jail, however, there comes a time when you stop

reading about crime and violence because they are boring. You have seen the faces of the killers and you have seen their victims. It is a world so familiar that there is no escape in reading about it.

Instead you crave what most newspapers and magazines carry as fillers. You cry over a story about a family where there is no incest, no wife beating, no child abuse, because such families are so rare in your world as to seem like fantasy stories. You are moved by a brief article that mentions an act of charity, of kindness, of selflessness. You linger over a picture of a smiling face because it has been months since you have seen anyone truly happy.

Jail is different. Jail is a place where insanity and mayhem reign supreme. Violence or the potential for violence is a part of daily life. You are polite and friendly, not because such an attitude is a proper one to have but because you never know when you are defusing the anger of a psychopath ready to explode in an orgy of destruction.

The only joy is when someone reaches out to you—for any reason.

When Nancy became my roommate I had reached my lowest point. She was a tall girl, big boned, and, in the time I knew her, gentle, kind and soft-spoken. Her parents belonged to an evangelical church and Nancy told me that she was born again in Jesus.

I didn't care about Nancy's religion. It was not important to me.

I am Jewish. I was raised in a Jewish family and, because it is believed that the religion is passed through the mother, my children are also Jewish.

This does not mean I have strong feelings about the practices of Judaism. I believe in God. Even in my darkest moments I did not question His presence. But I had no concern about the numerous strict laws that govern orthodoxy.

I was raised, and my family was raised, to be reformed. I took the kids to Sunday School until they reached thirteen and went through the rites of adulthood in my religion (Bar Mitzvah for the boys). Then it was up to them as to whether or not they attended Friday night services. Naturally, they didn't. But I didn't know any teenager who, given their choice, attended religious service.

I did not keep a kosher home. I enjoyed pork and shell fish. I did not see the dietary laws to be important in a modern society with better knowledge of food preparation and handling than the ancients had.

However, my casual attitude did not change the importance of certain holidays for me. The high holy days in fall, Hanukkah in winter, and the other special times were also family times. These were periods when we would gather together, share symbolic foods such as Matzo, and attend services. They mattered to me. My isolation from religious practices while in jail caused me great emotional pain. I longed to celebrate the traditions of my faith though I had previously had a cavalier attitude towards the routine activities such as going to temple.

Once I was in jail, isolated, I wanted the rabbi from my temple to visit me. I wanted someone from the Jewish community to reach out, to comfort me in much the same way that clergymen of Christian faiths visit prisoners. But, during that period, the Phoenix Jewish community had no outreach to the county jail. It was as though those of us who were Jewish had commited an unpardonable sin by being arrested. We seemingly did not exist, locked away and forgotten, a fact that added to my sense of emptiness.

This is not to say that Jews are callous, nor are they unfamiliar with prisons. The Old Testament is filled with stories of great men suffering in prisons. Often these were large pits from which escape was impossible without outside assistance. At other times these were actual prisons or special cell rooms built into homes or castles. But always it is clear that many people were being punished despite their innocence.

There are communities around the country where Rabbis visit the prisons. I later learned that one of the Federal penitentiaries in Texas even has such events as regular Wednesday night movies and special diets for Jewish prisoners. But not Phoenix; not at that time.

Christians feel strongly about visiting prisons, perhaps, as I later learned, because Paul, the most prolific of the known early writers and teachers concerned with the new religion after Jesus' death, spent so much time in jail. It is my understanding that in the book of Matthew, Jesus specifically mentions visiting prisoners. As a result, even in cities where many religious groups avoid the jails, there are always some groups, usually among followers of Jesus, who visit the inmates. The tragedy, as I found out, is that their mission is often warped.

It is easy to become a cynic about religion while in jail. Not only is there the loneliness I've described, there is also the taking advantage of the inmates by the large-scale television evangelists who write or contact prisoners. Many of these television evangelists are reaching what is literally a captive audience. They also are aware that at least a portion of the inmates have been involved with crimes where large sums of money are obtained. This may be from drugs, burglaries, strong-arm robberies, or similar activities. Even those inmates who plead poverty and use public defenders may have a stash of money hidden for when they return to the streets. And if they don't have access, someone on the outside not only can get hold of what they need, they can send it to whomever the prisoner designates.

One of those well known ministers with whom I had contact during this period wrote a letter to me which started in a manner that was deeply moving. He wrote:

"More and more as I serve God through this ministry

of His healing, saving and delivering power, I realize how much depends on our working and believing together . . . for each other and for the ongoing of God's work. Thank God you have let me know your needs. I go straight to prayer that God will bless your spirit through His Spirit. I'm also praying for each of your children.

" 'Lord, I come to You in Jesus' Name, Whose I am and Whom I serve, in behalf of my partner, Sister Lukezic. May You bless her, prosper her, increase her life, her health, her relationship with You, and may you bring her into a greater understanding of Who You are, how You work in her and through her, and who she is in You. God, bless Sister Lukezic and each of her loved ones. In Jesus' Name, amen and amen.' "

He continued wishing me well and encouraging me to study "God's Word." It was a touching letter that seemed personal, though when reading it later, it was obvious that this was a form that would work for many people, not just myself or someone in jail. There was nothing so personal in it that it could have been written specifically for me and/or my circumstances. But it was the second page that made me hostile.

The second page was all form, even to the point of having a facsimile address, not to me but to "Partner." It asked the minister to be aware of my needs on a special prayer sheet that I was to send to him along with a contribution.

The request for money was subtle. There was a box and a space for a dollar amount, along with the statement: "I plant this $ as a portion of my tithes and offerings and claim Malachi 3:10,11 in Jesus' Name."

Since many of the inmates who were serious about religion study the Bible, the passage was perfect. Often these were women who felt remorseful about their actions and genuinely wanted to change. They were trying to do right but were extremely poor. Often the little money they had was essential for use either for their legal defense, for commissary where they could buy necessary diet supplements, or to get started again after their release. They knew troubles and wanted God's love, so the reading from Malachi was one that could push them over the edge, getting them to contribute money best kept for themselves. The passage reads:

" 'Bring the whole tithe into the storehouse, that there may be food in my house. Test me in this,' says the Lord Almighty, 'and see if I will not throw open the floodgates of heaven and pour out so much blessing that you will not have room enough for it. I will prevent pests from devouring your crops, and the vines in your fields will not cast their fruits,' says the Lord Almighty."

Had I listened, as so many others did, my "blessing" would have been just another contribution to the controversial evangelist. And he was not alone, of course. There were many other "ministers," several of whom have been lately disgraced in sex and embezzlement scandals, who did the same thing.

By contrast, there was Nancy, my cellmate. Nancy and I were quite close because she, like myself, was different. She was well educated, from a good and caring family, and she tried to keep to herself in the jail. She did not use drugs, drink the bootleg hootch, or even smoke. She never swore and avoided the violence that was all around. Her family called themselves "Born Again Christians." They did not deny their daughter when she got into trouble. They accepted her problems, continued to love her, and accepted the fact that she had a debt to pay to society.

Most of Nancy's free time was spent reading, sometimes poetry, a love we both shared, and sometimes the Bible. Frequently she would ask to read to me, selecting passages that related to both prisoners and the troubled. The passages were from both the Old and New Testaments, and she always selected those that spoke of hope and God's promise.

Typical of Nancy's choices were sections such as Psalm 146 where she read, in part:

> "Blessed is he whose help is the God of Jacob,
> whose hope is in the Lord his God,
> the Maker of heaven and earth,
> the sea, and everything in them—
> the Lord, who remains faithful forever.
> He upholds the cause of the oppressed
> and gives food to the hungry.
> The Lord sets prisoners free,
> the Lord gives sight to the blind,
> the Lord lifts up those who are bowed down,
> the Lord loves the righteous."

Nancy took me through thousands of years of people suffering as she read the various passages, always showing the positive side, the ultimate triumph. I don't think I necessarily related my situation to what she was reading, yet I felt better for what I was hearing.

Frequently I would shut my eyes and let the words bring images to my mind that supplemented the types of coping imagery taught to me by the Debus psychiatrist. I felt happy, at peace, delighting in what I was hearing and the friendship I was being shown.

The sessions enabled me to forget my surroundings for a few minutes. Gone were the threats of violence. Gone were the thought of the inadequate meals, the memory of the daily horrors, such as the discovery of a roach in the center of a plate of spaghetti, the battered women who "fell" in the shower, the shared "fit" with the dull needle being jammed into a neck. I was hearing about the love of God from someone who came as close to being a friend as I had found in jail.

Not that Nancy was an angel. She, like the vast majority of women in Durango, was admittedly guilty of crime. In her case, she was an accessory to First Degree murder. She and her boyfriend were involved with the drug trade and had used a baseball bat to kill a supplier who had failed to keep his part of a deal. I don't know if she had been an active participant or just witnessed the murder and kept quiet about it. It didn't matter. She was guilty. She would eventually be moved to Perryville to serve her term. And the details were not something we discussed.

Nancy was involved with a religious cult headed by a woman named Sylvia. I did not know that it was a cult, nor do I think Nancy understood what was happening. She seemed to have been drawn into the group for the same reason that I eventually became part of them. The people who came to visit brought what seemed to be unconditional love.

There were two types of cult groups working in the prison system. One was the classic type where the followers believed that the leader was the reincarnation of Christ, or at least his modern day prophet. The other was led by someone who gained pleasure from the power he or she was given over the followers. Although I didn't know it then that was the case with Sylvia, the woman who led the group Nancy had joined.

Sylvia's followers came to the jail three times a week. Religious groups were allowed to visit with inmates without their visits taking up regular visitation periods. They were an extra diversion and, in many instances, a help for the inmates. When Nancy asked me to meet with the women, I agreed. It was something to do with people who were far more intelligent than I normally encountered.

"We know you're not a believer," I was told by Eleanore. "All we want you to do is hear God's word. We're here as friends. We want to help you. If there is anything we can do for you here or on the outside, all you have to do is ask. We truly care."

And I think that Eleanore did care. She seemed to be one of those genuinely loving people who felt that her group had the answer to helping others. She gave of her time and herself, touching me, accepting me, not worrying whether I was innocent or guilty. It was an unconditional love for others and I was deeply moved.

I decided to begin meeting with Nancy's group because I was so lonely, so desperate for companionship. We would sit around, read selections from the Bible, and discuss what we had read. Everything was carefully structured in the manner that Sylvia desired. I have since learned it was not particularly historically accurate. The interpretations were meant to increase my involvement with the group, gradually denying my family, friends, and even my attorney. Yet the information was presented in so loving a manner that I was blind to what was taking place.

The two meetings during the week brought me closer to the women. They believed in healing through the laying on of hands. If I said I had a headache, one of the women would hold my head, stroking me, praying for me. I would close my eyes and relax, focusing on the good feelings. For a few moments I would no longer be in jail. It was like being a little girl, when I would sit on my mother's lap, being touched, comforted, loved, knowing that nothing in life could ever hurt me.

Headaches and other stresses would vanish. The group openly rejoiced that Jesus had taken my discomfort and my own beliefs made me comfortable with the idea that God can heal. But, looking back objectively, I realize that my greatest pleasure came from caring human touch.

Before this the only touching I received in prison was from women who wanted a sexual relationship. They were seeking instant gratification, not offering genuine comfort. The group seemed my salvation and I looked forward to their visits.

Sunday services were different from the weekday

ones. These were attended by almost everyone in the pods. It didn't matter which denomination might be holding them.

The reason for the support was not always the spirituality of the inmates. Sunday services were open to everyone. Inmates from all four pods could attend. It was the one time during the week when drugs and other contraband could be exchanged with little risk. There were sexual liasons among women who had been separated. And there was a chance for friends to get together who were otherwise separated by the design of the jail. In addition, there were a few inmates who wanted to go to church, either because they felt a spiritual need or because they enjoyed the musicians who frequently performed with the religious groups.

At first I looked upon the services as theater and I watched the show. I enjoyed the music, a rare privilege in Durango. Today the inmates are allowed to have radios. When I was there, radios were banned. There was no way to hear music except when someone volunteered their time to come to the jail, and this usually meant Christian missionaries. Their concerts, even when their skills were limited, were rare treats.

Then, as I began to become more involved with the group, I stopped watching the people around me. I became a part of the service, one of the insiders, singing all the songs and reciting all the words. For the first time since I entered jail, I felt that I belonged to something. It was a special feeling.

I had been in the group a few weeks when Nancy asked me if I was "Born Again." I had heard the term used by people but never knew what it meant. Later I would learn that the origin is from First Peter in the New Testament. I would also learn that many evangelical Christians use the term to refer to an experience where they feel that their life is instantly transformed by God. It is a time when a new way to live suddenly becomes clear and they feel that they have been started on a new path that will bring them closer to the Lord. But my group did not think that way. They believed that they could make you "born again" and Nancy was going to show me the way.

We sat in our room, Nancy holding a cup of water. "I'm going to annoint you with oil," she told me, holding the water. Whether she was thinking symbolically or believed there would be a transformation of the water to oil, I did not know. I just closed my eyes, relaxed my body, and waited for her to proceed.

"Sha na na na . . ." she began. She was doing what she and the others called "speaking in tongues." The words came out like a chant and seemed to be unconnected with any language. They varied as she proceeded with the ceremony, but always they started with "Sha na na," the meaning of which was never explained.

Nancy touched my forehead with the water. Her fingers were gentle, soothing. I let myself further relax.

Nancy dipped her fingers again, then ran them down my arm. I felt a warm glow, delighted that someone was caring for me. It did not matter that the woman "anointing" me was a murderer. It did not matter that we were in jail. I was being touched, comforted, cared about by someone who was really a stranger even though we would share a cell for a few months.

"Sha na na . . ." The chanting continued. I stopped feeling the water and concentrated on the touch. Someone cared. Someone was reaching out to me. I would do anything to maintain such good feelings.

"Have you been born again, Joyce?" she asked, her voice in the same monotone she had used when chanting.

"I don't know what that means," I said, dreamily, my eyes still closed.

"How do you feel, Joyce?"

"Warm," I said. "Cared about."

"That's what it means to be born again."

"Then I must be born again," I said, pleased that I had accomplished what she and the others wanted for me.

"Hallelujah!" shouted Nancy.

The teaching became more intense, after I was considered one of them. I had not realized this, but they considered it a special prize to convert someone who had not previously believed the way Sylvia taught her followers. I was the new "star" and they were determined to keep me.

"Why are you worrying about your children, Joyce?" I was asked by Sylvia.

"Because I love them. I care about them. They're growing up without me. I'm in jail and can't be there to help them, to love them, to guide them. I don't know what will happen to them."

"Don't you believe in the love of the Lord?"

"Of course I do. Haven't I been born again?"

"Then give them up to God, Joyce. They're His anyway. Why do you have so little faith that you must be thinking about them all the time? See how the birds of the fields eat but do nothing to grow their food. The Lord provides for them. How much more will He do for you and yours if you truly love them."

"But I miss them, especially Eden. We're friends, maybe best friends. She's . . ."

"More of a friend to you than Jesus? Joyce, have more faith. If you love your daughter, you will leave her in the care of the Lord."

"I don't know . . ."

"Would it make you feel better if I check on them?" asked Eleanore. "Why should you have to contact them all the time? They need to be going to church. They need to be getting their own lives in order with the guidance of the Holy Spirit.

"If you really love your children, and if you truly love the Lord, then you will refuse to let them visit you in jail.

You don't need them and they don't need you. We all need Jesus and you have found him, Joyce. You have found him through us. We have the answers, Joyce. The church has the answers. Tell your children to go to church on Sunday and not waste their time coming to this den of iniquity."

"Yes," I said, and I believed. My children would know the love of God. My children would not be denied what I had found. I would cut them off from inappropriate ties to me, I would set them adrift in a stream of righteousness that would take them into a peaceful river of tranquility through the Lord, through the group, through Sylvia.

"Are you nuts, Mom?" asked Eden.

And I smiled. I prayed. I knew it was only a matter of time before the spirit touched her through Sylvia.

"I don't want those people coming here to see me. I don't want them taking care of me. I don't want to go to their church."

She would learn. I knew she would learn. So I cut myself off from the family, prayed to the Lord, and inside I was weeping, though I didn't know why.

"Why are you helping your lawyer with your case, Joyce?" Sylvia wanted to know.

"Do you worship your lawyer?" asked Eleanore.

"Yes, Joyce, is he an idol?" asked Nancy.

"He's the person who's getting me out of jail. I have to help him prepare my case."

"The Lord will provide for you, Joyce. If you need to send a message to your lawyer, we'll take it to him. But you must trust in the Lord. You've been born again. You must not rely on your lawyer. God will show him the way."

And so I stopped calling Thomas on a regular basis. I had been in contact with him every day or two, trying to help him prepare my appeal. There were many areas where he felt I needed to guide him in order for him to find needed information. But I came to believe that I was not being adequately spiritual when I concerned myself with the appeal. That was for God to handle, and if he wanted to work through my lawyer, that was for the two of them to decide. I should not be involved.

Isolation. Without realizing the magnitude of what I was doing I was becoming separate from everything that mattered to me. I was estranged from my children, uncooperative with my lawyer, and facing spending the rest of my life in the lonely hell of the penitentiary. Because of Sylvia's group the bitter truth of my predicament seemed distant, unreal. Yet I did not comprehend this. All I know is that one of them was always there for me. They promised they would take care of me. They made me feel good about myself in the midst of the other inmates, some of life's roughest losers.

My children were becoming increasingly worried about me. Eden telephoned the rabbi of the temple we had attended, though at this point there was nothing she could do or say that would get me to declare the depth of feeling I had for her. I felt guilty having ties with anyone but the members of Sylvia's group. They had shown me the way. I owed them. I had to do what they believed.

I made a court appearance while still a part of the group. I proudly carried my Bible, following the teachings of Sylvia. "The Lord has a special way of reaching you, Joyce. When you are troubled, take hold of your Bible. Grip the sides tightly in your hands, then open it quickly. Whatever page appears, that is where the Lord wants you reading. That is where he will have a message for you."

And I believed. Never mind that the Bible is not a series of anecdotes. Never mind that it is possible to open the Bible to a page containing nothing but genealogical history or obscure laws no longer followed by either Jews or Gentiles. Never mind that I frequently did not understand how the reading of some historic account I encountered in this manner had any connection with me. I prayed. I gripped the sides. I opened it quickly. I searched for meaning on the page that appeared. And I owed it all to Sylvia who taught me the way.

It was sick, but, during one of my hearings, the newspaper reporters caught sight of my magic Bible. They decided that I had found religion. They became convinced that I was guilty of murder, had repented and found the Lord. It was another story of sin, penitence, and redemption, or so they wanted to believe. And they loved reporting it.

The rabbi from my temple finally came to visit me at the jail, along with Ralph, a man about whom I knew nothing. He was a Jewish scholar, counselor, and, ultimately, a friend. His job was to visit the prisons throughout the state of Arizona, meeting with the inmates, talking with them, sharing with them. He did not believe in Jesus as the messiah, but he did accept those who did. He recognized that Christianity was a legitimate religion even if he did not accept its tenets. He also was an expert in cults and recognized that I was not following the teachings of Jesus. I was following the warped perversions of a power-hungry cult leader who used my vulnerability in prison to gain another convert.

Ralph gave me a series of scholarly books written for the layman. It discussed both religious issues and the ways cults perverted them. He took me back to my roots, my heritage, the God I had always known about, always loved; the God who was not magic and did not want human beings isolated from their loved ones.

Ralph also recognized my spiritual longing. He arranged to visit with me on Friday nights, to recreate the ceremonies with which I had grown up. He would bring in some candles and some wine, saying a prayer, lighting the candles, the two of us sharing small glasses of either Kosher wine or, when that was not permitted, sparkling grape juice. Then we would talk. Sometimes it was about religion. Usually it was about life.

Every Friday night I was special. This man was my psychologist, my counselor, my friend. He re-opened my life to my family, never making me feel guilty for having placed my trust in women who did not have my best interests at heart. He would not have cared if I genuinely believed in Jesus, but that was not the case. I had never converted to Christianity. I had never seriously considered Jesus as my savior. I was worshipping what amounted to a false god in Sylvia, going along with everything she told me because I was so desperate for someone to care for me.

Oddly, by losing my "friends," I found greater happiness within. Part of this was true spritualy, restoring my trust and faith in God without thinking that He would act while I sat back and sang His praises. I knew I had to be as much of a mother to my children as possible, even from within jail. I knew I had to help my lawyer present my case, that God's love was not going to result in Thomas having all the answers he needed from me. And I understood that people did care, even if they did not know enough to come to see me.

The other inmates recognized this special time for me and teased me about it. They were a little jealous of my wine, my moments of freedom with Ralph. They knew what I had discovered. When someone special comes to see you, someone who is not part of family or former friends, taking you into an isolated area, talking, sharing, you emotionally leave the confinement of the jail. For those precious couple of hours you can escape. The bars disappear, the walls melt, the barbed wire unmeshes. A smooth path to freedom beckons.

And I could joke with them. "Bring us back some wine, Joyce," they would shout. "Hold it in your mouth and smuggle it in."

"Eat your hearts out," I called back. "I drank it all and

I feel high as a kite. Come over here and I'll breathe on you, though. You can get high from my breath."

No one did, of course. They wanted the wine that I received so many Fridays. They wanted the taste of freedom that the visit provided. They were jealous, but in their own ways, I think some of them were pleased for me. One of their own, if only for a short time each week, had found freedom.

Nancy was transferred to the penitentiary and I was given a new roommate, the usual order of things in Durango. So I never did find out what she might have felt when I explained that what I had been doing was wrong.

The other women from the cult—the so-called loving friends of mine who did not care what I believed but only wanted to help—dropped me immediately. It was as though I was dead. They did not try to see me. They did not try to talk with me. They avoided contact with me, even if we were in the same area together.

It would seem that jails would welcome religion. Religion has a calming effect on inmates. It is a way of modifying negative behavior.

There was tremendous tolerance for religion when I was in Durango. That was why every type of group, including Sylvia's, could have such easy access. Yet when it came to the religious holidays, what we experienced was a mixture of tenderness and senseless brutality.

The second Christmas that I was in B Pod, a group of us decided we should have a tree. Naturally we couldn't bring in a tree from the outside. Even an artificial tree could have been used as a weapon. But all of us were involved with some form of handcrafts and it seemed possible to make a tree from paper cups.

We began saving paper cups well before Christmas. We worked out the design for the tree, then began stacking them in a way that would form it. I became an expert at tearing and shaping the cups to correct proportions for the tree and the star at the top.

We worked for hours, many of the women contributing intricately shaped paper creations. There is a great deal of talent in the jails, raw, untrained, but more skilled than anything you would expect. Perhaps it is because everyone has so much time on their hands. Or perhaps, for some of these women who were inarticulate and put down by men, their families, and the law, the one outlet has been through drawing, paper sculpture, or similar skills. Whatever the case, we took pride in our tree, a harmless arrangement of cups and intricately torn paper placed in a section of the pod where it was in no one's way and could not hinder security.

On Christmas Eve, right after dinner, we were in the day room, looking at the tree, talking, planning the festivities for the next morning. Christmas meant a real meal with turkey and other food that was out of the ordinary. There wouldn't be much, we realized from our past experiences. Many of the donated turkeys ended up on the tables of jail staff's families. But they would leave enough for the meal to be different, special, enjoyable. We were happy together, a rare occurence, when suddenly a whistle blew.

"Sit down where you are. Don't go to your rooms. Don't go to the bathroom. Everyone sit down on the floor in the day room. Now!"

Three men and two women entered, all dressed in uniforms, all of them strangers to our pod. They never used the regular guards for the dirty work. They didn't dare. There might be retribution or the fear of retribution, the latter being just as dangerous because it could cause the guards to over-react. These were outsiders and they came on like Hitler's gestapo.

We had had these experiences before. They were called when someone was known to have hidden drugs or weapons. Everything would be searched, the people found with stashes taken to solitary for punishment.

Sometimes the guards handling the searches were respectful of personal property. They would go through your belongings, violating your most personal treasures, but they would leave the rooms neat, your property undamaged. At other times the guards seemed to take delight in brutality, in doing what they could to hurt and humiliate. That Christmas Eve we faced the brutal guards.

To outsiders their actions may seem minor since none of the inmates were touched or physically hurt. But when your possessions consist of a few colored pencils for drawing, a photograph of a loved one framed within the cardboard torn from a matchbook cover and taped on the wall, a picture crayoned in a childish scrawl, or some similar objects, they become prized more than gold. Remember that such items were often all that we had. We frequently had no way to replace them, either because of cost or because of difficulties communicating with people on the outside. They were little things that made the rooms more bearable, that turned a cell into a fantasy of a home.

The guards tore the pictures from the wall, ripping them and trampling them with their feet. Sheets were torn from the bed, then stepped on, the guards knowing it would be several days before we could get clean ones. They were aware that, night after night, we would have to look at the footprints, remember the damage they had done, and try to rest with such thoughts being the last ones we would have before falling asleep.

Nothing was sacred. The inmates accepted that a certain amount of destruction was natural when guards were seeking hidden weapons and drugs. A book binding might be broken if a woman was known to slip her cachè within that part of the book. Or a jar of make-up might be emptied if the center might contain a small bag of heroin hidden by facial powder or some other item. That was to be expected. But not the destruction of photographs, of gifts from children, or of our Christmas tree.

The latter was what hit me the hardest. The tree was systematically crushed and broken into pieces.

At first the women were nervous. The drug users were glancing about, then whispering to each other. "Where'd you hide the stash? Is it safe?" "God, if they find my 'fit.' " "I got it on me. I don't know why. Had a feelin' is all." "They'll get it. They'll get it and put me in the hole."

But whatever the guards were seeking was not there or, if it was, they said nothing about it that night. They tore the place apart, destroyed our precious Christmas tree, and left.

I looked around and, like some of the others, began to cry. It was not a cry of self-pity or helplessness. We shed tears of rage. To try and stop them, even to attempt to talk them out of their destruction, would have resulted in harrassment charges against us. Our situation would have worsened in ways about which none of us wanted to think. Yet the guards were wrong. This had nothing to do with corrections. This had nothing to do with anyone trying to commit a crime from within the jail. This was a group of women, some wishing to celebrate the birth of Jesus, others just wanting to be a part of the festivities of a holiday season, who fashioned a simple Christmas tree and had it destroyed.

As I lay in bed that night, I heard the cursing. The women swore about the "pigs." The "shit heads." The "cock suckers" and "mother fuckers." They used all the foul language they could think of, but it sounded adolescent. There was no power in their words, no force to their anger. They were angry over a wrong that could not be rectified and they knew they were helpless.

The next morning the mood was different. We gathered together for our special meal, the turkey slices as small as they had been the previous years because so many of the donated birds had been stolen. But it was turkey and it was Christmas. Surviving hand-made or commissary bought presents were exchanged by a few of the women, and some received gifts from outside. We gathered together to sing carols. We ignored the brutal insensitivity we had encountered the night before. We carried on as though nothing had happened.

Yet inside, all of us were different. Inside there was a tiny ember of anger concerning the system that, for some like myself, still burns in the deepest regions of our souls. And for others the ember was a spark that, months later, would detonate explosions against guards, police, or other authority figures when these women were back on the streets. They would injure, maim, or kill in what, to casual observers, was senseless violence. But in their hearts it was revenge for a hundred wrongs, just one of which was the night they crushed our Christmas tree.

PART THREE

THE NEW TRIAL

Chapter 14

THE INVESTIGATION

Mary Durand looks like your high school best friend's mother, the one who was always puttering in the kitchen, baking cookies, urging you to try her latest recipe with a large glass of milk. She is the type of woman to whom you feel comfortable confiding your inner-most thoughts and fears. You can picture her sitting at the breakfast table, flour in her hair, the aroma of vanilla on her hands, listening intently as you tell her about your love life, your problems with your parents, your dreams of college or a job after graduation. She is overweight, gentle, settled. She is also a private investigator licensed by the state of Arizona, a former deputy warden in the prison system, and quite capable of holding her own should a situation unexpectedly turn violent.

In March of 1984 Thomas Thinnes approached Mary Durand about working on the Joyce Lukezic case. She and her partner, Ed Aitken, would be handling the investigation to learn whatever facts had yet to be discovered.

According to Mary, Thinnes told her, "There are four or five things I absolutely need you to do. The first thing is that it appears that the only piece of evidence against her is this guy Arnie Merrill. He said that he overheard a conversation between Joyce and Mr. Cruz in the office of Sun View Development. Let's find out what's going on in that office. Nobody took pictures. Nobody took samples of the wall.

"So the very first thing, after going up and meeting Joyce, was beginning to locate the physical evidence. We went out to the building which had been purchased. They had torn down the suite of offices that Sun View Development had occupied.

"Then I talked to the construction foreman, the project manager, and learned that the building was two sided with a large courtyard in the middle. They are doppelgangers, if you will. And he said the offices on this side are exactly like the offices on that side. The only difference is that the Sun View Development office had very lush paneling which adds another layer onto the wall.

"So we went to the opposite office, directly opposite Cruz's office, and cut out a section of the wall to prove that it was not, as Mr. Merrill had testified, flimsily constructed, that the doors were thick. And we got a description of the interior of the office from the people who tore it down. Apparently it was very plush carpeting, etcetera."

Mary took pictures of the wall, using her partner's hand to show the thickness. "We took pictures to show what the wall sections were like, put his hand up to show how fat the wall was. It was not what Mr. Merrill had testified that it was."

Mary also learned other details of the construction from the company that had purchased Sun View, including how much air, the best insulator, was between the walls. The information was never used, but it was one of the first actions taken during this independent investigation. It was also something that neither the prosecutor's investigator nor the original defense lawyers had ever apparently bothered to check.

"The other thing that Thinnes was concerned about was Joyce's mental health. She had been assaulted in jail and she was pretty depressed. And he wanted me to spend time with her just so she knew that he was out there, that he cared about her, that he was interested in her well being, and that she could call him, Craig, and me any time she wanted to.

"She was fearful. She was withdrawn. She was untrusting. I think she was scared to death. She had not been given the death penalty, but she knew that she would have been sentenced to it had the judge not granted the motion for a new trial.

"So here she was, this rather elitist kind of lady sitting in the Maricopa County Jail in a blue uniform, overweight, no make-up, and she couldn't quit crying. She was scared to death she was going to die. She really didn't know what to do. So I spent a lot of time just talking with her. Not doing investigations, just talking with her."

Mary explained that Thinnes was quite concerned about the effect jail would have on Joyce, especially after seeing Jean Holsinger destroyed by her imprisonment. He felt that if someone was on the street awaiting trial, the pressures had to be endured. But being in jail, helpless, unable to see her family, there was a chance that Joyce would be destroyed.

"At that point Ron disappeared. Here's a woman whose husband comes in, leaves $50 on her books (for commissary purchases), and splits, leaving her kids. She went crazy; she had enormous guilt feelings because she wasn't there with her kids.

"I felt that the majority of her depression stemmed from the fact that she was separated from her kids, and she wasn't sure she'd ever be able to get out there and mother them. She had tremendous guilt about the fact that they were out there alone. And angry at Ron. But she couldn't turn the depression into anger. She just cried. You know, 'Where is he? What's he doing?'

"At that point one of the decisions that was made was that we had to find Ron. 'Where is Ron? Why hasn't Ron ever been questioned? Why wasn't Ron called to help defend his wife?' All of these questions about Ron, the mysterious Ron. And it was at that point that I went looking for Ron. Ron wasn't around.

"I went to Ron's old bars, and Ron's old haunts, and tried to find Ron's old girlfriends, and talk to people who knew Ron. From *Sir Don's* (a popular nightclub) to this sleazy bar up in Cave Creek, to the *Ivanhoe*. But Ron was gone.

"First we heard he was in California, then we heard he was in Florida, and Texas. We tried to contact people who worked at Graphic Dimensions who knew Ron, who may have taken sides. We went to Chester's Bar . . .

"I'll tell you what astounded me. Joyce appeared, even in jail, to be a classy woman, to have some breeding, as it were. She and Ron hung out in some sleaze bars, bars at which I would not drink anything except out of the bottle because I wouldn't trust them to put it in the glass. I'm telling you, these bars were pits. You wouldn't go to them. I can't imagine her sitting there with him."

As Mary Durand continued her investigation, she felt that the only reports she could trust were the statements by Larry Martinsen, one of the police investigators. In Phoenix law enforcement, she explained, there was a say-ing—a perversion of the old line, "He lies like a rug." In Phoenix, the statement is, "He lies like a cop under oath." There were exceptions in officers like Detective Larry Mar-tinsen, whose integrity was unquestioned. Unfortunately, he was not the primary investigator in the case; Dan Ryan had that distinction. Mary Durand was aroused by actions that apparently reflected either incompetence or obses-sion, even at the cost of truth.

"I get offended by the feeling of omnipotence in the County Attorney's office—that you can do anything you want to get a conviction. You can lie. You can cheat. You can steal. You can alter. You can withhold Brady. You can suborn perjury. You can pay witnesses. You can . . . It makes me crazy when they do that!

"What makes me crazier is that they did it. They got caught, kind of. I'm not sure that there wasn't more that went on. I'm sure that's the surface. And what happened to them? Nothing. And my sense is that the County Attorney should bring charges against somebody that does that. I mean, if he's hired to uphold the law, the law is for everyone."

There is reputed glamour and excitement in being an investigator because of the way the movies portray their actions. In reality, the work is drudgery, checking records, reading reports, finding witnesses. It is as though someone took a jigsaw puzzle and scattered the pieces to the four winds. The investigator's job is to find all the pieces. The attorney's job is to put the pieces together into a picture that can be shown to the jury.

Thomas Thinnes and Craig Mehrens had several trials to review. There was Joyce's first trial, of course, but also transcripts from the convictions of the killers and Robert Cruz. All had testimony that had to be checked and compared. All contained possible clues to what had happened to Joyce.

The most critical aspect of the defense was the character of Ron Lukezic. In addition to proving Joyce's innocence, it became necessary to also build a case against the most logical suspect, Ron Lukezic. It was felt that a jury would feel more comfortable judging someone innocent if they also had a handle on who might have ordered so vicious a crime. The trouble was that no one had interviewed Ron Lukezic in any depth and he had never taken the witness stand in his wife's trial. The only direct testimony that could be used in relation to Ron was the testimony he gave during Robert Cruz's trial back in 1981.

Thinnes and Mehrens picked up a file box from Joyce's former attorney and, in the bottom, there was an envelope. Inside was a tape to which they listened intently. "The tape recording was of an investigator who was talking to this girl named Judy McKinney," said Durand. "And she was telling this story about how Ron Lukezic had been at a party, pulled up his shirt and showed her where some guy stabbed him or shot him in a home burglary. He boasted that he paid some black guys $500 to find him and kill him.

"Well, they played this tape for me and I almost had a stroke. I said, perhaps we should find Judy McKinney. I mean, I was being very facetious, but they said, 'as soon as possible.'

"Here we had a critical witness. They had the tape. Nobody had ever found her. I couldn't find a file back on her. I called the investigator who had made the interview. I called the lawyer who had talked to her—like eight times. He refused to call me back.

"So finally I ran into him (the lawyer) one day and I said, 'Where's Judy McKinney?' He said, 'Gee, I don't know,' and he walked away. It was unbelievable. So I began searching for her.

"She had left town, gotten married in Las Vegas. Her husband was in the CIA, I think. There was no Air Force recruiter or world wide locater, so I started calling air bases. And I think I called fifty Air Force bases, asking for him. And I tell you, when I found her, he was not listed at that base. What does that tell you?

"It was the toughest find. I never had such difficulty locating anyone. It took forever. But when I finally found out her new name, luckily she worked at an Air Force base. Had she not worked at an Air Force base, I never would have found her. Anyway, I called her, I interviewed her, and she came out and testified."

The initial telephone interview proved surprisingly rewarding. "I knew Ron Lukezic for a million years," said McKinney. "I think he's one of the all-time lowlifes of the world, if you want to know the truth.

"Pat and Ron were best friends since I've known

them. In fact Ron, when I first met him, was the general manager of what was called Allied Printing at the time. I mean, we're talking now probably fourteen years ago, and Pat Redmond was his printer. And they were always buddy, buddy.

"When Ron started his own company, Pat came in as his partner. I thought the world of Pat Redmond. I never knew how those two got along so well."

McKinney knew about the Redmond murders from friends in Phoenix, but she did not know that Joyce was convicted of the crime. She was told that there was going to be a new trial and that Joyce was facing the death penalty for planning the murder.

"I have no idea what happened," said McKinney. "I was shocked when I read the paper. I knew Pat and Marilyn Redmond for so many years and I thought the world of Pat Redmond. But I'll tell you something, the minute they went and arrested Joyce, and you know she's got three kids, I figured that Ron set her up."

Judy McKinney continued, explaining about the scar on Ron's chest. "He told me he was shot . . . He told me this story ten times . . . He had a scar on his chest where he said a black man had came in and shot him. And then he said he paid $500 to have the guy killed." Then, when asked if Ron told the story to anybody else, she said, "I'm sure he told it to everybody."

According to Durand, when the jury heard Judy McKinney in person, they were "quite struck by her testimony." It was an important statement from a key witness to Ron's character, yet the locating of the witness involved little more than endless telephone calls. Busy work. Intense. Boring. And Joyce Lukezic's life depended upon its success.

The prosecutor's office was as concerned with the trial as the defense. The original team of prosecutors had been replaced for both official and unofficial reasons by Larry Turoff. The official statement coming from the office was that there had been so much press involving the original prosecutors—press that was not favorable—that it was best to use different individuals. Off the record, individuals familiar with the case who worked within the department commented, "We got caught with our pants down. Merrill's statement was full of holes they should have checked right at the start. Ryan either perjured himself or was a fool. They just made such asses of themselves that no one wanted to risk what might happen with any more of them in the courtroom than necessary."

Turoff, the man who replaced the original team of prosecutors, appears to have been created for the part by a Hollywood casting agency. His face is stern, like an angry father facing his daughter's date after the couple has returned home two hours later than her curfew. He is heavy-set, his appearance a little like that of a detective in a 1940s gangster film.

Turoff's actions in the case were seemingly contradictory. He was uncomfortable with the idea of Joyce as the person who set up the murders, though his "by the book" attitude forced him to prosecute her based on the statements of others. Too many people had pointed the finger of guilt at Joyce for him not to take her to court. Yet he too eliminated two logical suspects, men who had not been fully investigated.

One such man was Arthur Ross, Joyce's brother, a man who knew everyone involved with the case, including the killers. He was a part of the Las Vegas dealings and theoretically had something to gain, if only a finder's fee, from Ron's and Pat's accepting the printing job. Whether the money was substantial enough for him to want Pat dead, or whether he was even capable of thinking along such lines, no one knew. Neither Dan Ryan nor anyone else bothered to find out. They made no serious effort to question him extensively, though he was named at least once as being involved. That accusation came from a man who, unlike Merrill, was *not* known to be a liar.

The second man was Ron Lukezic, who truly had the most to gain from Patrick Redmond's death. Ron not only got control of the printing business, he was free to engage in any type of activity he desired. Yet, again, there was a limited investigation culminated by an action that shocked outside observers. Without the case being fully resolved, without someone with a better motive arrested and convicted, Larry Turoff, Deputy County Attorney and Chief of the Major Felony Unit of the Maricopa County Attorney's Office, sent the following letter to Stephen Dichter, attorney for Ron Lukezic. It stated, in part:

". . . the following is the State's position and agreement concerning Ronald Lukezic as they relate to the above captioned matter (i.e. the case of the State v. Joyce Lukezic—the Redmond and Phelps Homicides).

"In exchange for Ronald Lukezic's testimony either at trial or at a deposition the state agrees to confer use immunity to him. That is, nothing he testifies to nor anything derived as a result of his testimony could or would be used against him by the State of Arizona.

"As I told you in our conversation, at this time the County Attorney's Office has no intention of charging Ron Lukezic with any offense arising out of the Redmond and Phelps homicide investigation. There simply is no evidence to warrant charging him.

"I trust the above states our understanding."

Later Turoff would sum up the case as the prosecution understood it at the time of the arrest and the time of the second trial. He explained that though Merrill's statements were strong, there was no confirmation until Wally Roberts came forward. He said:

"Wally Roberts knew both Joyce and Ron Lukezic, and he knew Pat Redmond. He had worked with all of them. He was a graphic artist working in the graphics business—the business they were in.

"He came forward and told us about a conversation he had with Joyce Lukezic . . . What he said was 'the Las Vegas business.' The background, at least as we put the pieces together and may or may not be the reason for the murders . . . It never made much sense *to me* (author's emphasis) but this is what everybody said, that Cruz had some method of obtaining . . .

"This is what we believe, what we said. I don't know if I believe he had a way of obtaining business. The story was that Graphic Dimensions, through Cruz by way of or through Artie Ross by way of Cruz, was able to get Graphic Dimensions as much Las Vegas business as either they could handle or they wanted to handle. The implication, of course, being that this wasn't going to be a bid situation. This was going to be done through a connection of Cruz.

"The business didn't come through. Both partners apparently decided not to do business with the Las Vegas interests. Wally Roberts apparently claimed to have spoken with Ron Lukezic about the business, and Ron apparently said to Roberts, 'I really don't want to talk about it here. If you come over to the house, I'll tell you what went on.'

"He went to the Lukezic home that evening. Ron wasn't there. He talked to Joyce and asked her about the business and said, 'I hear you're not getting it.'

"Joyce apparently, according to him, flew off the handle and started making statements which would indicate that she was deeply involved in attempting to get the business and that she wasn't willing to write it off."

The theory Turoff followed was that Joyce was somehow involved with all this through Cruz and her brother, despite the fact that all witnesses familiar with Graphic

Dimensions felt that Joyce had no interest or involvement. Only Ron Lukezic seemed most concerned, though Turoff stated: "I don't have any evidence that Ron Lukezic had anything to do with it. Whether or not he knew what was going on, or knew what went on after it happened, is questionable. I think he knew after it happened who did it. And it's possible he put two and two together and figured out why he did it."

Turoff explained that there was no direct evidence against Joyce except through the statements Arnie Merrill made, including his statement about what Cruz said. Oddly, there was at least as much circumstantial evidence against Ron Lukezic as there was against Joyce. There were the FBI memos, the statement by Campagnoni, the statement at the Redmond funeral, and even Wally Roberts' admission to his lack of credibility. More important, Ron could be shown to have the strongest motive for having his partner killed. Yet Larry Turoff granted Ron Lukezic immunity from prosecution and prepared to bring Joyce to trial yet again.

Turoff continued explaining: "Roberts tied it together. She made a statement to Roberts, at least this was his testimony, when she asked him about the business, the business is not lost, that it is Artie's deal, and Pat has stood in the way or has been in the way of the business long enough. And she's going to have him wasted.

"In addition, there's some reference, totally unrelated to the Graphics Dimension business, but not unrelated to Cruz . . . There is some mention made to Roberts that he testified to about a request that Joyce made to him that he could get rid of, I think, something like ten pounds of coke that she was going to have brought in by way of a Chicago connection.

Then Turoff commented that there was no evidence that she was connected with anyone from Chicago, especially organized crime figures. "The only connection she had was through Cruz, and I'm not even certain how much of a connection that was. But those are the two aspects of the case that involve Joyce Lukezic."

Despite the seeming contradictions between the prosecutor's reasoning and the facts in the case, Turoff felt he had to go to court. Yet even the testimony of Wally Roberts bothered him, as he explained.

"Roberts, by his own testimony, is an alcoholic or was an alcoholic. I guess once you're alcoholic, you're always an alcoholic. He's an alcoholic and a drug addict. And he had been very friendly with both Lukezic and Redmond, but I guess in a more lucid moment he started to think about it, and to think about what she said to him and decided to tell us about it.

"He said he had been dry both as far as alcohol and drugs are concerned for some while prior to coming forward, but he had gone to New York on a real bender before then.

"As I recall, there was some testimony from him that he had discussed it with a sponsor in AA, and supposedly the guy said go ahead, tell what you know. That may have been his reason for it."

Turoff admitted that there were changes in Roberts. "Before he began his testimony in the case, although not recanting, he seemed to lose the desire to testify and attempted to disappear. And in addition, he attempted to qualify his testimony by indicating that because of his alcohol and drug addiction, he sometimes merged things together, and that he didn't consider himself to be a reliable witness."

Turoff made a judgement call about Roberts. He felt that the information Roberts had provided was accurate. Only the attempt to tone down the impact was "bullshit." Yet at no time did the prosecutor's office investigate where Roberts had gone when weighing his decision to testify.

His connection with Ron Lukezic and Ron's father was not brought out.

"(Roberts' testimony) coupled with Merrill's statement about being in the office of . . . I can't remember the name of the office now . . . the office owned by Artie Ross, Joyce Lukezic's brother—land development or land sales office. He said he went there to meet with his brother, and this was after the first attempt on Redmond, early in December . . . He said he went to that office to meet with his brother who he said was a friend of Artie Ross and Bobby Cruz, and while there, Joyce Lukezic came into the office and went down to Artie Ross' office where she met with Bob Cruz and demanded to know when Pat Redmond was going to be taken care of. According to Merrill, Cruz told her he would be dead by Christmas."

Turoff was asked about Artie Ross, obviously a key person in the murder if the prosecutor's scenario was accurate. Joyce had nothing directly to gain by murdering Pat Redmond. She would not inherit the business if Ron died. She would not get the business if there was a divorce despite her reputed angry statements because, as she well knew, in the community property state of Arizona, both she and Ron would separate retaining what they owned when they entered into the marriage. The only benefit could come through Artie Ross and there seemed to be a hint that Ross must have known something in advance. Yet, according to Turoff, Artie Ross had disappeared.

There is no statute of limitations on murder. If anyone wanted to find Artie Ross, his business interests, lawsuits, and other factors would make him easy to trace. But the same people who were determined to send Joyce Lukezic to the gas chamber were unwilling to take the extra measures needed to locate and investigate Ross, by their own admissions a key player. In fact, when pushed, Turoff said, "I don't have any evidence that he had anything to do with the murders. I know that we had everything we were able to get. I don't know that Ross had any more information than Ron Lukezic, and if he did, it came about after the fact, after it happened. He, like Ron Lukezic, could have been concerned for his own safety and decided to make himself scarce."

Once again an illogical noose was tightening around Joyce's neck. For Joyce to be the villain in the case, she had to have something to gain. There could be no gain through inheritance if Ron was also murdered. There could be no direct benefit in that Joyce knew nothing about the printing business, had a proven history of not being interested in the printing business, and knew enough about business in general to know that without knowledge, she would run it into the ground. Therefore, Joyce had to be doing everything for her brother, Artie Ross, whom the prosecutor felt knew no more about the murders than Ron Lukezic whom he claimed was innocent. Joyce was being tried in Wonderland and, like the mythical Alice, the queen was shouting for her head.

Equally frightening was the selective use of evidence. Merrill probably lied from the first interview with Ryan. Ryan should have checked out these "so-called" facts, but obvious lies went uncorrected. Information about Joyce's being at the New Year's party, coldly watching the news about the murders, making statements that were incriminating—when, in reality, she was never at the party but standing in the cold, talking with police—should have been a red flag. If Merrill would lie about an event where many people could, would, and did contradict him, why should he be trusted where there was only his word against hers?

There was the "overheard" conversation at the office. Mary Durand made an effort to determine whether or not a conversation could be heard. If anyone else bothered, they undoubtedly discovered the same facts as Durand and her partner, that nothing could have been heard the way it was described. Either Dan Ryan did not check, implying poor preparation for the case, or the statement was false and the information was suppressed. Either way, the prosecutor handling the case should have demanded that so important a clue be proven true or false.

Chapter 15

THE FIGHT

"I never cried in public. Everything was always fine to somebody on the outside. I kept all my problems inside. As upset as I was, I could be finished with something and Thomas would leave and I would be hysterical in jail because of something he's asked me.

"It was Craig who said, 'Why can't you show that you're human, Joyce?'

"And I said, 'Maybe it's my pride.'"

Joyce Lukezic was fighting for a sense of personal dignity; her attorneys were fighting for her life. The other people arrested for their involvement in the murder of Patrick Redmond and Helen Phelps had had their trials. The killers were on death row, the same place to which Joyce would be sent if convicted of arranging for the murders. She had already lost once in court. It appeared that the results of that first trial might be repeated.

Joyce had been broken in body and spirit, yet she remained impassive, unwilling or unable to show the grief and agony she was enduring. Not to strangers. Not even to her attorneys.

Oddly, the guards were the first to accept Joyce as a person when she was awarded a date for a new trial. She had been in the jail for more than a year. She had caused no trouble, provided no help. She had simply made herself a part of the population, marking time, trying to stay alive.

266

She had not been caught participating in the bootleg alcohol operation, though all the inmates were suspected of being involved at one time or another. She had avoided being a snitch, avoided witnessing anything other than the "accidental falls in the shower." The times she carried drugs, she did so to avoid problems within the system, never becoming a part of the drug underground. Some guards seemed to like her as much as they liked anyone. Others felt she might as well not exist. And all of them seemed equally brutal about her possessions when they looked for contraband.

Until she was granted a new trial.

"No one said anything. No one wished me well. There was no obvious change except that they stopped breaking up my things when they searched for contraband. Sometimes they didn't even bother with my room when they made their searches and that was the first time that had happened. There was no question that they were treating me differently, but not so anyone would think I was a snitch or something that would get me in trouble.

"I think they were afraid of me. They were afraid of what I would say in court about them. I had filed grievances against them, especially after they tore apart that Christmas tree we made from the paper cups. I don't think they were certain I was innocent or guilty. They just knew that an inmate going to court could say something that would hurt them. Most of the women went directly to the penitentiary where no one cared how they had been treated in Durango. This was different and they wanted to protect themselves."

The change in treatment could not alter how Joyce would be seen by the jurors. The way she held in her emotions, the limited sleep, the refusal to go outside in the sun, all had made her look worse than before. There were circles under her eyes. Her skin was grey. The tension and fear had made her face taut, hard.

Her lawyers' first concern was Joyce's outward physical appearance. Joyce had always dressed casually. Her medical work required uniform type slacks and she liked to work around the house in jeans. She had never been comfortable in dresses and skirts, purchasing only those she had to have for some special event.

Joyce also wore her hair in a pixie cut with the bangs coming low on her forehead. It was the same style that entertainer Liza Minelli had adopted. On Minelli the hair style looked fresh, attractive, youthful. On Joyce, it looked like a style you might encounter on a woman who was earning her living in alleys, working as a mugger. However, it was also a style easy to maintain in the jail where the only hair cuts came when they were permitted to use a safety razor and could take a little extra time to also trim their hair with the blade.

Thomas Thinnes and Craig Mehrens arranged for professionals to come to the jail to change Joyce's appearance. They had told her that they were going to do something, but she figured that they would just have her daughter, Eden, pick up a couple of new dresses. What she did not expect was the loudspeaker announcement:

"Joyce Lukezic, come to the door of your pod." There was a pause, and then the guard making the announcement turned her voice into a parody of a snobbish butler announcing the arrival of the Vanderbilts at a posh party held by Lady Astor. "Your beautician is here."

"My first reaction was just, 'Huh?'" said Joyce. "My beautician? And the way they announced it. They didn't have to use the loudspeaker. They normally just came to the pod and got you. The guard wanted to have some fun with me and let everyone know what was happening."

Then Joyce saw them. Craig Mehrens appeared in his usual, perfectly tailored suit, accompanied by a young man in his late twenties or early thirties. The youth wore tight jeans and a white shirt. His sleeves were rolled up and the shirt had two or three buttons undone so his chest was exposed. He was extremely handsome and the total effect was raw sexuality. He was also rather nervous as the women spotted him and started whistling and shouting at him.

"Wiggle that ass over here, baby!" "Isn't he cute? You ever been eaten by a real woman, honey?" "You can cut my hair, baby. All of it."

"The hair dresser was wonderful. He was sexy, very nice, and from the Boston area originally so we had much to talk about. The three of us went to a little room off the big gym area where we could have privacy while he worked.

"There was something special about having my hair done, something that was like a taste of freedom.

"And the cutting of my hair . . . I was a suburban mother again, going to the beautician. It was an experience that millions of other women encounter on a regular basis, yet one of which I had been deprived for months.

"At the same time I was a little scared. I had to wet my hair first, then he explained that he was going to style my hair. I thought there was nothing wrong with the way I looked. I wore the same style for years and was comfortable with it. Finally I just told myself that I had been locked up for more than two years and there was nothing more anyone could do to me that I could not endure. Besides, he had cologne on. He smelled delicious. He smelled like a man. And he smelled free. That was appealing; very appealing. 'Chop away,' I told him.

"When he was finished, he shaped it with styling mousse, again something that had become unfamiliar. I could not see what I looked like, could not learn until I would appear in court, because there was no mirror in the room. However, Craig was delighted, so I knew the change was what he wanted."

It was over too soon for Joyce, who, impulsively,

reached up and stroked his neck with her hands. "I want to take the smell of your cologne back to the other women," she explained to the startled hair dresser. He laughed, not fully understanding, yet recognizing that whatever the reason, it was important to Joyce.

Joyce returned to the pod, a queen. The prisoners gathered around, smelling the cologne on the palms of her hands, smelling the styling mousse on her hair, admiring how she looked. They were both jealous and happy for her. The lingering perfume smell reminded them of what it was to be normal, to be free to come and go on the streets, to be able to experience so simple a pleasure as a visit to a beauty shop or enjoying the physical presence of a man who carried no night stick, badge or gun.

For Joyce, the new hairstyle was a radical departure from what she had known in the past. She felt like a Barbie Doll and scorned her appearance. "I thought it looked disgusting. It wasn't me and I didn't like it. I went through a crowded room and emerged this little person in a white frilly dress. That's how I felt," she said. "And then I realized that that was the point. Thomas and Craig thought I looked too harsh. They wanted something that looked different. But I was just appalled. It took everyone telling me how much they liked it for the next couple of days before I was comfortable with it."

A day or two passed. The excitement of her haircut had almost died down, when there was another announcement over the PA. It was the same as before except that this time the visitor was "my make-up consultant."

"My make-up consultant. . . . ?"

This time the visitor was a woman who was part of the Plaza 3 Modeling and Talent Agency of Phoenix. The agency was a large, respected organization whose training program legitimately trained young women for modeling careers. They also booked the girls and, occasionally, were involved with the active Phoenix film industry. The staff was knowledgeable about make-up, clothing, and color, all factors that would influence Joyce's appearance in the court.

The consultant made a number of suggestions. She brought out a salmon pastel type of rouge, a lipstick Joyce hated because she never wore lipstick of any type.

Joyce felt like a school girl playing with make-up for the first time. The consultant showed her how to use a light touch, to change her face without calling attention to the make-up she was using. She learned professional techniques for making the most of her appearance, given time to practice over and over again. There were no crayons, no moistened magazine pages, and no one telling her she had to stop. Craig was concerned that she would be skilled enough to handle the task herself before she went into court. Joyce was delighted to be able to play in a way she thought was lost to her forever.

Next the consultant used swatches of colored fabric which she and Craig studied, then noted so that Eden could use them as guides when shopping for her mother. There were still more than two weeks before the trial and Joyce was in need of a better skin appearance. She was told to get as much sun as she could before the trial. For the first time she was comfortable going outside.

Joyce, however, still did not want to be in the large yard that held so many obvious contrasts. There were grass, sky, birds, and large spaces. But there were also guards, barbed wire, fences, and other noticeable security measures, endless reminders that she was in jail.

Instead, Joyce chose to go to a patio area that was kept open during the summer. It was actually a concrete surface about the size of a large bedroom. There were still high walls and barbed wire, but it was less traumatic. Joyce took advantage of the location to get as much sunlight as possible, still returning inside for a shower before most of the other women were back.

Eden had returned from the year with her father and agreed to handle the shopping for Joyce's clothing. Her first time in the stores she followed the color scheme the consultant created, but bought designs she knew Joyce would like. The attorneys told her to return everything and try again.

The second time Eden made purchases according to the taste of the consultant. Arrangements were made to leave the clothing and make-up, along with a 5×7-inches mirror, in an anteroom at the court house. It was the area where Joyce would go each morning before the trial, applying the make-up and changing from the prison garments. Her watch and some studs for her ears would also be there.

One of the outfits was a beige jacket and a wrap-around skirt, neither tight nor flared, but similar to the more modest styles made popular in some of the fashion magazines. A second suit was peach, a third white, and the fourth, also beige, but with a mid-calf skirt. She also had several blouses, some half slips, bikini panties, bras, nylons, and perfume.

"It was like going into Cinderella's house and finding the fairy godmother had been there," said Joyce. For more than two years she had been forced to wear jail clothing without make-up, perfume, or jewelry. The clothing looked and felt institutionalized. "The minute I walked into the anteroom, I began touching the clothing. I held each piece, running my hand across the fabric, holding the materials to my face. The smells. The feel. I had almost forgotten what it was like."

There were notes with the clothing as well, notes that would appear daily from Eden. They were reminders to pay attention to her appearance, a subtle way of telling

Joyce that she had to act differently from the way she appeared during the first trial. "I love you. Smile." "These are the clothes you'll be wearing when you come home. Smile." As Eden handled the cleaning and replacement of Joyce's clothing, she also provided the one constant support Joyce enjoyed throughout the trial.

Joyce was amazed that the clothing fit perfectly since no one had measured her and her weight had increased somewhat while in jail. She also was amused to discover her awkwardness in the shoes that Eden had purchased. They were low heeled, yet she began clunking about as she first tried to walk in them. She was as awkward as a little girl trying on her mother's shoes for the first time. The time in prison had caused her to forget how to balance herself in the heels.

When Joyce was finally able to see herself in a full length mirror, she felt that she looked similar to Mrs. Leonard, a neighbor down the street from where Joyce's family once lived. Mrs. Leonard was the perfect housewife and mother, a woman who was born to play that role. Her clothing was frumpy despite the fact that it was well made and expensive. Her hair was always slightly disheveled from the heat of the kitchen stove where she would endlessly bake cookies, pies, and cakes for her family. If one of her children fell and hurt himself, if company came to her home, or if a neighbor dropped by for a minute to borrow a cup of sugar, Mrs. Leonard would offer each in turn something to eat, something to drink, acting the nurturing mother under any and all circumstances. Her actions seemed almost a stereotype, yet she was sincere and everyone accepted her for being a relic from a previous time.

"Thomas wanted Mrs. Leonard in the courtroom and that's the way he had me dress," Joyce later recalled. "I guess he knew best, but they weren't the clothes I would have picked out for myself."

Everything was moving smoothly. Everything was in readiness. Only a week remained before the trial and Joyce was sitting in a cell with some of the inmates, women who considered themselves her friends.

The women had heroin with them, using a "fit" one of them had successfully hidden from the guards. They were talking and nodding, but Joyce did not care. She was nervous about the trial, filled with hope, feeling comfortable with women who were helping her pass the time before she had to face the jury. What she did not know was that one of the women there had been sexually aroused by her. The woman was hoping to have a relationship with Joyce.

Suddenly the woman grabbed Joyce around the neck in a hold that felt like something a police officer would use to arrest a violent, struggling prisoner. Before Joyce could react, the woman immobilized Joyce's head long enough to squirt heroin into Joyce's nasal passage. Then she released Joyce, waiting for the good times to begin.

What the woman did not realize about heroin is that one of the reasons fewer people become addicted to it than become addicted to cocaine is that there are two common reactions the first time you have it. One is a "high," the good feeling that encourages its use with greater frequency. The other is what happened to Joyce—she became violently sick, vomiting continuously until everything was out of her system.

The woman was shocked. She wanted a relationship, not to possibly kill Joyce. She helped Joyce to the bathroom, then helped her back to her room and left, leaving Joyce nauseated both by the drug and the life she had been forced to endure. That whole night she lay awake, unable to sleep.

The prosecution of the case was being handled by Larry Turoff. He laid out the case as he felt he had to pursue it in the courtroom, explaining:

"You got to prove the homicides first. Then you have to prove her connection with it, so you prove her connection by her statements."

There were problems with the case, Turoff explained, "all kinds of problems. One is credibility because you don't have any physical evidence that she did anything. What you have is the testimony of witnesses as to what she said.

"You don't have a lot of corroboration. Arnie Merrill was eighty to ninety percent of the case against her. And Wally Roberts was the other portion of the case—ten to twenty percent. But she could have been saying this, you know, 'I'm mad. I had no intention of doing anything. I'm just mad at my husband and Pat Redmond because this was going to be some lucrative business. And I don't know why it's turned down, so I'm making statements and I don't figure anybody's going to do anything. I didn't ask Bob Cruz to kill him, and Arnie Merrill's lying when he says I did.'

"You have her word against Merrill's, and if you don't have a hell of a lot of corroboration, it doesn't fly."

Turoff continued, "After a while I got to know Cruz somewhat, and I feel that he may have . . . if she said, 'Geez, I'd like to see Pat Redmond taken care of.' And because of this business, wheels might have been generated in his own mind that 'I can get the business out of her.' And even though she was not serious, or may not have been serious, or there was no indication that she was serious, she might have been taken as serious. You know, if I (Cruz) take care of this thing, she's going to get some of the business and I'm going to get it from her. Or I can squeeze her out. Or I can squeeze her and her husband out. Or it might just be that I'll show up as a big man, that I can get a job done that she's indicated she wants done."

False Arrest

Reviewing the case, Turoff commented, "First she was convicted. There was a lot of things in the first trial that should not have gone in, a lot of prejudicial things that were kept out, that should have been kept out. I still don't understand why the judge allowed it in. But apparently he saw the error of his ways somewhere along the line.

"You have to go to court (against Joyce) because you do have people willing to testify about her involvement. But it's a weak case. Whether you get a conviction, it's up to the jury. It's probably something where once Wally Roberts came forward, we had some cooboration of Arnie Merrill. We weren't going solely on his (Merrill's) testimony. We just about had to (go to court). Rather than make the decision we're not going to do it, you go to court and see what happens. Let the jury decide."

Then he added, "If you didn't do anything, you might be subject to criticism."

When the trial began, Joyce had to face the seating of the jury. This was a complex process for everyone involved. For Joyce it was especially traumatic because this was the second time she'd endured it all.

First came the submission of written questions to the jury to try and weed out the most obviously unfit. The jurors would be present during questioning to determine who would stay and who wouldn't, so if somebody made a derogatory remark that could influence the others, all the jurors called would have to be released and a new group impaneled. As Thomas Thinnes commented:

"The worst thing in the world to do is to get seventy people in the courtroom and then the judge impanels twenty-four and has twelve more waiting back here and you ask the question to juror number six, 'Have you read about this case.' And juror number 6 says, 'Yeah, I read she's a guilty son-of-a-bitch,' and all seventy of them have to leave. So we submitted written interogatories, questions to the jurors so we could sort those."

A large selection of potential jurors was called, questionnaires submitted to them to get a sense of their attitudes and potential reactions. Joyce's lawyers wanted to know if potential jurors had read about the case; if they knew about the conviction. Knowledge of the conviction was seen as an important point because Thinnes had every intention of using that fact. He wanted to show that the reason Joyce was convicted was because she was "sold down the river." Then he planned to show the reasons why.

"We first went through the written and put plusses, minuses, graded them, put a scale on them of what you think," said Thinnes. "And, sure as hell, when you see the person and compare it with the written answer, you're like 180 degrees off in some cases. You think, boy, this bitch is going to be tough and it turns out to be a nice, elderly looking, clean cut woman you had pictured as some ogre."

Thinnes and his partner, unlike many other lawyers, do not work with professional jury selectors. They work from what they call their "gut" instinct. In order to do that, there were some warning signs of problems they tried to anticipate. "The red flags we looked for were some prior knowledge of the case, what they had read and what they had heard, and what conclusions they had formed.

"You come into court and I ask you, as a prospective juror, 'Have you read about this case?'

" 'Yes.'

" 'Have you formed any opinions from the articles you've read?'

" 'Not really. I only read the headlines or I only read the first paragraph,' which you know is bullshit.

"What I try to do, when I ask people about reading and forming opinions about the case, is to try to find a contemporary subject that has been in the same newspaper as this one. And the best example I can think of is when I had a trial in Tennessee. It was a front page article about my client being arrested for attempted murder, and he's shown shackled, being led into court by the popular sheriff in that community. Ask the jurors if they had read about the South Korean airline 007 that was shot down and what kind of opinion did you form after reading about that?

" 'Oh, those fucking Communists,' etcetera.

" 'Now also in that paper was an article about my client. You remember reading that, don't you?'

" 'Yes.'

" 'Now you formed an opinion that you felt pretty safe because this guy was in custody.' We get a lot more honest answers if you approach it from that direction. So what we were concerned about was people, not who had read about the case, or heard about it, or saw television about it. I'm concerned if a guy says, 'Look, I read about it. I heard about it on TV. And, by God, I'll try my hardest to disregard that crap and listen to the evidence and what comes out on the witness stand. I'll try my hardest.'

"I'll take that juror over any juror who says, 'I only read the headline. I didn't form an opinion. I don't listen to television. I don't listen to radio. I don't let anyone form my opinion, etcetera. So you kind of look at not only what they write, but how they answer some of these obvious questions.

"All we wanted was people who would presume she was innocent. That's how the questions were structured."

There was one handicap for both the prosecution and the defense. In Phoenix the judge asked the questions from a battery of questions submitted by the attorneys. The judge could ask some of them, all of them, or questions only of his or her own choosing. Thinnes tried to pose questions that might elicit some emotions when the jurors responded. The defense lawyers wanted to be able to feel that the jurors would give their client a fair trial, presuming Joyce innocent at the start, then listening closely to the evidence presented.

" 'You ask the question, as you sit here right now as a juror, would you be satisfied if you were sitting in the defendant's seat and the defendant was in your seat, would you be satisfied with the way you feel to have you as your juror?' Having read about the case, having formulated some opinions . . . I mean, obviously, if she's found guilty by one jury, there are people who have some pretty strong opinions and we're going to have to overcome that."

It was important for the defense to have the judge point out that fact, to caution the jurors to disregard the previous trial and the conclusions. They were going to have to divorce themselves from the past and limit themselves to listening to the evidence being brought in the courtroom. "And a number of the jurors would say, 'I will try my best.' That's all you can ask for.

"The guy who says, 'Hey, no problem. Shit, I don't care if the jury's found her guilty. This is a new ballgame . . .' It's the way they answer the questions. It's really feeling rather than words. All you want out of a juror is a fair shake."

The most obvious bias among jurors will result in their elimination "for cause" right at the start. Thinnes gave as an example a juror whose brother was convicted twice in courts. The juror hates cops and believes the system "sucks." Such an individual will be biased towards the defense right from the start, something the prosecutor will not tolerate.

"What I try to look for is somebody who has enough guts to stand up and give an honest answer, because what I am also looking for is a foreman, a potential foreman for that jury. And you want an individual who would probably lead rather than follow. The housewife who gives you name, rank and serial number, and says she has five kids, and doesn't answer any other question is somebody you know is going to be a follower. So if you have a fairly strong leader, I pick the foreman when I pick the jury.

"If I see a woman who is Irish and kind of gives you a side glance when you're giving answers, and grimaces, I don't want her because she isn't going to follow you. So you got to watch the byplay. You got to watch how they react during recess. Which of them pair up together. Which of them go to lunch together. You got to watch that. You got to watch the jury all the time because they're watching us."

The effort to "soften" Joyce's appearance was not good enough to make her seem the gentle housewife and mother. In addition, Thinnes did not feel that the evidence gave her that image. "She worked. She had her own business. She was at home in the evenings, making supper and that, but I think if we tried to portray her as a mighty domestic who was always at home with the kids and stuff like that, that was bullshit. We had to sell her as a business woman who was trying to maintain her own business, and keeping her financial affairs separate from her husband. And also raising a family.

"So we're looking for jurors—business people, women who are in business for themselves, or have ventured in the business world. . . .

"Joyce is tough for men to relate to. She's tough because I think some men find her challenging to them, which is something that we had to look out for." He was afraid that such men would find her guilty "just to put her in her place."

"We have not used . . . I haven't . . . a psychologist or any of these so called experts at picking juries. I think the best barometer you've got is your 'gut.'"

Joyce tried to remember everything Thinnes was telling her. She knew she should not try to make eye contact with the jurors and that she dare not get into a staring contest with them. "I was told to look away if I made contact with them," she explained.

She was also told to show emotions. She dared not hide her feelings.

During the second trial, Joyce was aware of what could happen to her, aware of the courtroom. She was terrified, but no longer in shock. There were no illusions left after nearly three years in jail. She knew that an innocent person could be sent to death row. She knew that she had everything to lose.

Things were different this time around. The court reporter, the bailiff, and several of the security guards were the same people as before, but this time their attitudes were different. They were friendly for the most part, supportive. Several of them talked with her briefly, wishing her luck, when the judge and jury were not in the room. When the trial took place, they remained neutral, never showing their feelings. They made certain that their attitudes could not be seen by the jury trying the case. However, when the courtroom was clear and a comment could be made, they expressed their support.

Marilyn Redmond came to the trial to watch the opening statements by the prosecution and the defense. It was unclear how she felt towards Joyce. She was not interviewed and did not attend the trial as an observer except at the very beginning and the very end. In between she had a friend sit in and watch.

Larry Turoff, the prosecutor, came on like an aggressive bulldog. He frequently used the trick made famous, first by Richard Nixon during his "kitchen debate" with Kruschev in Moscow and later by John Kennedy, where he would take his finger and point it accusingly at Joyce. The action is a subtle one, the person observing being given the subconscious impression that the prosecutor was in charge, knowing Joyce was guilty and determined to put her where she belongs. It is an action that immediately makes the other person seem weak and defensive, leaving the jury with the thought that the defendant must be guilty.

Thomas Thinnes was determined to show that Joyce had no motive for the crime, that others, especially Ron Lukezic, were the ones who had to be behind the murders. He wanted the jury to understand that Joyce had been railroaded into a jail sentence she did not deserve. If his approach worked, Turoff's image would change from that of someone filled with righteous indignation and a determination to see justice done, to that of someone attempting to railroad an innocent person into jail.

Joyce did not realize that Turoff had mixed feelings about prosecuting the case. He was not entirely convinced Joyce was guilty. If anything, he felt that she was either innocent or someone who knew what happened after the fact, not someone who was actively involved. He also hated the fact that he had to use the witnesses available. They were not credible, yet their statements were such that he was forced to try and build a case.

Joyce was frantic, "I was actively involved in my second trial. I had a big yellow steno pad and I would write notes when someone on the stand was lying. I'd put down that that was not what was happening, not what was said. I'd be writing furiously and Thomas would put his hand on my shoulder to try and calm me. 'Don't get so excited. Don't worry. I know. I know,' he'd whisper. 'I'll get them on the cross-examination.' It was comforting." It was also an action that the jury noticed, a physical closeness that gave the jury the impression that Thinnes was comfortable with his client.

There was great tension for Joyce, especially when she was on the witness stand. "I remember that I had a handkerchief I was holding and twisting the ends. I would twist them tighter and tighter until the whole thing could stand up on end."

Yet despite the tension, Joyce was not withdrawing into her shell as she had during the first trial. When she was on the witness stand, she would sometimes turn to the jury and make a comment before fully answering the prosecutor. She felt as though they were there with her, not strangers observing a play as had been her reaction at the start.

She also felt that Larry Turoff, the prosecutor, was going to send her to jail if possible. He would hang her with every trick he could use, regardless of his feelings. This made her frightened but wary. Thinnes had taught her not to answer a question instantly, to pause, to think, to be certain she had her facts straight instead of instantly blurting out anything that came to mind. This was especially helpful with Turoff who kept trying to twist her answers.

"He would ask me something like, 'Did you know so-and-so?' and I'd answer, 'Well, I saw him once.' Then he'd come back with, 'Then you knew him and you also saw him.' He twisted my words. I had to stop him and tell him that that was not what I had said."

There were small triumphs throughout the trial. Arnie Merrill had lied during the first trial, but Joyce had not remembered just how he had handled himself. This time she realized that he was looking straight at both the prosecutor and the defense lawyer when he gave his testimony. "I didn't know how he could do that: to lie looking someone in the eye, I mean. I never knew anyone like that.

"I made eye contact with that man purposely, hoping that as Thomas asked him a question he would look at me and maybe the truth would come out; maybe he wouldn't lie. You know everybody can lie. I cannot look at somebody's eye and not tell them the truth. I'll look away. I'll look . . . anything. I don't understand their capability. I just stared him down so many times, he would give me a dirty look. I did nothing but stare at that man. And I was so happy with Thomas for doing what he did to him. And I mean, he was crucifying him. If I had been lying like him, I don't think I could have taken it as well as this man took it from Thomas. Coming back with another lie and another lie and another lie . . .

"I was happy inside. Even from the position I was sitting in, I was pleased. He was such a slime, and Thomas showed him as a liar."

There were other triumphs as well. Cathy Fox had gained a tremendous amount of weight. She was a beautiful woman when Joyce first knew her and when she was in love with Joyce's brother, Arthur Ross. Her figure was excellent, her posture was straight, and she was the type of woman who made heads turn as she walked down the street. But since she first testified against Joyce, she had obviously changed dramatically. To Joyce she was a "blown-up balloon with no neck," no trace remaining of the beauty Joyce had seen in her.

"It made me feel good to know that she had suffered for her lies. She was free and I had been in jail. But she was paying a price for what she had done and it made me feel better to see it. I didn't dwell on it. I haven't thought about it since. But at the time, I felt good about it."

Yet Joyce was still horrified by how someone could lie in order to destroy another person's life. "It was as though these people were prompted to give the answers they did. I couldn't understand that. It wasn't a game. It wasn't charades. And it wasn't, 'Oh, after we're finished, we're all going to go home.' It was a deadly serious thing."

Despite her shock Joyce went on the offensive, reacting to what was taking place, making notes, alerting her attorney. The jury were responding favorably, something neither she nor her lawyer realized at the time.

Having read through the newspaper clippings on the case, and having seen the trial transcripts, Joyce realized that the witnesses who were lying seemed to be quoting from the old newspaper reports. It was as though they were parroting the speculations they had read and turned them into "facts" in order to attack Joyce. She could understand such a reaction from close friends of Pat Redmond, friends who were emotionally shattered by his loss. But not by people who should have been neutral, and thus able to tell the truth.

Despite the shock and the anger, Joyce felt less emotion than she expected she would. Thinnes had told her who the key witnesses against her would be. Merrill she knew and hated. Others, such as Wally Roberts, evoked no emotion. Roberts was so pathetic that he even admitted he did not know what was the truth and what was not. He was a man whose tremendously talented and promising life was over because of his addictions to drugs and alcohol. She had no feelings for or against him as he gave yet another discredited statement on the stand.

Thinnes decided to bring character witnesses for Joyce's defense, despite the danger of leaving the prosecution open to bring in hostile witnesses to her past. One of these was her aged uncle, a man who had made the trip from Sun City where he lived alone. He was close to ninety years old, partially disabled from a disease that affected his muscles and made him walk with difficulty. His life revolved around frequent trips to the race track where he enjoyed watching, only occasionally placing a $2 bet. He had known Joyce all her life and was the type of man who an observer instinctively knew would not lie. Everyone in the courtroom seemed to sense that if Joyce had done something wrong, and if he knew it, he would tell others that fact. He was incapable of deception, even to save a beloved family member.

The uncle spoke kindly of Joyce, making it clear that he felt it was impossible for her to have done the horrible acts of which she was accused. Then, when he finally left the witness stand, he started out of the courtroom, pausing only long enough to raise his hand and wave to her. It was a moment that was deeply emotional and, for the first time in public, Joyce lost control. She buried her head in her hands and wept for the love he had shown her. The tears were over quickly, pressed to the back of her emotions, but the jury had seen them, known they were genuine, and been moved by the testimony.

Eden's testimony also evoked a deep emotional response from Joyce. Eden had graduated from high school and was attending Arizona State University and working part time for a local department store. She had borne burdens that most adults could not handle and she had never complained. Joyce saw her as a child in a woman's body, and she knew the pressures were extremely difficult. Eden tried to be brave, yet looked terrified of being on the witness stand. Her hands moved constantly as she endlessly twisted and shredded the tissue she was holding. Joyce wanted to touch her, to hug her, to comfort her, but that was not possible until Eden's testimony was complete and there was no chance of her being recalled to the stand. After that, during the break, Joyce was allowed to hold her daughter for a few minutes while the judge and jury were out of the room. It was not much, but it was more than they had had, and to Joyce it meant everything.

There was an unusual mix of people in the courtroom. Some were regulars, elderly individuals and couples who watched trials as their daily entertainment. They were retired and enjoyed seeing the living drama that courtrooms allowed.

Others who had never seen a trial before were rather uncomfortable. Two different classes of what appeared to be high school students attended a few hours of the trial. They were apparently in an American Government or similar civics course. Visiting the murder trial was a way for them to see the justice system in action. They appeared to have been briefed concerning what was taking place, but their visit shocked Joyce.

Part of her concern was the nature of the trial. There was sex, violence, and greed all being discussed. Perhaps it was no worse than many of the shows on television, yet it seemed a rather harsh way to learn about life.

The other concern was more personal. "They were just babies and they were all staring at me. I kept wondering what they were thinking about me. I felt very uncomfortable with them."

There was little new that came out in the trial except for information that had not before been available. Nine months earlier, in September of 1984, Marilyn Redmond had made a deposition against Ron that could now be used in the case. She brought out alleged crimes Ron had commited. One of the questions Marilyn had been asked was:

"Now, you've talked about over the twenty years you've known Ron Lukezic, while you mentioned something about stealing from the company and padding customers' accounts. Would you tell me what you meant by that?"

And Marilyn had answered:

"Bill Nicholson, from Rocky Mountain Bank Note, told Pat that Ron had padded his account. The last couple of years Pat was alive Bill Nicholson dealt with Pat only. Bill Arliskas, who owned Able Carton & Die, had a problem with Ron owing him several hundred dollars, and he did not pay that." Then she stressed that this was during a period when the company was solvent and there were no financial problems that might prevent the payment.

Later in her testimony, Marilyn was asked, "To your knowledge, have any criminal charges ever been filed against Ron Lukezic regarding the incident in question (the murders)?"

"No."

"Have you ever sought to have any criminal charges filed against him?"

"Yes."

"When did you first do that?"

"As soon as I was able to talk after the incident."

"And at that time you felt, in your own mind, that Ron was at least partially responsible for the incident?"

"Yes."

A little later she added, talking about Ron:

"Then he came to the funeral with a shoulder holster and a gun because he was afraid and cried on half a dozen people's shoulders, 'Oh, my God, what did I do?' And they're all afraid to testify because we've asked several of them. They're not in the criminal proceedings at this point (September 17, 1984).

"He knew the minute it happened what happened and why. And everybody in town knew it."

It was unclear by her statement whether or not she thought Joyce was guilty, though she commented, "His wife is being convicted. How could you live in the same household and not know your wife is planning to have your business partner murdered? It would have been a lot easier if I hadn't lived for all concerned, wouldn't it."

There were also statements by Arnie Merrill, both during his trial and the trial of the killers, which were contradictory. Over the time that had elapsed since Joyce's first trial, additional testimony had added to the weight of her innocence.

Yet Joyce had lost before. Though the defense styles were different and Thinnes felt himself to be a far superior courtroom attorney than Larry Debus, everyone realized that there could be no certainty about how the case would resolve itself. Many of the people testifying seemed more sympathetic to Joyce. It was as though, in Joyce's mind, people were trying to word their statements in a totally objective way. They seemed to understand what had happened to her and the penalty she faced. They wanted to be certain that the facts presented were accurate and would not mislead the jury.

Joyce felt the judge, Rudolph Gerber, was the "most uncaring, biased, working for the prosecution only judge that God ever created." But she was also reacting to remarks her lawyer made under his breath when rulings went against him. She had no idea whether Thomas was frustrated in not gaining what he wanted or had genuine concerns about prejudice against her.

Finally it was time for the closing arguments. "Again I felt I was in a theater. Marilyn Redmond came in and took a seat in the front row with her friend. Then Larry Turoff began walking back and forth, talking about how vicious I was, how cold blooded. He kept coming over and pointing his finger at me, and I hated it."

The way the court system works, the prosecutor speaks first, presenting the reasons for the defendant to be found guilty. Then the defense attorney makes his statement. Finally the prosecutor has a chance to make a few more remarks in rebuttal.

Thinnes talked for several hours, as had Turoff. He discussed the motive in the case, stressing that Joyce had no reason to have Patrick Redmond killed, that Ron Lukezic, alone, could and did profit from the death. He showed that Joyce could not inherit the business from Ron even if Ron also should be killed. He stressed the obvious illogic of even charging Joyce with a crime since there was no reason why she would consider such violence.

Gradually Thinnes either became tired or he used the idea of exhaustion as a way of influencing the jury with his arguments. He explained that he was afraid to leave the floor. He was afraid to sit down. He stressed the fact that he knew that Joyce was innocent, that he recognized that this was his last chance to show the jury the truth of that knowledge, and he was afraid that he was not going to be adequate. They had to know. They had to understand. He could not fail the innocent woman they saw before them.

"It was a brilliant performance, whether what he said about being so exhausted was true or the result of carefully planned strategy. He gave the jury the impression that he cared about me, that I wasn't an evil person he could not touch. It was an image that, had Larry Debus been the type of defense attorney to work the same way, might have gained me my freedom after the first trial. Yet none of us knew if it would be enough.

"Waiting for the jury to make its deliberations was a nightmare. I was exhausted as it was. Trial was conducted four days a week, the fifth day left for the preparation work the lawyers needed to handle each week.

"In order for me to be ready for the van that transfered me from Durango to the court house, I had to get up at 2:30. Then I could wash, fix my hair, and get prepared for the early trip. Another hour would have to be spent putting on the clothing and make-up in the ante-room before the trial. By the time the judge dismissed everyone for the day, I had been up twelve hours. Yet my day wasn't ended. Vans went from the court house to Durango on a very specific schedule. A court case that ran a little longer than normal, and that happened with some frequency during my trial, resulted in my missing the bus. This meant being kept in a holding area until it was convenient to return me to the jail, something that might not occur until 11 o'clock at night. It was not unusual for me to have to function on just three hours' sleep, only a flow of adrenaline getting me through the day.

"The medical staff was frightened by what might happen to me with the pace I was forced to live. They did nothing to ease my travel problems, but they loaded me with medication for my heart, my skyrocketing blood pressure, and my nerves. I had medicine ranging from tranquilizers to tablets to take in the event of an angina attack.

"I had no rest except on weekends when I would collapse, sleeping as much as possible between meal times.

"The waiting period was a tense one. I was able to obtain a copy of George Orwell's novel, *1984,* which I had missed reading in high school. The book fascinated me and helped pass the time.

"Thomas could not handle the situation quite so calmly. He constantly paced the floor when he was with me. He also told me that the longer the jury is out, the better it is for the defendant. A jury that comes back almost immediately usually finds the defendant guilty.

"What Thomas didn't say was that something was wrong. The members of the jury were arguing loudly in the room reserved for their deliberations. The sounds carried into the hall and through the judge's chambers. We could hear them even in the courtroom, though we could not tell what they were saying. They also asked for clarification regarding the case and to see several documents.

"Finally we realized that we were facing a possible hung jury. Too many days were passing; the arguments were too intense. We felt it was eleven to one against me. We believed we had touched someone's heart. We had made one person believe I was innocent. If that person held out, there would be a hung jury and a new trial. If that person caved in to the pressure of the others, it would be twelve against me and I would be sentenced to the gas chamber.

"I was terrified. I felt fate was in the hands of one man or woman, someone whom I did not know, had never seen before the start of the trial. I had thought that the case was presented better this time around. Certainly my appearance was better and the interaction with the attorneys must have accounted for something. I would have to live with the fact that Arnie Merrill had been believed. I would have to . . .

"And then it was over. It was a hung jury and the judge had to declare a mistrial. But the hung jury was not what it seemed. It had been a ten to two decision with the ten members refusing to yield in their belief that I was innocent.

"Innocent? They believed in my innocence? Ten jurors wanted me to go free, to end my nightmare?

"I was joyous. I was facing another trial. I was not safe from the gas chamber. But ten people, the majority of the jurors, believed me, believed in me.

"There was more good news. Thomas talked with the jurors, learning more about the hold-outs. One was an older woman, embittered by a divorce and apparently the victim of a husband who threw her over for someone else. For some reason she had become convinced that Ron and I were in all this together. We had made an elaborate scheme where the Redmonds would be murdered, we would get the money, then go off together and live happily ever after. In her fantasy, I was going to join Ron wherever he was hiding, then we would live the good life on blood money.

"It was an irrational belief with no connection to the evidence presented by either side, yet she was unshakable. The second hold-out was a young man barely out of high school. Either he was weak, wanted to support her out of respect for his elders, or truly believed in my guilt. I may never know which is true. All that is certain is that he voted with her, the two acting against all the others.

Later Thomas was talking about going before the judge to gain my release on bond. He was certain that with the jury that much in favor of me, and with the new trial likely to take place that fall, I could leave the jail that had been my home for more than two years and nine months. But that did not matter at the moment. The adrenaline that had sustained me was gone. The stress that had threatened my heart in the past resulted in complete exhaustion. For the first time in weeks I could relax, and when I did, I could think of nothing but bed. The van took me back to Durango where I could express neither joy nor sadness. I collapsed on the bunk, sleeping almost around the clock. I knew Thomas was working to get me out. I knew there was a chance I finally might be back with my family. Yet at that moment all I could do was stretch out on my bunk and sleep."

PART FOUR

FREEDOM

Chapter 16

THE FINAL ORDEAL

Thomas Thinnes was upset with the jury's being dead-locked, but optimistic about Joyce's release. He explained to her that he thought he could get her released on an "O.R. bond"—own recognizance. She would pay no money, post no bond. She would sign a paper guarantee-ing to appear in court when a new trial began. She would be responsible for herself, a trust she had not been given in the past. The closeness of the decision was such that he felt a judge would release her based on her promise to appear for trial.

At first Joyce did not understand. She had not been found innocent. She had been returned to jail. Life was continuing as usual.

Then, gradually, she realized what her attorney was telling her. She might be able *to go home.* The fact that she had not been found guilty, the fact that the jury voted ten-to-two for acquittal, all of these things could result in the judge releasing her pending a third trial.

Home.

To Joyce it was a house that no longer belonged to her, children who were no longer children. She remem-bered where she had been living when she left the Madi-son Street jail and she relived that experience in her mind.

She would go to that house, go to the kitchen, sit on the chair, and wait for her children to come racing home from school. Her older son and daughter were in high school, her younger son in junior high. All of them were little, rushing to her, vying to see who would sit on her lap, all of them being embraced by her.

They would kiss and laugh and hug each other. They would share a meal, perhaps talking into the night. They would show her their school work. She would help them with their studies. They would be a family again, Joyce and her three babies, all sitting in the kitchen.

Hour after hour she lived the fantasy. Thinnes alerted her that there would be a hearing in another day or two. There was a good chance that the forty-eight hours following her second trial would be the last she would have to spend in jail. There was a chance that she would be allowed to walk the streets, a free woman, until the matter could be decided once and for all during the third trial.

"I was so high, my feet never touched the ground," said Joyce. "As low as I had fallen when I was suicidal and in jail, that's how high I became when I knew I might get out. I think had the judge not released me, I would have killed myself."

But the judge did release Joyce. It was a simple decision based on the presumption of innocence as a result of the hung jury. She put up no bail. She simply promised to appear for the third trial.

"I was driven back to the jail without handcuffs, without restraints of any kind. The detention officers took me in their private car, Mary Durand traveling behind in her own vehicle.

"They brought me in the back door. Then they got a stack of clothes, whatever clothes I had come in with three years ago. They handed me this plastic bag and they went to get my personal property. And they brought me back to the building I had been housed in, with the bag in my hand.

"The clothing all fit. It was loose. It was also stiff. It stunk. It was disgusting, but I was free."

Joyce was wearing a slightly flared pair of Levi's and her son Eric's Brophy Bronco Football T-shirt from his high school. She also was wearing Sheriff's Department underpants and a bra, both of which she burned the moment she returned home because the under garments had been marked as property of Maricopa County. Although she remembered Eric as being little, the T-shirt went down to just above her knees. The clothing had been held without airing for two years, nine months, and seventeen days.

"I went back into the pod to my room. I think I was the only inmate ever to be allowed into her old room wearing street clothes. I mean, who knows what I might have been smuggling.

"The other inmates were crying. They had been watching the news about my trial. They were rooting for me the whole time.

"I was trying to put my things together. All I wanted was my pictures and my letters. Everything I had saved, that I had treasured, that meant so much, I gave away. Pens, stationary, commisary, I gave away to whoever needed what.

"I hugged. I kissed. I cried. I told lots of people, 'Don't worry.' I mothered who I could before I left. And just the tears rolled down. Just the tears rolled down so . . . I think I became the humblest person in the world that day.

"When I got to go outside, inmates from all four pods went to their windows. The women were pounding on the glass, applauding, each with a clenched fist raised in the air, a salute of triumph.

"I was crying. I was smiling. I wished them all luck."

And then there were the reporters. They were a sea of faces, overwhelming. Microphones and small cassette recorders were pushed towards Joyce. There were harsh lights, apparently from the television cameras, and the whir, click, whir, click of motor driven still equipment recording her every move for the next day's newspapers. Voices called to her. "How do you feel, Joyce?" "What's it like to be going home, Joyce?" "Are you happy, Joyce?" "Over here, Joyce?" "Look at the camera, Joyce."

Mary Durand moved in front of Joyce, holding her arm, guiding her through the mass of reporters. Joyce was barefoot, tears streaming down her face, in shock, overwhelmed by so many people, by freedom, by the fact that she was going home. She said nothing to the press, could say nothing. She let Mary lead her to a car, grateful to see the door lock, hear the engine begin moving her away from Durango.

At first Joyce just enjoyed the sunshine, the fresh air, the sky as Mary drove her away from Durango. Then she realized that this was the first time in almost three years that she had been able to look out a window that did not have bars on it. There was nothing to obstruct her view. Everything was fresh, alive, free. She looked at cars, at people, at traffic lights, buildings, grass. "I kept swiveling in my seat, turning constantly from side to side.

" 'Do you like music, Joyce?' Mary Durand asked me as we were driving.

" 'Yes,' I told her.

" 'Then turn on the radio.'

" 'Can I?' I asked, surprised. And Mary cracked up.

" 'What are you asking me for? You're not in jail anymore.'

"Hesitantly I touched the control knobs. I was afraid to do something I shouldn't do."

Mary explained that they were going to see Eric first. Jason was in Massachusetts with his father and Eden was working, unable to come home for a few hours. But Eric had been living with some friends and would be expecting her.

"I couldn't have eaten if I wanted to. I couldn't have gone to the bathroom if I needed to. My nerves were in a tight ball."

Ironically, Eric was staying with a couple with whom Mary Durand had been friendly long before she knew of Joyce. They were both on their second marriage, each having a child by the previous relationship. They had learned to love each other's children and simply made Eric their third son. They reached out to him constantly, understanding his anger, his fears, his frustration, working with him any way they could. They helped him with his homework, talked with him about dating, and tried to do the same type of parenting they were doing for their own children. He was withdrawn, angry, yet they accepted that fact, reaching out to him constantly, yet letting him set the boundaries for their interaction.

Eric had been told to expect his mother. The couple who had taken him into their home waited outside with their two sons, but Eric was nowhere to be seen when Mary and Joyce arrived at the house.

"I was afraid to get out of the car. I was afraid to go in. I couldn't understand why he wasn't outside when everyone else was."

The couple with whom Eric was living told Joyce that he was waiting for her in his room and she should go into the house.

"The door was closed and I go inside. There was my son, this big, huge whatever, lying across the bed, reading a magazine. I opened the door. I looked at him. I closed the door and I said, 'Hi. What's new?'

"I said, 'So what are we reading? Do you have homework?' I tried to keep talking but I didn't know what to say. We tried to carry on a conversation.

Neither could touch the other. They spoke in inanities, somehow talking, saying nothing, desperate to reach out, yet each afraid of rejection. Then, quietly, they touched, holding one another. "I really didn't think you were coming home," said Eric, his voice a frightened child in the body of what seemed to have become a man overnight. Joyce could not yet face the fact that they had been apart almost three years.

"And we talked . . . oh . . . for another two hours. We talked about school, if he was dating. We talked about things like you'd talk to a distant cousin. I kept telling him how much I missed him and how much I loved him. I kept saying, 'Eric, look at me. Eric, talk to me. Eric, I'm here, what can I help you with?

"I just rambled. I didn't know what to say. I just kept rubbing his head, playing with his arms. He was so big. I think I rambled for about three hours before I could get him to give back. Never I love you, but a smile, yes. And a hug and a giggle.

"He giggled. And you know how it's like a nervous giggle?

"When I got done, he told me he would come over where Eden was staying later. And he walked me to the door of his room and gave me a big hug and a kiss. But he still wouldn't come out . . ."

The couple with whom Eric had been staying walked Joyce to the front door and said, "Don't worry. He's going to be okay. Just give him some time."

"During that time Eden had been called and was waiting for me at the house of a former neighbor with whom she had been living.

Mary Durand drove Joyce to Hayward Avenue, past the house where she had once lived, to the home where Eden was staying. Eden came rushing out to see her mother, a big smile on her face. They hugged. They kissed. Then Eden grabbed as many bags as she could and took them inside. Mother and daughter would be staying together in the home until such time as Joyce could get an apartment.

"It was dinner time, and Eden said, 'Okay, Mom, if you could get anything in the world you wanted to eat, what would it be?' And I wanted a tuna fish sandwich. I had been craving tuna."

Eden made the sandwich while her boyfriend at the time, a youth named Art, went to McDonald's to get burgers and fries for the two of them. "We talked like I had been on vacation and come back and she had clothes to show me or a letter she had gotten. We talked half the night."

Eric joined them as he promised, the three of them talking. But Eric returned to where he was living, seemingly pleased that Joyce had come to see him first, yet not ready to change his circumstances. Then, alone with Eden, Joyce discovered that freedom could be as terrifying in its own way as living in jail had been.

For almost three years Joyce had slept in the light. There were routines that had to be followed, bed checks made. Darkness was something Joyce had forgotten, and the desert region where she and Eden were living could be almost black at night. Even worse, Eden had closed the door to the bedroom they were sharing, making Joyce feel trapped and disoriented.

Eventually Joyce turned on the bathroom light and opened the door in order to feel comfortable enough to get some rest. Yet sleep remained uneasy. The sounds of the house were terrifying for her. They were different than the sounds to which she had become accustomed in the jail. In jail, a change in sound from the routine means that someone is coming to give you a beating, to rape you, to murder you. Joyce had learned to react to the abnormal as a means of survival. But suddenly the abnormal was the normal, a fact that could not help her stop the adrenaline rushes that caused her to frequently awaken, staring around the room, seeing if she would have to defend herself.

"I remember when the phone rang and startled the hell out of me.

"Eden and I stayed in the house. Maybe it was a week before I could go out. I didn't want to go out. I was afraid to go out. Everything was too much. I felt like everything was closing in on me.

"The trees were so close. There was so much traffic. Even in the streets, there were kids or the dogs running around. There was so much going on. It was so busy. I was very, very, very uncomfortable.

"I remember the first time—maybe it was six or seven days later—that Eden and I went grocery shopping. I was paranoid because I had been on TV and I really didn't want anyone to see me, so I wore glasses. And then there's the grocery aisles . . . I got nauseous and I thought everything was going to cave in on me, and I made Eden take me home."

There were too many people and they all made her nervous. There was constant movement and she could not determine where to focus her attention. Everything had been controlled in prison, familiar. The life had been hell, but it was one to which she had adjusted. She was frightened by the fact that a world in which she had lived all her life could no longer be handled without becoming nauseated—like someone's getting airsick.

"I was terrified the phone would ring and everyone would say, 'Ha, Ha. It was all a mistake. The game's over and you've got to come back.'

After a week of rest, I told Eden I had to start going over to Thomas' office to prepare for the third trial.

"The first thing Eden asked was, 'Can you drive?' I nodded, but said embarassedly, "But I no longer have a valid license." She told me I had to go and get one right away.

"We drove down to the Bureau of Motor Vehicles where I applied for my license. And they were so nice. They gave me a temporary. They all knew who I was. They wished me luck. They took my picture. And I went home.

"The next morning I got into Eden's car. I wanted to take a drive by myself. Dawn was just breaking. There was no traffic. I drove around the streets for what was a good hour, then I drove towards Prescott; afterwards I drove to a place that was just woods." The location was in the mountain country of Arizona. Joyce pulled the car off the road, parking it amidst tall sheltering pine trees. It was an area she had visited in her mind thousands of times during the relaxing exercises the psychiatrist had taught her. Only now it was real.

Stepping outside, she walked to a spot where she could sit on the ground and look towards Phoenix, miles in the distance. She listened to the birds, smelled the grass, felt the earth beneath her fingers. She wanted to be alone, needed to be alone.

As a young girl, Joyce used to drive for miles as a way of trying to think. She was not certain if she had returned to those times, those feelings, or if she just needed to be and feel free. For the first time in three years, she was at peace.

Taking trips became easier once she could drive herself. Her fear of strange places remained, but routine seemed easier. Always she wore sunglasses to reduce the chance of being recognized, yet her story had been so frequently in the newspapers and on television that strangers often spoke to her by name.

Surprisingly, most people were friendly. Only once, when she and her attorneys were asked to go on a local radio show, did she experience real hate. "You got off because you're a rich bitch who can afford those top attorneys," one caller declared. "And there were others who insisted I bought my way to a freedom I didn't deserve. But those were the exceptions. I was scared all the time, but almost everyone was decent."

Joyce sensed major changes in herself, though she did not realize to what a degree at first. Some of the experiences were normal, such as the delight of realizing that she no longer had to stand at attention by her door once an hour so the guards could check to see she was still there. Others were more surprising.

"The most special, special, special thing is opening the refrigerator and seeing all kinds of food in there. If I wanted something, I knew I could have it.

"I listened to the birds. That was special to me.

"I went out to the pool. That was special to me.

"I looked up at the sun. That was special to me.

"They were just non-expensive, free things that any person can do and not think anything of it.

"Before I went to jail, if there was food on the table, I didn't think twice about it. There simply was food on the table. If I had to go out some place, I could go. If I woke up in the morning and the sun was out, it was like every other day. And now nothing has ever been the same. I have never felt the same as before I went to jail.

"I know that, like people behind the Iron Curtain, my freedom, my rights can be taken away. For the longest time, I thought it was the greatest thing in the world to go to the laundromat to do clothes. Joyce, who always had a maid and a washer and dryer. It was so wonderful. It was so special for me. They were my own clothes and I didn't have to wash them in the sink.

"Just the ability to pick and choose was exhilarating."

Sometimes freedom was overwhelming. Joyce could not go into a supermarket alone. She needed someone to help her. Not only was there a seemingly endless array of food, there were different brands of the same product. She didn't know which to choose, which would taste better. Or whether she should take one of everything, to sample all the tastes, to experience the freedom of more choices than she had remembered possible.

Sleep became easier with each passing day, but it was troubled. She would sleep restlessly. She would talk in her sleep. She would dream constantly, though, fortunately, she did not remember the nightmares.

Eventually Joyce moved with her two children into a small apartment. It was in a rural area of Phoenix, trees and grass planted all around, a Dairy Queen within walking distance. She could still afford some of the comforts she had once taken for granted. She had not turned over all her property to her attorneys as yet. That would come with the third trial. So she had an income from the New York holdings that enabled her to have her own place, a home she finally could again share with Eden and Eric— though Eric stayed there only when he was between apartments of his own. He was still adjusting to the chaotic changes in his family's life. He was talking more, touching and accepting touch, but he was only fully comfortable living on his own. He had a job, was going to school, was twenty years old, having survived without others since he was in his mid-teens.

Joyce and Eden got two kittens and brought them home. One was a stray and the other was obtained from the humane society. Joyce felt a kinship and a need satisfied by her contact with the animals. She began going to the humane society and the pound on a regular basis, an action she has continued to the present, in order to pet the animals, love them. "They're so poor and desperate. They need love. They need this. They need that. I just go and play with whatever."

"The most boring things for someone else now gave me pleasure, such as going for a ride, going to Luke Air Force Base. One day I went with Eden to Sun City and picked grapes. I picked twenty-one pounds of grapes. I felt like a little wine maker. I froze some. I gave some to whoever I could.

"Near the grape vines there were a lot of cows. I parked the car and walked through the pasture with Eden. That's the kind of things that were really meaningful."

Despite the pleasure, there was the painful need to prepare for the third trial. Joyce had to go regularly to Thomas Thinnes' office to plan for the strategy. He was concerned that she was still holding in too much emotion. He wanted her to stop acting as though she was afraid someone would condemn her if she was caught crying or reacting in anger. He arranged to have her talk with a psychiatrist, but she stopped seeing him after five sessions. Instead of guiding her through her feelings, he was the type who listened to her, came to conclusions about why she behaved the way she did, then presented her with an analysis of who she was and why she was acting the way she did.

"I needed to be able to talk out a lot of things, so maybe it was the man, the doctor, I didn't feel comfortable with. I didn't feel he could help me.

"I was very dependent. When anyone asked me to do something, I was very obedient. When they asked me to do something, I did it."

Fortunately Joyce's neighbor and friend, the woman who had been caring for Eden, was always available to her. They were comfortable together, talking about the normal problems of daily life. It was a natural relationship. The fact that she had been in jail did not matter, nor was it the focus of their talks unless Joyce brought up the subject.

Eden also spent time talking with her mother. She needed to know about Joyce's experiences. There were incidents when Eden had visited the jail and seen that her mother was bruised, yet Joyce had acted as though nothing occurred. There were times when Joyce had been demanding, treating Eden like her personal slave, seemingly trying to make her daughter feel guilty unless she did Joyce's bidding. All of these had to be discussed. Eden needed to know what Joyce had endured and Joyce had to understand the unrealistic pressures she had placed on her daughter. Together they relived the jail experience, Joyce coming to grips with her emotions and Eden gaining a more meaningful relationship with her mother.

While Joyce was discovering and savoring her freedom, she had no idea how concerned her lawyer was about the third trial.

He felt one of the reasons Joyce went to jail after her first trial was because of her seeming lack of emotional involvement. She had thought of the experience like a television drama. She and the jurors were the audience of a Perry Mason courtroom special. She felt they somehow knew who was lying and who was telling the truth. They were amazed at the attempts to mislead. Or so she thought. Only later had she come to understand that she was not a viewer, but a participant. No one shared her knowledge of the truth, and the person who told the best lies won.

The atmosphere of a murder trial is not that far from what Joyce mistakenly believed during that first experience. A courtroom is a theater, a fact recognized in England where not every lawyer is able to make an appearance before a jury. There they divide attorneys between barristers and solicitors. The barristers are the actors, the individuals who are both skilled in the law and have a sense of the theatrical. They know they are putting on a show and they hone their acting skills to the fullest.

The United States does not make that distinction, which is the reason many lawyers are excellent when advising clients but cannot win cases before a jury. The best trial lawyers recognize the need for having as much acting ability as legal knowledge if they are to set foot in a court-room. One criminal defense attorney in Maryland will do anything from "accidentally" dropping a law book when an opponent is making a telling point, to "goosing" his unresponsive clients; so the jury thinks the suspect is upset about what is being said in court.

Thomas Thinnes was well aware of the show business aspect of the legal system and, like any good performer, worked hard at preparing his presentation. He needed to be able to register shock, surprise, anger, frustration, and dozens of other emotions in response to the answers elic-ited from witnesses. He also needed to be able to remem-ber exactly what each witness said in order to use their words against them or to use those words to benefit his client.

It was easy for Thinnes to prepare for an initial trial. Bright, articulate, a skilled strategist, he had no trouble handling a case the first time. Sometimes his emotions were genuine. Other times he was reacting in a way that might influence the jury in favor of his client. He was al-ways able to concentrate on everything that was taking place, making notes, remembering, constantly shifting among the bits and pieces of testimony he was hearing day after day in order to present the best possible case.

A mistrial changed everything. A mistrial meant that the same evidence, the same witnesses, the same case had to be presented a second time. Maybe the strategy would be a little different. Maybe something seemingly unimpor-tant the first time would take on extra significance the sec-ond time around. There could be a surprise or two, though it was doubtful. Usually the second trial is identical to the first, and there is the problem.

Lawyers get tired. It is difficult to force the same en-thusiasm when having to discuss again the same facts about the same individuals. Even worse, it is hard to remember what was said during the testimony of a witness who had been questioned before. Are the facts ones that were introduced the previous week or the previous trial? If they were mentioned in the previous trial, the current jury will not be familiar with a key item of evidence. Thus there is a greater than usual need to concentrate on the testimony.

Thinnes was not comfortable with what he was facing. He had come close to winning the previous trial, ten of the jurors seeing the facts the way he felt they existed. The new trial would be more difficult. He had doubts about whether or not he could do better. He did not want to see Joyce return to jail because he was not skilled enough to present the facts in a way the jury could understand and accept.

Like Thinnes, Joyce was exhausted by the end of the summer. She realized as the new trial approached that she had been free in name only.

What if the judge had second thoughts? What if Dan Ryan had influence in ways that would result in her being sent back to jail? It would be legal to cancel the release arrangement and force her to stay behind bars until the trial was over.

Joyce could never relax. She would look searchingly at faces wherever she was, to see if anyone was a police officer coming to take her back to jail. She kept glancing in the rear view mirror of her car to see if anyone was following her. She slowed her car as she approached the driveway of her apartment to see if there were men and women lurking about, ready to arrest her.

There were also the press and the public. There were people who were sympathetic. There were people who ignored the trial, who did not even remember her after seeing her face on the evening news, in the Arizona Republic or the Phoenix Gazette. But there were people who thought she was still a rich bitch who had beaten the system with the best lawyer money could buy. Such people hated her, wanted to spit on her, see her hurt. There could be a crazy among them, someone who would do her physical harm if given a chance.

Apprehension filled her, drained her. She had been released on her own recognizance. There was no bail money. Her remaining property had not been confiscated pending the forthcoming trial. There were no holds on her so strong that she might not run.

After several weeks of freedom, Joyce had grown accustomed to her bedroom, to her own kitchen, refrigerator, toilet. She could sleep in the dark. She no longer jerked awake at the slightest sound, desperate to protect herself from a rape or beating. The survival instincts she had honed in jail dissipated as she adjusted.

Yet jail was always in the back of her mind. And, if she lost in court, prison, probably death row and a solitary wait for the gas chamber.

The sessions with Thomas Thinnes went well. She was impressed with the depth of his research. He focused on the key witnesses against her—Wally Roberts, Arnie Merrill, Cathy Fox, Sandy Perez—and felt he could expose their stories as being lies, half-truths, and innuendoes presented as fact. He had been studying the other trials related to the case as well since all of them were interrelated and there was always a chance that a witness in one of them would change his or her story when testifying in another.

Thinnes had cross referenced everything that was taking place, organizing all the depositions, exhibits, and statements from previous trials in cardboard file boxes. He would bring the boxes into court, selecting those containing the testimony of the witnesses who would be on the stand that day.

To Joyce the actions all seemed reassuring. Everyone seemed to have the trial under control.

But then, she remembered, they did before. They did when Larry Debus said that if she had to serve a day in jail, he would do the time for her. But she had gone to jail alone. Larry Debus had deserted her. And Thinnes could desert her as well. And she might have to go back to jail, possibly forever. She couldn't stand it happening to her again. Quickly in her mind she began to formulate plans.

She had to run. It was the only answer. She spoke Spanish, not fluently but enough to get by in Mexico. Later she could fully master the language.

Not that she looked Hispanic. Still, she was dark and, with the right clothing, the Spanish, a change in hair style . . . She could pass. She could get across the border.

She tried to get hold of herself, to stop her fantasies. Nobody hid out in Mexico, anyway. That was television. The land was too poor, the rural areas too hard for a stranger to penetrate unless the person talked Spanish. Even then, a new person entering a village was always suspect. In some communities they would be seen as an unwelcome drug dealer trying to corrupt the young. In other communities, where drugs were the major source of income, the stranger would be seen as a rival, someone who was trying to muscle in on the wrong territory. Either way they were likely to be killed.

Another fantasy cropped up. But not a woman. Women weren't involved with drug trafficking. Women weren't a threat. The police didn't look out for women except for a little sexual pleasure at the end of a working day.

And became more intense. She could go into Mexico without arousing suspicion. She could slip over the border, go to a rural area, live her remaining years in peace.

There was a woman Joyce knew, a domestic who had worked for her and others over the years. The woman knew how to smuggle people. She knew how to get them across the border so they could work in the United States without a green card. If she could take someone into this country without being stopped, how much easier it would be to take someone out of the country!

She knew the woman would be agreeable. Joyce would pack a few clothes in plastic bags. She would take only essentials. She would dress in a manner that would blend with the other women, a scarf on her head casting additional shadows to further darken the appearance of her skin. Then they would drive across the border, Hispanic women acting as driver and additional passengers.

Perhaps Joyce would be asked nothing. Perhaps she would have to speak and use her fluent Spanish. Or, if her accent might be noticed too easily, she would be a deaf mute, the tragic result of a family in poverty unable to gain proper medical care when she was a baby. So sad, the others would tell the border patrol. Such a tragedy, they would stress in Spanish. Such is life. The lack of speech and hearing were Joyce's cross to bear. The care of their beloved sister, so helpless, so lonely, would be their burden.

There would be words of sympathy, a nod of understanding, a friendly wave across the border.

And then freedom. Nobody would pursue her in Mexico. Nobody would threaten her ever again. She would live a quiet life, surviving as best she could. Without bars. Without fear. *Without her children . . .*

The fantasy faded. Eden was almost a woman. She might marry. She had been having a serious relationship with one young man. She was nearly twenty, a time for marriage, for having children of her own.

A mother belonged in the hospital with her daughter at the time of giving birth. A woman who has a baby should be present when that baby bears a child of her own. Yet Joyce would be in Mexico.

Back and forth her thoughts ran. Eden could visit. Jason. Eric. They all could come. It would not be far. One hundred or so miles to Tucson. Another sixty or seventy miles to the border. Wherever she stayed in Mexico would be within an easy day's travel for the family.

They might be followed to the border, of course. Their licenses might be noted. The Mexican police alerted.

But probably there would be no cooperation. The United States' relations with Mexico were strained at best.

There was also bias against the Mexicans by the American law enforcement organizations. They saw Mexico as corrupt, uncaring, unwilling to work on joint legal problems. Usually they were only concerned with establishing relations for major concerns—mass murder, gangs that preyed on the innocent on both sides of the border, major drug traffickers who had not paid off the police. A woman wanted for conspiracy, even one facing the gas chamber in Arizona, would not be seen as a priority for anyone. And, after a while, she would be forgotten entirely by the Mexican authorities.

The only question was timing. She did not want to flee before her trial. She did not want to be seen as admitting to guilt. She would attend the trial, witness the proceedings, then leave just before the verdict was announced. So long as she was free to come and go to the court house this time, there would be no effort to remove her to jail until the jury returned. Then, if she was found guilty, she would be immediately handcuffed and taken from the room to the waiting van.

Until then she was safe. Until then she could hold her children in the comfort of their home. She would talk with them, explain her decision, make all the arrangements, pack her bag. But she would not flee. She would have her day in court, knowing that the truth would not come out, yet hoping she might sway just one more person.

The jury selection went as before, though this time Joyce paid more attention to the men and women who would be determining whether the state decided she should live or die. There was one young man whose father was a police officer in the midwest. He explained that he was for the "good guys," and Joyce became frightened. Larry Turoff, the prosecutor, was delighted with the comment, determined to have him on the jury. Thomas Thinnes and his partner were split as to whether or not his attitude was a good one or a bad one to go against. Joyce was certain he would be pro-police, regardless of the facts. She knew she dared not have him, then was frightened when he was allowed to stay.

Another man also terrified her. He looked similar to her husband, Ron—only more sinister. He reminded her of Adolf Hitler. He looked like a determined man who would happily drop the cyanide capsule into the gas chamber himself. Again the man was accepted.

I'll be able to leave, she reassured herself, as the jury was impaneled. I'll go to Mexico. I'll . . .

This trial was different for Joyce. Perhaps it was because she was physically and mentally exhausted. Perhaps it was because she had resolved her future and no longer cared what happened, just so her ordeal would end. It was hard to tell. All that was certain was that a very different woman suddenly was on the witness stand.

"I tried to keep from being emotional," Joyce said. "It was so embarrassing. At one point I just buried my face in my hands and cried. The judge had to call a recess while I composed myself. I guess I was just too tired to hold it all in."

Larry Turoff did not recognize the change until it was too late. A prosecutor sees a lot of tears. A prosecutor knows that guilty people weep with as much ease as innocent ones. Sometimes they cry from remorse. More frequently their tears are from frustration. They got caught, a situation they never expected, and their emotions overwhelm them. Whether or not Turoff thought Joyce's tears were from frustration at being caught or the frustration of being innocent when no one had believed her is unknown. Whatever the case, he continued to use the same badgering manner of questioning as he had in the past.

Suddenly Joyce could take no more. He had asked the questions before. She had answered them truthfully, carefully, accurately. Why did he not believe her? Why did he make her say the same things over and over again when he knew she was telling the truth, knew she had not once changed her story? She talked to him directly, ignoring the jury, no longer concerned with how she looked or sounded. She had been needled, verbally abused, beaten down, locked away. She wanted it to end, to finally end.

Her emotions were ones of helplessness rather than aggression, frustration rather than anger. She was like a child who had become overwhelmed by the abuse of parents she was too small to fight or change. In that instant of rebellion everyone in the courtroom could see the real Joyce Lukezic, the gentle woman, the caring mother, the helpless victim. The hardness within her personality was suddenly seen as veneer that could be stripped away at the slightest touch. This was not the face and voice of a killer. This was a woman in trouble through no fault of her own. It was also the first solid breakthrough for the defense, the first time they had been able to show the woman, not the facade she had so carefully been taught to nurture over the years.

Arnie Merrill was another surprise. Merrill had been testifying in trial after trial related to the case. Twice in the past he had appeared to testify against Joyce. He had been on trial himself. He had spoken against Cruz, McCall, Bracy, Hooper . . . There had been appeals. There had been depositions. His words were recorded in depth, yet the past had nothing to do with the present until Thinnes worked out a way to destroy him through those very same words.

Thinnes had spent hours going through the statements, looking for contradictions in testimony. He noticed how over and over again, Merrill changed his stories. What were "facts" one day were discarded another in favor of a radically different statement, often the complete opposite of the previous remarks, yet still alleged to be the "truth." Thinnes made note of every change, listing the exact words, the date, the circumstances. Then he made a massive chart he brought into the courtroom when it was time for Merrill to take the witness stand.

Thinnes began quietly, simply. Merrill was asked a question, he gave his reply, then Thinnes asked him what he would say about a person who said something different.

Merrill, curious, listened as Thinnes quoted a completely contradictory statement without attributing the source. Merrill, unaware at first of what was happening, calmly said that anyone who would say something different than what he had just said was definitely a liar. The words Thinnes quoted were lies. And that was when Thinnes explained that he had quoted Merrill's own words, giving him the date and circumstances.

This approach was repeated three or four times before Merrill understood what was happening. He was in trouble for the first time since he had first taken the stand three years earlier when the trials originally began. His lies had been discovered, recorded, thrown back in his face.

There were discoveries about Dan Ryan as well. He had helped Merrill obtain a job as a chef in Casa Grande, Arizona, a job where Merrill had proven both dishonest and incompetent. When Merrill falsified his background, claiming that he had trained in New Orleans, Ryan acted as a reference, furthering the document of lies that was enabling Merrill to remain unpunished, unchanged.

Other key witnesses were handled in much the same manner. Larry Turoff's faith in Wally Roberts' confirmation of Arnie Merrill's statements disintegrated almost as completely as Arnie Merrill's credibility during cross-examination. Roberts not only fell apart on the witness stand, his testimony hurt the prosecution's case while strengthening the belief that Ron Lukezic might have been the person behind the murders. Then, on October 16, 1985, Craig Mehrens, Thomas Thinnes' partner, took on Roberts, asking him how long he had known Ron Lukezic.

"Since 1974."

"Prior to Mr. Redmond's death on New Year's Eve of 1980 was Ron acting like a gangster?"

"Correct."

"You have made that comment before; correct?"

"Correct."

"He was always talking about shooting people?"

"Right."

"And in 1979 he asked you about robbing a couple of people in Scottsdale?"

"Yes."

"You were asked by Ron to rob—to help him rob some people in a Scottsdale motel for a quarter million in diamonds with some automatic weapons?"

"He asked me if I'd be interested in holding up two diamond merchants, that he got information from Artie Ross where they were going to be and that they'd be armed and if I would do it he would supply me with automatic weapons so that I could handle it."

"Did you turn that down?"

"Correct."

"Did Mr. Lukezic, Ron Lukezic, ever make any remarks to you about harming Tony Sampson?"

"Yes, he did."

"What did he say?"

"He—Ron had done a printing job for Tony, I knew Tony very well, and Tony had not paid Ron and Ron felt hustled and conned. It wasn't that much money, it was only maybe $1400, $2400, but Ron wanted Tony's address to know where Tony lived so he could have somebody go over and break his legs."

"As a matter of fact back in this period of time prior to Pat's death Ron was hanging around with people that led you to believe that Ron's killing someone was about the next thing that he might do?"

"Correct."

"Now there is no question in your mind, is there, that Ron Lukezic on several occasions told you that this Vegas business would be worth seven—up to and including at least seven—million dollars to Graphic Dimensions?"

"That's correct."

"And if he were to have testified that it was only worth $27,000 would he have been violating his oath to tell the truth?"

"Correct."

The questioning continued with more interesting statements, not only against Ron Lukezic but also about the attorneys who eventually represented Joyce in her first trial.

"Let me take you back then to May of 1981. I think you told us yesterday that you were telling people and have told people, Ed Nell, Ken Mossar, Dave Seigel that Ron Lukezic had his partner Pat Redmond killed?"

"Correct."

"You then went on a bender, came back in June of 1981 and had your meeting with Ron—Ryan and Midkiff; is that correct?"

"Correct."

"At that meeting you mentioned some statements concerning Joyce that you did not tell them, and this is not in the police report, that you believed that Ron Lukezic had his partner killed; is that correct?"

"I don't remember at that point. I don't remember what that police statement was."

"When you testified at this deposition where you lied and Ryan winked at you, you did not—and you reviewed your police report before; correct?"

"Correct."

"At that deposition you did not testify under oath that you believed that Ron Lukezic had had his partner killed, did you?"

"No."

"Now at some point in time you then sought out Ron Lukezic for help; is that correct?"

Roberts then testified that he was in Connecticut and that Ron and his attorneys, Larry Debus and Mike Kimerer, paid for his flight and hotel room, as well as putting up his dog. Later he met with Mike Kimerer and Ron Lukezic, then spoke briefly with Debus while Ron was in the room. Because of those meetings, and because of statements by Ron, he believed the same lawyers representing Ron Lukezic had also defended Joyce Lukezic in the first trial. It was a statement that seemed casual, though it would later become the basis for further aspersions against both Ron and the lawyers who had been shown to seemingly have a conflict of interest in the case.

Roberts told of going to the Turquoise Motel in Center, Colorado, for a while, the trip paid for by Henry Lukezic, Ron's father. Later Ron talked Wally into returning to Phoenix to testify against Joyce.

"And when you gave that testimony at that first trial you didn't testify you thought that Ron Lukezic had his partner killed, did you?"

"Nobody asked."

"Ron's lawyers didn't ask you; did they?"

"No, they didn't."

Roberts' testimony again showed how weak the prosecution's case against Joyce was and how seemingly foolish they had been for relying upon him. The statements he made not only worked in Joyce's favor, they were further indicators that an investigation should have been more thoroughly made into the actions of Ron Lukezic.

There were a few surprises in the other testimony. One was the presence of a police officer who had been at the Redmond home the night of the murder. He claimed to have seen Joyce the night of the murder as she stood around outside the house. He said that he asked her if she knew the people who lived in the house and she said that she did not, an obvious lie. Then she turned and walked away.

The statement was an odd one in light of the fact that other officers questioned Joyce extensively and their statements were in the police records. All of them had her cooperating fully, talking about Pat and Marilyn Redmond. There was no attempt to hide her connection with the couple.

To emphasize the seeming dishonesty or confusion on the part of the police officer who had not heard Joyce speak in court, Thinnes asked him how Joyce spoke. The officer explained that she spoke normally, with no trace of an accent.

What the officer meant was that Joyce had what is known as a general American accent. It is the voice most newscasters use. It is free from regional variations in speech patterns.

The problem is that Joyce is from the New England area and has a very strong accent to the ears of anyone not from that region. She frequently does not pronounce the letter "R" in a word, for example, so that her brother, Arthur's, name is stated "Ah-tha." Similar pronounciations occur with such frequency that anyone hearing her voice and not from the Boston area will instantly remember it.

The police officer spoke with a general American accent in a state where most individuals who have English as their first language either have the same accent he used or speak with a slight southern drawl. Had he heard Joyce speak, he would not have forgotten. The jury had heard Joyce speak and they did not forget the police officer's incorrect statement.

The trial lasted four weeks. Some witnesses from the past were not able to come or had successfully hidden from subpoenas. Their testimony was obtained from previous trials and depositions, then read into the record. Even Ron Lukezic's statements from the McCall trial became part of the testimony, his words at that time contradicted by witnesses in the courtroom.

When the jury filed out to begin deliberations their faces seemed impassive. No one was able to tell what their verdict would be. It was time for Joyce to make the final decision about whether or not she would go to Mexico.

"I knew when I was on the witness stand that I could not do it. I wanted to leave. God, how I wanted to leave. I didn't think I would survive in prison. I thought I would die there. I thought I would commit suicide or just give up. My heart wasn't strong. I knew I couldn't take it.

"But if I went to Mexico, I couldn't be present when Eden married or had a baby. She would have to give birth without her mother. I wouldn't be able to see any of my grandchildren, not even in Mexico.

"I would be a fugitive from the law. There would be telephone taps on all my children, twenty-four hours a day. My sons and daughter would be followed everywhere they went. And when they married, their spouses would be followed. Dan Ryan and the other investigators would spare no expense to track me down. I was going to be a hunted fugitive, haunted by my past, never able to lead a normal life again.

"In the end they would get me. I knew that. They

would follow Eden and her baby when she went into Mexico to visit me. They would watch as I was once again handcuffed and put into chains before being taken north to the penitentiary. They would witness my being placed in solitary confinement before going to death row. I was too important a criminal for anything else to happen.

"And that was when I decided to stay. I would face the jury's finding me guilty. I would accept the fact that the men and women who had lied about me were walking free while I, who was innocent, would be in jail. Perhaps there would be a future appeal. Perhaps I would be one of the few women to be executed in Arizona. It no longer mattered. In jail I would be near Eden. In jail I could at least be a part of her life without living in fear. And if I died, no matter what awaited me, it had to be better than continuing this nightmare.

"That night I told Eden of my decision. I explained matters to the woman who was helping me.

"I don't know what they thought. Perhaps they were frightened. Perhaps they were relieved. It did not matter. They accepted my decision, Eden loving me no matter what I did, trusting that my judgement would ultimately prove correct."

"I waited at Mary Durand's home. She lived close to the court house and no one would mind if I was there. She had become a friend, a trusted confidante, a person who could make me laugh and make me feel safe. Yet she and I both knew that she considered herself an officer of the court. If the jury found me guilty and I decided to run, she would do whatever was necessary to bring me in. She was a totally honest individual.

"The call, when it came, required that we race back to the court house to hear the decision. Mary drove me, hurrying as fast as possible, then having difficulty finding a parking space because there was some sort of reception going on. I never did find out what was taking place. I only saw dozens of judges and lawyers having refreshments and talking among themselves. In addition, there were news crews from every radio station, television station, and newspaper in the area, as well as some who felt the story was so big that they had been dispatched from other cities.

"Everyone rushed at me as Mary cleared the way so we could get back inside. I think they were shouting, but I was deaf to their words. All that mattered was hearing the verdict.

"As I moved through the doors I was shocked by what I saw. First, there were two guards from the detention center. The judge had ordered them to be present and ready to return me to jail. It was a melodramatic touch that conveyed to me his belief in my guilt. He had been the judge at all three trials and either he was convinced I had conspired to commit murder or he assumed that the jury would hang me regardless of the truth. It was an action that further eroded my confidence in the future.

"Then there were the spectators. All the judges and attorneys from the surrounding courtrooms and the gathering came to witness the judgement. They were crowded into the seating and standing areas as the reporters also moved inside. I was chilled by what was taking place, horrified, unable to do anything but watch.

"The jury filed back into the room, their expressions blank. I felt that they would be happy if they let me off. They would be smiling, perhaps giving me a quiet 'thumbs up' signal.

"They would be pleased to send me to jail if they thought I was guilty, of course. But I knew people didn't smile under such circumstances. I was likely to be sentenced to death. All the jurors had said that they believed in capital punishment. It was not fitting, proper, and dignified to express delight in such a sentence; so their faces would be properly blank. Again it was a clue to my fate.

"And then the foreman spoke. He was the man who looked like Ron, a man I had watched occasionally during the trial as he sometimes stared at me, glaring, having already judged me from the first.

" 'We find the defendant not guilty.' "

In the movies there is a moment of hesitation, then a scream of delight and the defendant starts hugging and kissing her lawyer, her family, the judge and the spectators. Sometimes the courtroom breaks into spontaneous applause as the prosecutor slinks off into the night.

Real life is quite different. Joyce had been broken in body and spirit. Her heart condition was so aggravated by her ordeal that she was on several forms of medication to prevent a major heart attack. Her emotional reserve had been shattered. She had accepted prison, accepted the slow death she knew would result if she went back.

And now the jury had believed the truth. They had found her innocent.

Joyce has no idea what happened in the moments that followed. Those in the courtroom who were near her tell a more complete story of what took place. They remember a sound which some said would haunt them the rest of their life.

It was a moan, a keening sound. It was a sound of pain, a cry to God so deep that it sears the soul, demanding comfort for an agony so great that it will stretch into eternity.

And then Joyce buried her head against her attorney's chest and wept. She clutched his jacket, soaked his shirt, "ruining his clothes" as she later said.

As she began to gain control, some of the jurors spoke with Joyce. The foreman congratulated her, letting her know that he believed her almost from the start of the trial.

Then the youth she had feared came over. He was beaming with happiness. "Can I give you a hug, now?" he asked. "I wanted to hug you before, but it wasn't right. We knew you were innocent, but we couldn't show our emotions. We were afraid that would be wrong; so we deliberately kept our expressions blank when we came in. We didn't want to do anything that would hurt you."

"And with that he gave me a big hug. I thought I could read the jury. I had been afraid of these people. And they had believed me. They had believed me!"

Somehow she was taken from the courtroom. Somehow she ended up back in her attorney's office where she was handed a glass of champagne.

A television crew was given access to the office as Joyce's mood changed to one of elation. She began talking rapidly, suddenly fascinated by the reflector system the technical crew was using to light the room for the television camera. "I've never seen reflectors like that," she told the reporter. "So that's how they control the shadows on your face. They look like little balloons over the light. And you adjust them. That's so fascinating. That's . . ."

Lightheaded now she smiled, feeling detached, heady. She had handled all the pain she could take. She had shattered the reserve that once dominated her life and would never be the same again. But she could not reveal any more of her deepest emotions. Not then. Instead she was genuinely delighted to find her attention diverted, to be able to witness the behind-the-scenes activities involved with a location interview. And when she spoke to the reporter, her voice was softly modulated, her words filled with happiness, her face animated.

She had endured. She had triumphed. She was free.

EPILOGUE

The instigator of the murders of Patrick Redmond and Helen Phelps remains at large. The two most logical suspects, Ron Lukezic and Arthur Ross, are free. No further investigations into the case have been instigated.

Ross now makes the east coast his home. He remains close to his sister and had made arrangements to financially assure an appeal if she lost the case. His business success has been such that he is a wealthy man and most people involved with the case seriously doubt that he had anything to do with the murders.

Yet Ross was named by people who were involved with the case. Ross might have been in a position to receive either a substantial finder's fee or on-going income from helping to arrange the deal that would generate the Las Vegas printing business for his brother-in-law. He had a motive and he had no emotional attachment for the Redmonds. He also knew or had met every person involved with the murders, including the killers.

Dan Ryan's vendetta against Arthur Ross, at least as it existed in Ross' mind, may have been one reason why Ryan pushed so hard to have Joyce arrested. It is believed that he was counting on Ross' love for his sister to be so great that he would step forward and confess his guilt to save Joyce.

The truth is something else. Ross was terrified of being railroaded into jail. Innocent of the crime or guilty, he was not ever likely to want to replace his sister in prison. The fact that he is almost certainly innocent does not change the situation that exists. Ross had motive and opportunity yet was never investigated. Joyce had neither motive nor so complete an opportunity as her brother, yet she was prosecuted to the limits of the law, her case making three trips through the court system.

Ron Lukezic, the man who had everything to gain and nothing to lose from the murders, keeps a low profile. At this writing, he is believed to be in the Denver, Colorado, region. He keeps in close contact with his mother in Phoenix and has testified in the trials of some of the other people involved with the killings. He refused to respond to requests, made through his mother, for an interview. Yet whether Lukezic is innocent or guilty, the actions of Larry Turoff have ensured that he will never face the ordeal his wife, whom he abandoned, had to experience. And if he is guilty, the fact that he can not be charged means that he committed the perfect crime.

Dan Ryan became a private investigator who periodically worked for Wackenhut Security in Phoenix. According to the manager, Ryan was not an employee but operated under their license when they needed freelance work done. Ryan was contacted through Wackenhut, then telephoned to say that he would not talk and would not explain why he would not talk. Thus the record has had to speak for him and the record shows a man who went far beyond the legal system he swore to uphold in order to satisfy his obsession about Joyce Lukezic, the person he sought to convict of murder. Even more frightening, this former FBI agent, former agent for Alcohol, Tobacco, and Firearms, former investigator for the Maricopa County Attorney's office may have had strong reasons to suspect Ron Lukezic's guilt all along. That is certainly the implication of the FBI memos on the case, making his vendetta against Joyce even more difficult to understand.

The initial lawyers for Joyce continue in private practice and continue to handle major cases. Each maintains
that he did the best possible job, and each seems uncomfortable with the other's comments.

Arnie Merrill was last known to be living in the east
with one of his children, the others allegedly wanting
nothing to do with him.

Joseph Brownlee, the first prosecutor, is in private
practice. His partner at the time, Mike Jones, eventually
became a judge. Larry Turoff awaits retirement, accepting
his prosecution of the innocent Joyce Lukezic as something that had to be done, given the law and the comments
made by others connected with the case. Larry Martinsen,
the primary police detective involved with the preliminary
investigation, refuses speculation on the case. He is curious about the truth, judging none of the principals as innocent or guilty but keeping an open mind about them all
until the day comes, if ever, when the truth is known for
certain. He is also the only person heavily involved with
the case who has come through all the trials with the reputation of being honest, thorough, without malice, and
trusted for both his testimony and his attitude.

For Joyce Lukezic, life will never be quite the same.
After her acquittal she had to face life with mixed feelings.
She has no time for bitterness, though the intense sadness
of what she endured is always just below the surface. She
cries easily now, her face softened, her heart heavy. She
has triumphed over personal adversity, though at the cost
of her children being emotionally scarred, one way or another, for the rest of their days.

There was the offer of a telemarketing job when Joyce
won her final battle, a job she took. She was paid $5 an
hour, then proved so reliable that eventually she became
supervisor at $30,000 per year. Her efforts were successful,
ensuring the company's survival far longer than a poor
cash flow situation should have allowed. When the firm

went out of business two years after she started there, she was credited with being one of the reasons it had not folded sooner.

From telemarketing Joyce went to work for the state of Arizona, working with people in financial crisis. In both jobs she has come across women she knew in jail, occasionally hiring one or two when still with the telemarketing company, in order to give them a new chance in life. Tragically she also has had to fire all those she had known. "They talked like they wanted a job and I think they wanted to be like everyone else. But they could not change. They were still involved with drugs and prostitution. They saw the job as a place to rest, to talk, to continue their street activities. I had to fire them when they didn't work or tried to bring drugs to the job. It was so sad. I wanted them to know my happiness. I guess they were just not ready to change."

It is not with her business life that Joyce suffers the greatest pain, though. It is with her children. Eric was just shy of his sixteenth birthday when Joyce was first arrested, Eden a year younger. Jason, the baby of the family at ten and a half, had no comprehension of what was happening, his emotions buffeted by his stepfather's leaving with another woman, his mother's going to jail, and his natural father's living in Boston.

Each child was of an age where the emotional trauma of Joyce's imprisonment mingled with other aspects of what they were experiencing in their daily lives. Eric was rebellious, testing the limits of childhood as he grew rapidly into adulthood. He was in a period of rejection, trying to establish his own identity, yet needing the stability of a family base, of routine, of love and acceptance. This period would have been difficult for him at best. With the disruption in his life, he became sullen, withdrawn, expressing his anger in his music. He did not date, did not seem to want to be vulnerable to another human being. All the adults who had been close to him disappeared.

Eric was also self-conscious about the trial of his mother. He was mildly disabled in a way that had caused him discomfort from the time he was seven. He had been playing with some friends as they flew what was called a bat kite. The wind was not right and the kite dipped and soared in an irregular manner as it tried to stay aloft. Suddenly it began to drop as Eric watched. Before he could get out of the way, it struck his eye, gashing the lids and taking his sight on one side.

The remaining eye compensated for the loss of sight in some ways. The peripheral vision of that eye increased dramatically. He developed excellent depth perception. He obtained a prosthesis that looked so natural that it was almost impossible to tell he had sustained such a loss. Yet seven-year olds can be cruel. He was teased and made the center of attention from time to time.

As a teenager, his physical imperfection caused him more pain. Teens think that they are immortal and looks are a major factor in popularity. He was a handsome young man, tall, athletic looking, a good student interested in marine biology. Yet he was not perfect. Just as the most popular girl in a typical high school is determined, in part, by whether or not she will fall victim to acne, hair with split ends, or the ability to keep current with fashions that change daily, so an artificial eye can be seen by a teenaged boy as a deterrent to all manner of future success. Eric had to cope with the fact he had a prosthesis, a mother in jail, *and* the normal pressures of being in high school. The combination was overwhelming, causing him to withdraw into himself.

Joyce feels her children's pain intently:

"Eric and I were further estranged by the fact that he could almost never bring himself to visit me in the hospital or in the jail. He had seen hospital rooms too often when his eye was bad. Anything that reminded him of an institution was beyond his ability to cope. He had to avoid them for his own emotional sake.

"Eden coped well on the surface. Her emotions were in turmoil, but she had had an experience the others lacked, an experience that gave her greater understanding. She had been with me the day of the arrest. She had witnessed the shock, the sense of helplessness, the horror of what took place. She had been to the jails, the courts, the hospital. She knew that my ordeal was something I did not want, but could not help or avoid. She had been my victim, but she had also been my friend. Her personal hell did not separate us.

"Jason was different. He was too young to understand jail.

"I remember when I came home from the Madison Street jail, I was holding him on my lap when he said, 'Mommy, I hope you won't have to go back to the slammer.' It was a statement that made me want to laugh, to cry, to hug him and hold him and tell him everything was going to be all right.

"But it wasn't going to be all right and I knew it. I had to prepare for a trial that I wasn't necessarily going to win. Certainly there would be little time I could spend with him and my agreement with my ex-husband was such that a summer visit was normal. Jason left for Boston and I prepared for the trial. I had no idea that it would be more than three years' time until I was free.

"Jason had a difficult time in Boston. He had always been his father's favorite, but his father did not understand parenting. We had been divorced far too long, and seeing the kids for a week or two at a time was not the same as raising them full time.

"My ex-husband tried to show the children his love through buying them presents. Jason became interested in the guitar and asked for lessons after we eventually were re-united. He had a simple instrument and took it with him to Boston for a visit. He returned with an acoustic guitar of a quality only a professional could play. Yet Jason's interest was that of the amateur. The instrument discouraged rather than encouraged him.

"But I am getting ahead of myself. Jason and his father were suddenly in a difficult position. Jason was reaching puberty, experiencing raging hormones, radical emotional changes, and all the normal difficulties of coming of age. His school work would vary in quality depending upon what might be troubling him on any given day. He felt abandoned by me, too young to realize that there was a major difference between a sentence to the 'slammer' and two weeks paid at Club Med. He was still of an age where his parents seemed gods, in total control of every aspect of life. To him, I was in jail because I wanted to be in jail. I could come home if I wanted to come home. And I sent him away, not because I was living a nightmare but because somehow he was not good enough.

"Jason's father had to take on a child experiencing all these feelings when he had previously lived alone for all but a couple of weeks during the year. For a period Eden lived there, too, and she acted as a surrogate mother for Jason. Once Eden left, though, whatever buffer existed between Jason and his father ended.

"My ex-husband's hopes for Jason were great. He believed in Jason's abilities. He knew our son was bright, had tremendous potential as an individual. Eric was working part time in restaurants, had formed his own band, which was earning money and giving him a creative outlet as a song writer. He was going to college to study marine biology. Eden was also working part time, going to school in preparation for a career in business management. His father felt that Jason's potential had to be just as good. It both was and is. Unfortunately, Jason was going through a time in life when nothing is quite normal under the best of circumstances. On any given day he could be part child, part adult, and part rotten little kid in addition to needing special nurturing because of his sense of being abandoned by me.

"I had learned about life with teenagers having experienced the changes that two of them went through, not to mention their friends. My ex-husband had none of that preparation. He didn't know when to encourage, when to be firm, and when to ignore Jason's behavior. As a result, he became frustrated, angry, and occasionally used violence to try to assert his control. Jason became surly, argumentative, ready to push all adults to the limit in order to be knocked down.

"I don't know if Jason was deliberately taunting. The angry response might have given him a sense that he was loved, that someone did care what happened. I don't even know if he came to genuinely hate his father, blaming him for all manner of personal pain over which his father had had no control, taunting him because of that anger. All that is certain is that his home life in Boston was miserable, yet neither he nor his father were able to say anything. They both knew that nothing could be done.

"At the same time, Jason was developing a life in that eastern community quite different from the one he had known in Phoenix. By the time he came home to me for good, he would have spent a third of his years in Boston. Phoenix, the place I considered home for myself and the children, was a strange place for him.

"Once I got out of jail I began calling Jason regularly, sending him cards and notes for special occasions. He did not want to come to Phoenix, even though I had retained full custody of the children throughout my ordeal. My ex-husband never challenged the custody agreement even though, when I was jailed for murder, it would have been easy to declare me unfit. Instead, he opened his home to his children when they wanted to be there and tried to parent. I will be forever grateful for his efforts, just as there will always be some pain for the conflicts that caused Eden and Jason so much discomfort.

"Finally, in the summer of 1985, Jason agreed to come for a two week visit. He flew out and I met him at the airport.

"I thought I knew what to expect. The airlines know how to handle little children. He would be seated on the plane until all the passengers were off. Then a flight attendant would go to him, give him a set of wings he could proudly pin on his clothing, take his hand, help him with any carry-on luggage, then escort him down the aisle, out the cabin door, and into the waiting area. He would break away from her, running to hug me, and I would take him in my arms, loving him, holding him, as I verbally confirmed my identity with the attendant.

"I had already prepared for his return at home. I had stopped by the grocery store and picked up all the special foods that children delight in. I purchased 'Fruit Loops,' 'Count Chocula,' and other cereals that were probably 90 percent sugar and would rot his teeth. But I didn't care. I had my child back for two weeks and I would spoil him rotten with all the wrong foods and all the loving attention I could give him.

"My little boy never returned. There was no stewardess holding his hand and guiding him up the ramp towards where I was waiting. That child was gone to me forever.

"The Jason who walked toward me was tall, well over six feet, as big as his brother, almost as much bigger than me as I was taller than he had been when last I saw him. I recognized him instantly, of course. I would know his eyes, his face anywhere. He was still my baby. He was only a teenager, but he had almost become a man.

"Again, nothing was right. The cereals might have been baby food, considering his age and all. Yet at least he enjoyed them. Like all teenagers, he was at a stage where he hadn't lost the pleasures of childhood, the delight in what had once been forbidden fruits. At the same time, he was too old to admit such things and would rather 'die' than be caught either requesting or buying such things. However, since I had gone to so much trouble to bring it into my home, the least he could do was eat it. And he did so with relish.

"There was no responding to my touching, though. He accepted my hug, my kissing, with stoicism. He had not forgotten me. We had talked and corresponded. He was my son and I was his mother, yet we were also strangers to each other. I might have been a delightful, doting maiden aunt he once spent time with, but had not taken very seriously for many years.

"It mattered, but it didn't matter. I had accepted the fact that reuniting with my children would be difficult. I had seen the problems with Eric who at least was older, better able to understand what had happened. I could not expect less with Jason.

"That first night I could not sleep. I kept getting out of bed and walking across to Jason's room, standing at the entrance, watching him. To me the moments were precious, to be cherished, even if the first visit was less joyous than I had hoped. A couple of times I took pictures of him with my camera. He was so deeply asleep that the flash did not disturb him. He probably would not have understood had he awakened.

"I knew not to push anything. We talked; we went out to eat; I took him to movies; we went to the mall. Some things he enjoyed; some things bored him. I felt as though we were on a blind date, wanting desperately to please each other, yet uncertain how to do it. He would say something to see how I would respond. I would say something to see how he would respond. Occasionally we would laugh. Occasionally we would have awkward moments of silence. And in the end the visit was mutually unsatisfying.

"Jason came for periodic visits over the next year, not returning for good until fall of 1987. By then his relationship with his father had become intolerable for him. He wanted to move in with a friend, then decided, because of opposition from my ex-husband, to come back with me.

"This time Jason was more willing to be touched. He hugged me, was pleased to see me, was comfortable coming home. We still were not close, though. There were still many things he did not understand.

"Jason's return also created dissension with Eric. Jason returned at approximately the same age Eric had been when I went to jail and his world fell apart. Eric had received no nurturing from his family from the time he was sixteen into adulthood. Now he had to watch me interact with his brother, showing him the love he never experienced. There was tension, anger, jealousy, and perhaps a touch of self-hate.

"Jason needed special attention, because he was still coping with what occurred. There were times he wanted to be treated exactly as he had been before my arrest, having me tuck him in and say the things that parents and children share during early childhood. At other times he was very much a young man, wanting to be treated with the respect his newly developed maturity required.

"Eric watched our interaction and it hurt him. The boys would often argue, pretending they were teasing, yet it was obvious that they were each hoping the other would take the comments one step too far. It was as though they each had a chip on their shoulder and wanted the other to knock it off. Fortunately, the closest they came to violence was when they would wrestle, using more force than friends and less force than their anger might have allowed. I had to break them up and, at times, marks on their bodies would indicate that they had tried to hurt each other. Yet there were always boundaries they did not cross, boundaries I could live with as they adjusted.

"Eventually I was able to talk with Jason, truly talk. I helped him come to understand what had happened to me. I helped him realize what it was like for a mother to have a ten-year-old child who needed an adult for guidance. I showed him that I had no choice except to call on his other parent. Had it not been for his father, he might have been placed with a family of strangers. His sister and brother, though old enough to appear adult to him at the time, were not mature enough to keep everyone together in the house. They were also kids, old enough so that he looked up to them, but not old enough for the three to survive on their own.

"I have had to adjust to the adult Jason has become. One day he asked me to get something from his wallet and I discovered a condom inside. Now I know that many teenaged boys buy a condom and carry it in their wallets as a sign of manhood. They claim that they need to be prepared when they are on dates, but the condom ages, the package blackens from being carried and the elastic becomes brittle from disuse. Carrying it is a rite of passage, though they may be virgins for months or years after they buy it. However, Jason made it very clear to me that he had used them before and was being responsible about sex.

"First Eden, then Jason. I chose not to pursue the issue any more, nor did I ask Eric about his love life.

"The fact that Jason was able to talk has been a tremendous help. Eric has yet to be able to do that.

"I keep trying to reach Eric, to get him to share his pain, his fears, his anger, and his hopes. I am extraordinarily proud of his successes. His music has become softer, gentler, more in line with the folk songs of my youth than the angry violence of the early songs of his band. He is doing well in school. He is reasonably self-sufficient, living on his own. While he can't talk directly with me, when he sends me a card for my birthday or some special occasion, he will often write a poem that shows such love, tenderness, and pain that I want to cradle him like a baby, delighting in him and comforting him.

"Oddly, Eric does reach out when he is sick. He comes home every time he doesn't feel well. He seems, at these times, to be like a wounded animal who slinks off to the safe, familiar, dark, quiet cave where his mother lives to mend. It is an action we never discuss, yet one that gives me hope for our future together.

"The public reaction has been mixed. When I went to work for the telemarketing company, the owner knew who I was, though I thought I had fooled him by using my previous married name instead of keeping Lukezic. I did not realize that he did not care and was willing to give an innocent person a chance. However, one of the women who worked there was not so compassionate. When I gave a co-worker a ride in my car because she needed a way to get home, the other woman warned her to avoid me because I had been in jail for murder. I was hurt when I discovered that, though the pain was eased when we eventually became friends.

"Eden reached full womanhood after going to South Africa for a year of college not long after I was released. My brother, Arthur, still had a business there, a business he later sold. He invited Eden to stay with him, to have the experience of going to school abroad.

"We talked about it, though this time I did not feel selfish, self-pitying, and angry about the separation. I knew it would be good for her. She was becoming serious about a boy and, though I did not know how serious, I had visions of her getting married, settling down, then regretting never having traveled or done anything because she tried to grow up too fast.

"She went. The trip had two results. One was that it gave her an intense understanding of racial hatred under the apartheid system. Because she was white and living on Arthur's rural ranch, she traveled with a handgun for protection because she was potentially subject to random violence. Yet her sympathy was with the black majority and she came to understand the pain of both sides, her horror resulting in school papers on the issue that showed sensitivity and anger over what the blacks were experiencing.

"The second result was the young man who is now her husband. She moved in with him towards the end of her stay, coming back to the States to get married. They are both hard working, completing their education and, oddly, her husband appears to be planning a career in the printing business. His specialty is silk screening. Fortunately that is where the only similarity with Ron ends, but the coincidence is one that still causes me to sometimes laugh, sometimes causes a clutch in my chest. The two of them are quite happy with each other.

"Since I have gotten out of jail I have had to testify in the appeals of the killer in the case. I still am uncomfortable when someone recognizes me because of the past notoriety and does not come to know me as a person. There is also the attitude that no one goes to jail for a crime they did not commit, an attitude that is not so hostile as the one towards the 'rich bitch' who bought her way to freedom. Still, it hurts when I experience it, hurts to know that I may continue to have people judge me for where I have been instead of learning the truth.

"What will tomorrow bring? I have no idea. Writing this book has helped to put the past in perspective, to deal with the emotions, to move forward with my life.

"There is pain. There will always be pain. I have been hurt too many times to think about another marriage, another period of risking being vulnerable to someone else.

"Yet there is a joy with life I never knew was possible. I take nothing for granted. I revel in the sound of a bird singing in the morning. Each new sunrise, each sunset, these are experiences to treasure. I taste my food, savoring the rich variety of flavors. I feel the varied materials that have been made into my clothing. I delight in the variety of people who walk the streets, in simple acts of kindness. I love the animals that abound, the flowers, the creations of God in the country and of man in the city.

"I have an appreciation for life that I never realized I was lacking. I weep with sorrow for the time lost, for the damage to my innocent loved ones. Yet each new day brings me happiness that in those dark days would have been beyond my comprehension.

"I am free."

Joyce Lukezic now works for the state of Arizona, Department of Appeals, seeking justice for those, like her, who have endured unjust punishment.